PRIVATE PILOT'S HANDBOOK
of Aeronautical Knowledge

FEDERAL AVIATION AGENCY
Flight Standards Service

1965

For sale by the Superintendent of Documents, U. S. Government Printing Office, Washington, D.C.   20402.   Price $2.75.

Foreword

The *Private Pilot's Handbook of Aeronautical Knowledge* contains essential, authoritative information used in training and guiding private pilots, but until now found in several different publications. Applicants for private pilot certification, flight instructors, and flying school staffs have often suggested that the Federal Aviation Agency issue this type of material under one cover. This handbook responds to those requests.

Much of the information in this handbook is based on subject matter included in the FAA booklets *Path of Flight, Realm of Flight, and Facts of Flight.* These publications have been available to the aviation public for over a decade and have been very popular. This new handbook, however, tells the private pilot for the first time how to use to his best advantage: (a) *Airman's Information Manual,* (b) data in FAA-approved Airplane Flight Manuals, and (c) basic instruments required for airplane attitude control.

All subject areas in which an applicant for private pilot certification may be tested are covered in this handbook, except the area of Federal regulations pertinent to civil aviation. Private Pilot Certificate test items are always based on current regulations, as amended. Up-to-date, applicable regulations should be purchased and studied by each certificate applicant as nearly as possible to the examination date. All FAA regulations are sold at the Superintendent of Documents, United States Government Printing Office.

This handbook was prepared by the Flight Standards Service.

Table of Contents

I. Principles of Flight

CHAPTER	PAGE
1. Forces Acting on the Airplane	1
2. Function of the Controls	9
3. Loads and Load Factors	11

II. Weather

4. Weather Information for the Pilot | 15
5. Nature of the Atmosphere | 16
6. Significance of Atmospheric Pressure | 18
7. Wind | 20
8. Moisture and Temperature | 31
9. Results of Condensation | 34
10. Air Masses and Fronts | 40
11. Aviation Weather Forecasts and Reports | 50

III. Navigation

12. Navigation Aids | 59
13. Aeronautical Chart Reading | 61
14. Measurement of Direction | 63
15. Basic Calculations | 69
16. The Wind Triangle | 72

IV. Aircraft and Engine Operation

17. Airplane Structure | 78
18. Engine Operation | 80

V. Flight Instruments

19. Pitot-Static System Flight Instruments | 87
20. Gyroscopic Flight Instruments | 92
21. Magnetic Compass | 95

VI. Aircraft Performance

CHAPTER	PAGE
22. Weight and Balance	97
23. Aircraft Performance	98

VII. Flight Information Publications

24. Airman's Information Manual | 105

VIII. Flight Computer

25. Slide Rule Face | 129
26. Wind Face | 138

IX. Radio Communications

27. Radio Communications | 144
28. Radio Guidance in VFR Flying | 148
29. Emergency Radio Procedures | 154

X. Flight Planning

30. Preflight Planning | 157

Appendix I

Selected Exam-O-Grams | 161

Appendix II

Answers to Exercises | 174

Illustrations

FIGURE   PAGE

1. Relationship of forces in flight 1
2. Cross-sectional view of an airfoil 1
3. Relationship between flight path and relative wind 2
4. The angle of attack is the angle between the chord and the flight path 3
5. The angle of attack is always based on the flight path, not the ground 3
6. Flow of air through a Venturi tube 4
7. Curvature of airfoil and layers of undisturbed air act as the constriction in a Venturi tube 4
8. Difference in pressure between upper and lower wing surfaces produces lift 5
9. Relationship between relative wind, lift, and drag 5
10. Flow of air over a wing at various angles of attack 6
11. Use of flaps increases lift and drag 7
12. Lift and drag increase with an increase in angle of attack 7
13. Effect of altitude, temperature, and humidity on takeoff run and rate of climb 8
14. Axes of rotation 9
15. Conventional arrangement of controls (red) is shown at left. The airplane surfaces that respond to the controls (red) are shown at right 10
16. Effect of ailerons 11
17. Effect of elevators 12
18. The load on the wings increases when the angle of bank increases. The rate of increase is shown by the length of the white arrows. Figures below the arrows indicate the increase in terms of plane weight. For example, the load during a 60-degree bank is 2.00, twice the weight of the plane in level flight 12
19. Effect of rudder 13

FIGURE   PAGE

20. Effect of trim tabs 13
21. Load factor chart 13
22. Stall speed chart 14
23. The troposphere and stratosphere are the realm of flight 16
24. Barometric pressure at a weather station is expressed as pressure at sea level 17
25. Atmospheric density at sea level enables a plane to take off in a relatively short distance 19
26. The distance required for takeoff increases with the altitude of the field 20
27. Station model showing method of recording atmospheric pressure by upper-right group of three digits. The numeral 203 indicates pressure of 1020.3 millibars. Change within preceding 3 hours is shown in tenths-of-millibars immediately below 21
28. Heat at the equator would cause the air to circulate uniformly, as shown, if the earth did not rotate 21
29. Principal air currents in the Northern Hemisphere 22
30. Circulation of wind within a "low" 23
31. Use of favorable winds in flight 23
32. Convection currents from on-shore winds in daytime 24
33. Convection currents from off-shore winds at night 25
34. Avoiding turbulence caused by convection currents by flying above the cloud level 26
35. Varying surfaces affect the normal glide path. Some surfaces create rising currents which tend to make the pilot overshoot the field 27
36. Descending currents prevail above some surfaces and tend to make the pilot land short of the field 28
37. Turbulence caused by obstructions to normal flow of air 29

38. Planes approaching hills or mountains from windward are helped by rising currents. Those approaching from leeward encounter descending currents 30

39. Speed and direction of wind are shown on weather map by wind arrows and isobars 30

40. Above: Flow of air around a "high." Below: Isobars on a weather map indicate various degrees of pressure within a high 30

41. Station model showing method of indicating wind direction and speed. The wind is shown to be from the northwest, with a speed of 25 knots 31

42. Station model showing temperature and dew point. The temperature is shown to be 50° F., the dew point, 47° F. 32

43. A chart used for converting degrees Centigrade to degrees Fahrenheit and vice versa 32

44. Cumulus clouds as they appear at low, intermediate, and high levels 33

45. Stratus-type clouds at various altitudes 35

46. Various types of bad weather clouds 36

47. Cross-section of a cumulonimbus cloud (thunderhead) 37

48. Weather map symbols used to indicate sky cover 39

49. Basic weather symbols used on weather maps 40

50. Typical station model report on printed daily weather map.. 40

51. Sample plotted station model using official weather code.... 40

52. A warm front: (upper) cross-section; (lower left) as shown on weather map; (lower right) as reported by teletype sequences 42

53. A cold front: (upper) cross-section; (lower left) as shown on a weather map; (lower right) as reported by teletype sequences 44

54. Weather map indication of wind shift line (center line leading to low) 45

55. An occluded front: (upper) cross-section; (lower left) as shown on a weather map; (lower right) as reported by teletype sequences 46

56. Three stages in the development of a typical occlusion moving northeastward 47

57. Development of an occlusion. If warm air were red and cold air were blue, this is how various stages of an occlusion would appear to a person aloft looking toward the earth. (Precipitation is green.) 48

58. Cloud formations and precipitation accompanying a typical occlusion. (Details of the third stage of development series shown in figure 56.) 49

59. Section of typical weather map showing methods indicating weather facts important to pilots 50

60. Key to aviation weather reports and forecasts 52

61. Index of sectional charts 60

62. Altitude, form and slope of terrain as indicated by contour lines and numerals (U.S. Geological Survey) 62

63. Meridians and parallels—the basis of measuring time, distance and direction 63

64. When the sun is directly above the meridian, the time at points on that meridian is noon. This is the basis on which time zones are established 63

65. The compass rose enables the pilot to determine direction in terms of points of the compass and degrees of arc 64

66. Courses are determined by reference to meridians on aeronautical charts 64

67. Magnetic meridians are in black, geographic meridians and parallels in blue; variation is the angle between a magnetic and geographic meridian 65

68. A typical isogonic chart. The black lines are isogonic lines which connect geographical points with identical magnetic variation 65

69. In an area of west variation a compass needle points west of true north; in an area of zero variation it points to true north; in an area of east variation it points east of true north 66

70. The relationship between true heading, magnetic heading, and variation in areas of east and west variation 67

71. Magnetized portions of the plane cause the compass to deviate from its normal indication 67

72. Compass deviation card 68

FIGURE		PAGE
73.	Relationship between true, magnetic, and compass heading for a particular instance	68
74.	Motion of the air affects the speed with which airplanes move over the earth's surface. Airspeed, the rate at which a plane moves through the air, is not affected by air motion	69
75.	Airplane flight path resulting from its airspeed and direction, and the wind speed and direction	70
76.	Effects of wind drift on maintaining desired course	71
77.	Establishing a wind correction angle that will counteract wind drift and maintain the desired course	71
78.	Principle of the wind triangle	72
79.	The wind triangle as it is drawn in navigation practice. Blue lines show the triangle as drawn in figure 76	72
80.	Steps in drawing the wind triangle	73
81.	Finding true heading by direct measurement	73
82.	Finding true heading by the wind correction angle	74
83.	Pilot's planning sheet and visual flight log	75
84.	Computations for a round-trip flight	76
85.	Steps in constructing the wind triangle and the various measurements for a true course of 110°; wind 20 mph from 225°; airspeed of 100 mph	77
86.	Preflight inspection should include at least: (1) propeller; (2) engine; (3) landing gear; (4) wings and fuselage; (5) control surfaces and controls; (6) weight of baggage and passengers	79
87.	Four strokes of the piston produce power: (A) Fuel mixture (light blue) is drawn into cylinder by downward stroke. (B) Mixture (darker blue) is compressed by upward stroke. (C) Spark ignites mixture (red), forcing piston downward and producing power that turns propeller. (D) Burned gases (light red) pushed out of cylinder by upward stroke	81
88.	Formation of ice (white) in the fuel intake system may reduce or block fuel flow (red) to the engine	84
89.	Pitot-static system with instruments operated from it	87
90.	Sensitive altimeter. The instrument is adjusted by the knob (lower left) so the current altimeter setting (30.34 here) appears in the window to the right	89
91.	Vertical speed indicator	89
92.	Airspeed indicator	90
93.	Airspeed indicator showing color-coded marking system	91
94.	Model gyroscope	92
95.	Turn and bank indicator	93
96.	Indications of the ball in various types of turns	93
97.	Heading indicator	94
98.	Attitude indicator	94
99.	Various indications on the attitude indicator	94
100.	Magnetic compass	95
101.	Before takeoff, be sure the load is distributed correctly to assure proper balance. Flight can be very hazardous if the center of gravity is not within the allowable CG range	98
102.	Koch chart	99
103.	Takeoff performance data chart	101
104.	A cruise performance chart	102
105.	A landing performance data chart	103
106.	Air navigation radio aids	106
107.	Good operating practices	107
108.	Medical facts for pilots	107
109.	Radar	108
110.	Wake turbulence	109
111.	Departure procedures	110
112.	Enroute procedures	111
113.	Arrival procedures	111
114.	Landing procedures	112
115.	Glossary of aeronautical terms	114
116.	Abbreviations	115
117.	Sectional chart bulletin	116
118.	Lake, island and mountain reporting service	117
119.	Special notice	118
120.	Oil burner routes	119
121.	Notices to airmen	120
122a.	Airport/facility directory legend	121

FIGURE		PAGE
122b.	Airport/facility directory legend	122
122c.	Airport/facility directory legend	123
123a.	Airport directory	124
123b.	Airport directory	125
123c.	Airport directory	126
124.	Airport/facility directory	127
125.	Three scales and speed index. Arrow #1, miles scale; arrow #2, minutes scale; arrow #3, hours scale; arrow #4, speed index	129
126.	Slide rule face of a flight computer	130
127.	Wind face of a flight computer	130
128.	Assigning values to the graduations of the scales	131
129.	Finding total flight time when ground speed and distance are known	132
130.	Finding ground speed when flight time and distance flown are given	133
131.	Finding total available flight time when amount of fuel and rate of fuel consumption are known	134
132.	Estimating amount of fuel to be used when estimated time enroute and fuel consumption rate are known	135
133.	Sector of computer used for true airspeed computations	136
134.	Finding true airspeed when temperature, altitude, and indicated airspeed are known	137
135.	Converting knots to miles per hour (33 knots equals 38 mph)	138
136.	Important parts of the flight computer wind face	139
137.	Wind triangle as it should be visualized in this discussion	140
138.	First step in wind triangle solution—place wind direction under true index and measure up from the grommet (along center line) a length equivalent to the wind speed. Place dot at this point	141
139.	The next step in wind triangle solution—place true course under true index and adjust sliding grid so the true airspeed circle lies under the wind dot. Then read ground speed and wind correction angle	142
140.	A typical VORTAC station	148
141.	VHF transmissions follow a line-of-sight course	149
142.	Cockpit installation for a typical VOR receiver set. The vertical needle and "TO-FROM" indicator are combined into a single instrument (upper left). The course selector is the adjustable dial (bottom center)	149
143.	VOR receiver instrument indications for various positions of an airplane relative to its desired course and the VOR station	150
144.	Quadrants and courses of an LF/MF radio range. (Note: On sectional aeronautical charts, the "N" quadrants are outlined by lines along the range courses.)	152
145.	A typical air marker	154
146.	If you are lost and the airplane radio is not operating properly, fly a triangular pattern. If only the transmitter is inoperative, fly the pattern to the right (bottom). If receiver and transmitter are inoperative, fly the pattern to the left (top)	156
147.	Flight plan form	159
148.	Back of flight plan form	160

SECTION I—PRINCIPLES OF FLIGHT

1. Forces Acting on the Airplane

The airplane in straight-and-level unaccelerated flight is acted on by four forces—*lift*, the upward acting force; *weight*, or gravity, the downward acting force; *thrust*, the forward acting force; and *drag*, the backward acting, or retarding force of wind resistance. Lift opposes weight and thrust opposes drag (fig. 1). Although these four forces are acting on the airplane in any attitude of flight, only their relationship during straight-and-level flight will be discussed. (Straight-and-level flight is flight at a constant altitude and heading.)

Drag and weight are forces inherent in anything lifted from the earth and moved through the air. Thrust and lift are artificially created forces used to overcome the forces of nature and enable an airplane to fly. The engine-propeller combination is designed to produce thrust to overcome drag. The wing is designed to produce lift to overcome the weight (or gravity).

In straight-and-level, unaccelerated flight, lift equals weight and thrust equals drag. Any inequality between lift and weight will result in the airplane entering a climb or descent. Any inequality between thrust and drag while maintaining straight-and-level flight will result in acceleration or deceleration until the two forces become balanced.

Before discussing these four forces further, let us examine some of the terms used extensively in this section.

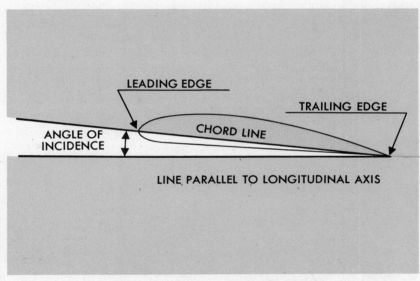

Figure 2. *Cross-sectional view of an airfoil.*

Airfoils   An airfoil is a device which gets a useful reaction from air moving over its surface. In our discussion we will consider an airfoil a device which, when moved through the air, is capable of producing lift. Wings, horizontal tail surfaces, vertical tail surfaces, and propellers are all examples of airfoils.

For convenience, we will use a cross-sectional view of a wing in our discussion. Generally the wing of the type of aircraft the private pilot will fly looks

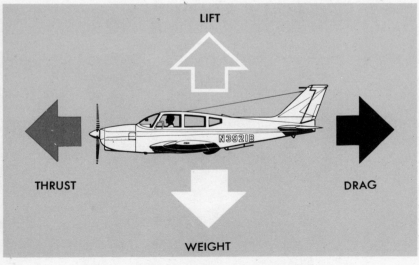

Figure 1. *Relationship of forces in flight.*

1

in cross-section like the one in figure 2. The forward part of an airfoil is rounded and is called the *leading edge*. The aft part is narrow and tapered and is called the *trailing edge*. A reference line often used in discussing airfoils is the *chord,* an imaginary straight line joining the extremities of the leading and trailing edges.

Angle of Incidence   The angle of incidence is the angle formed by the *longitudinal axis* of the airplane and the chord of the wing. The longitudinal axis is an imaginary line that extends lengthwise through the fuselage from nose to tail. The angle of incidence is measured by the angle at which the wing is attached to the fuselage. The angle of incidence is fixed—it cannot be changed by the pilot.

Relative Wind   The relative wind is the direction of the air flow with respect to the wing. If a wing is moving forward and downward, the relative wind moves backward and upward (fig. 3). If a wing is moving forward horizontally, the relative wind moves backward horizontally. If a wing is moving forward and upward, the relative wind moves backward and downward. Thus, the flight path and relative wind are parallel but travel in opposite directions.

Relative wind is created by the motion of the airplane through the air. It is also created by the motion of air past a stationary body. An airplane parked on the ramp with a mass of air (the wind) flowing over its surfaces is subject to relative wind.

Relative wind can likewise be created by a combination of the motions of the body and the air. An airplane on the takeoff roll is subject to the relative wind created by its motion along the ground and also by the moving mass of air (the wind). For this reason, takeoffs should be made into the wind.

It is important, however, to remember that during flight *only the motion of the airplane produces a relative wind—the direction and speed of the wind have no effect on the relative wind.* Wind direction and speed only affect the movement of the airplane over the ground. During flight, the actual flight path of the airplane determines the direction of the relative wind, the relative wind flowing parallel and opposite the flight path.

Angle of Attack   The angle of attack is the angle between the wing chord line and the direction of the relative wind (or between the chord line and the flight path) (fig. 4). The angle of attack should not be confused with the angle of incidence. The angle of incidence is determined when the airfoil is designed and is that specific angle of attack at which the ratio between lift and drag is the highest. For example, if the angle of incidence is 2°, the wing would be mounted on the fuselage so that the angle between the longitudinal axis of the airplane and the chord line of the airfoil is 2°.

Remember, the angle of incidence is fixed but the angle of attack may be changed by the pilot and is based on the flight path (fig. 5).

Bernoulli's Principle   To understand how lift is produced, we must examine a phenomenon discovered many years ago by the scientist Bernoulli and

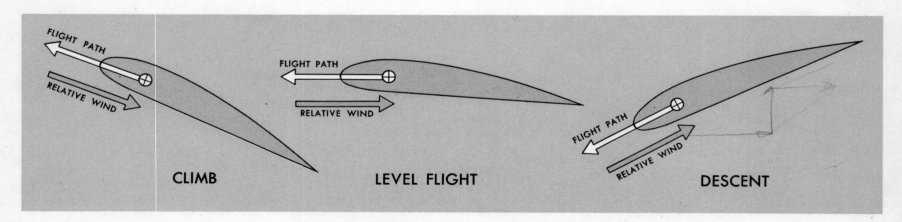

Figure 3. *Relationship between flight path and relative wind.*

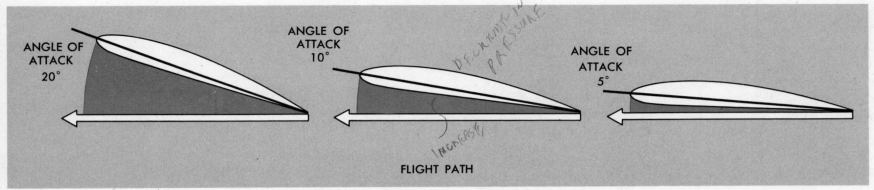

Figure 4. *The angle of attack is the angle between the chord and the flight path.*

later called Bernoulli's Principle: *The pressure of a fluid (liquid or gas) decreases at points where the speed of the fluid increases.* In other words, Bernoulli found that within the same fluid, in this case air, high speed of flow is associated with low pressure, and low speed with high pressure. This principle was first used to explain changes in the pressure of fluid flowing within a pipe whose cross-sectional area varied. In the wide section of the gradually narrowing pipe, the fluid moves at low speed, producing high pressure. As the pipe narrows it must contain the same amount of fluid. In this narrow section, the fluid moves at high speed, producing low pressure. (See fig. 6.)

An important application of this phenomenon is made in giving lift to the wing of an airplane, an airfoil. The airfoil is designed to *increase the velocity of the airflow above* its surface, thereby *decreasing pressure above* the airfoil. Simultaneously, the impact of the air on the lower surface of the airfoil increases the pressure below. This combination of pressure decrease above and increase below produces lift. (See figs. 7-9.)

Lift   Probably you have held your flattened hand out of the window of a moving automobile. As you inclined your hand to the wind, the force of air pushed against it forcing your hand to rise. The airfoil (in this case, your hand) was deflecting the wind which, in turn, created an equal and opposite dynamic pressure on the lower surface of the airfoil, forcing it up and back.

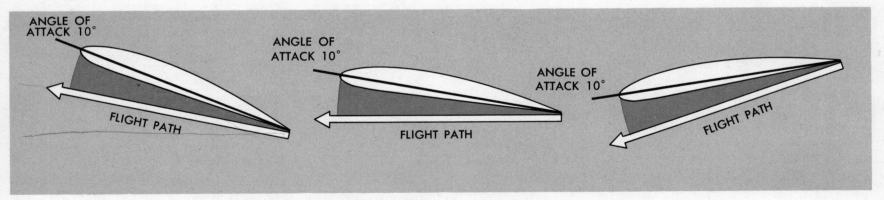

Figure 5. *The angle of attack is always based on the flight path, not the ground.*

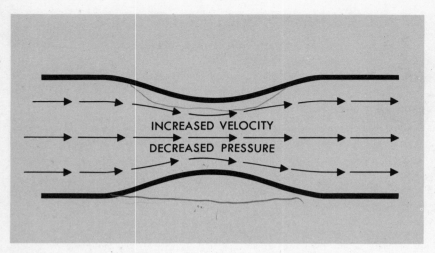

Figure 6. *Flow of air through a Venturi tube.*

The upward component of this force is lift; the backward component is drag.

Relationship Between Angle of Attack and Lift   As noted previously, the angle of attack is the acute angle formed by the relative wind and the chord line of the wing. At a zero angle of attack, the pressure below the wing would be equal to the atmospheric pressure. In this case, all of the lift would be produced by the decrease in pressure (less than atmospheric pressure) along the upper surface of the wing. At small angles of attack, the impact or positive pressure (above atmospheric pressure) below the wing would be almost negligible, most of the lift still being produced by the decreased pressure above the wing.

As the angle of attack is increased, the impact, or positive, pressure on the lower surface of the wing will increase. Also, the pressure above the wing will continue to decrease (so long as the air continues to follow the curvature of the wing) because the effective camber (curvature) of the airfoil is increased, requiring the air to travel a greater distance. According to Bernoulli's Principle, it must, therefore, travel faster, producing a greater decrease in pressure. The combination of increasing positive pressure below the wing and decreasing negative pressure above the wing results in a greater pressure differential between the lower and upper wing surfaces. This increased pressure differential results in a greater upward force, or greater lift. It also results in greater drag.

When the angle of attack increases to approximately 18° to 20° on most airfoils, the air can no longer flow smoothly over the wing's upper surface because of the excessive change of direction required. It is forced to flow straight back, away from the top surface of the wing, from the area of highest camber. This causes a swirling or burbling of the air as it attempts to follow the surface of the wing (fig. 10). The particular angle of attack at which this burbling of air begins is the *burble point*. At this point, the turbulent airflow, which has appeared near the trailing edge of the wing at lower angles of attack, suddenly spreads forward over the entire upper wing surface. This results in a sudden increase in pressure on the upper wing surface which, in turn causes a sudden and large loss of lift with a sudden increase in resistance (drag).

Relationship of Thrust and Drag in Straight-and-Level Flight   During straight-and-level flight at a constant airspeed, thrust and drag are equal in magnitude. When the thrust output of the propeller is increased, thrust momentarily exceeds drag and the airspeed will increase (provided straight-and-level flight is maintained). However, the increase in airspeed will also cause an increase in drag. At some new and higher air-speed, thrust and drag forces again become equalized, and speed again becomes constant.

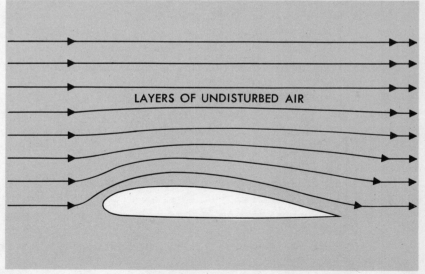

Figure 7. *Curvature of airfoil and layers of undisturbed air act as the constriction in a Venturi tube.*

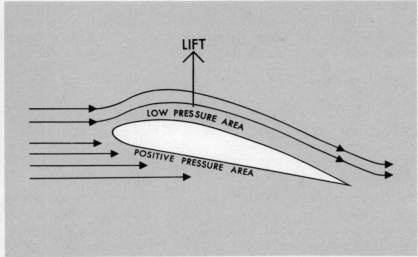

Figure 8. *Difference in pressure between upper and lower wing surfaces produces lift.*

At some point, the thrust output will reach its maximum. The airspeed will increase accordingly until drag equals thrust, when a constant airspeed will prevail. This will be the top speed for that airplane in that configuration and attitude.

When thrust becomes less than drag, the airplane decelerates to a slower airspeed (provided straight-and-level flight is maintained), where the two forces again become equal. Of course, if the airspeed becomes too slow, the airplane will stall. With an increase in airspeed, drag increases very rapidly —as the square of the airspeed. If we double the airspeed, we have four times as much drag.

Relationship of Lift and Gravity in Straight-and-Level Flight Lift, the upward force on the wing, always acts perpendicular to the direction of the relative wind. In straight-and-level flight, lift counteracts the airplane weight. When lift is in equilibrium with weight, the airplane neither gains nor loses altitude. If lift becomes less than weight, the airplane will enter a descent; if lift becomes greater than weight, the airplane will enter a climb. (Once a steady state climb or descent is established, the relationship of the four forces will no longer be as depicted in figure 1. However, for all practical purposes, lift still equals weight for small angles of climb or descent.)

Factors Affecting Lift and Drag

A number of factors influence lift and drag—wing area, shape of the airfoil, angle of attack, velocity of the air passing over the wing (airspeed), and density of the air moving over the wing. A change in any of these affects lift and drag, and the relationship between lift and drag. Each means of increasing lift also causes drag to increase.

Effect of Wing Area on Lift and Drag The lift and drag acting on a wing are roughly proportional to the wing area. This means that if the wing area is doubled, other variables remaining the same, the lift and drag created by the wing will be doubled. The only way the pilot can change the wing area is by use of certain types of flaps, such as the Fowler flap, which extends backward as well as downward, increasing the wing area.

Effect of Airfoil Shape on Lift and Drag As the upper curvature, or camber, of an airfoil is increased (up to a certain point), the lift produced by the airfoil increases. High lift wings have a large curvature on the upper surface and a concave lower surface. Wing flaps cause an ordinary wing to approximate this condition by increasing the curvature (camber) of the upper surface and creating a concave lower surface, thus increasing lift on the wing (fig. 11). A lowered aileron accomplishes this by increasing the curvature of a portion of the wing. Of course, drag also increases. The raised aileron reduces the lift on the wing by decreasing the curvature of a portion of the wing. The elevators can change the curvature of the horizontal tail surfaces,

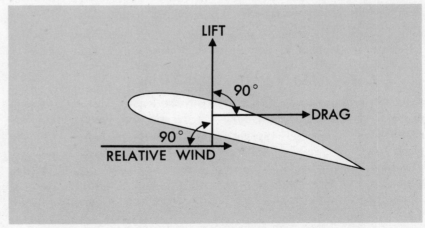

Figure 9. *Relationship between relative wind, lift and drag.*

5

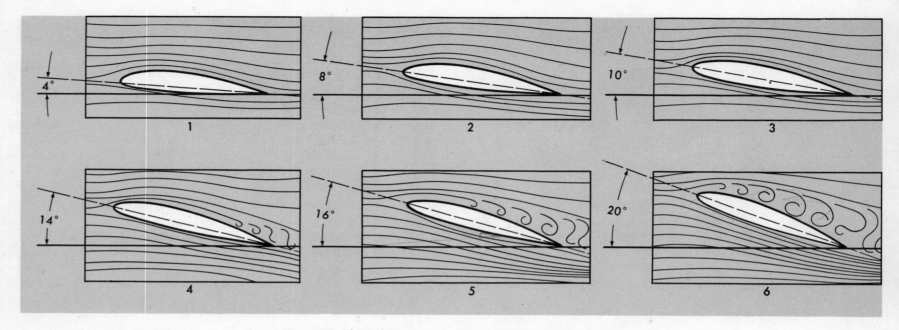

Figure 10. *Flow of air over a wing at various angles of attack.*

changing the amount and direction of lift. The rudder accomplishes the same thing for the vertical tail surfaces.

If ice forms on the wing, the shape of the airfoil is altered. Many people believe that the weight of ice forming on an airplane wing at high altitudes or in cold weather makes icing a flying hazard. This increased weight is only a small part of the danger of icing.

As the ice forms on the airfoil, especially the leading edge, the airflow is disrupted. The ice changes the camber of the wing and destroys the airfoil shape, designed to give the airplane its greatest efficiency (highest lift to drag ratio).

Even the slightest coating of frost on a wing can prevent an airplane from taking off. The smooth flow of air over the surface of the airfoil is disrupted and the lift capability of the wing is destroyed. This is why it is extremely important that *all frost, snow, and ice be removed from the airplane before takeoff.*

Effect of Angle of Attack on Lift and Drag   The effects of the angle of attack on lift have already been discussed. As the angle of attack is increased, both the lift and drag are increased, up to a certain point (fig. 12).

Effect of Airspeed on Lift and Drag   An increase in the velocity of the air passing over the wing (airspeed) increases lift and drag. Lift is increased because (1) the impact of the increased relative wind on the lower surface of the wing creates a higher or greater positive pressure; (2) the increased speed of the relative wind over the upper surface means a lowered pressure there (Bernoulli's Principle); and (3) a greater pressure differential between the upper and lower wing surfaces is created. Drag is increased, since any change that increases lift also increases drag.

Tests show that lift and drag vary as the square of the velocity. The velocity of the air passing over the wing in flight is determined by the airspeed of the airplane. This means that if an airplane doubles its speed, it quadruples the lift and drag (assuming that the angle of attack remains the same).

LOAD HIGH VENTURI TUBE
HIGH
↓ PRESS

Effect of Air Density on Lift and Drag Lift and drag vary directly with the density of the air—as the air density increases, lift and drag increase; as the air density decreases, lift and drag decrease. Air density is affected by several factors: Pressure, temperature, and humidity. (See Exam-O-Gram No. 11, appendix I.) At an altitude of 18,000 feet the density of the air is half that at sea level. Therefore, if an airplane is to maintain its lift, the velocity of the air over the wings (airspeed) must be increased or the angle of attack must be increased. This is why an airplane requires a longer takeoff distance at higher altitudes than under the same conditions at the lower altitudes (fig. 13).

Because air expands when heated, warm air is less dense than cool air. When other conditions remain the same, an airplane will require a longer takeoff run on a hot day than a cool day (fig. 13).

Because water vapor weighs less than an equal amount of dry air, moist air (high relative humidity) is less dense than dry air (low relative humidity). Therefore, when other conditions remain the same, the airplane will require a longer takeoff run on a humid day than on a dry day (fig. 13). This is especially true on a hot, humid day because then the air can hold much more water vapor than on a cool day. The more moisture in the air, the less dense the air.

DRY COLD AT SAME LEVEL

Less dense air also produces other losses beside the loss of lift. Engine horse-

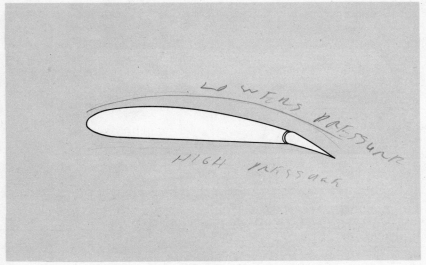

LOWERS PRESSURE

HIGH PRESSURE

Figure 11. *Use of flaps increases lift and drag.*

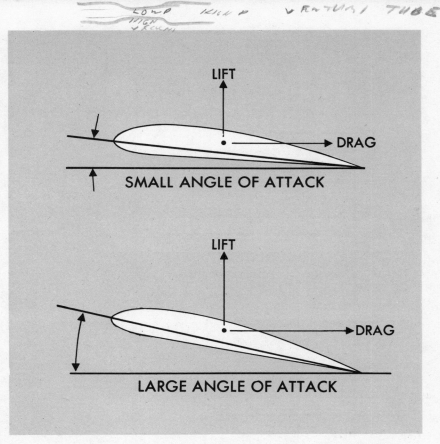

Figure 12. *Lift and drag increase with an increase in angle of attack.*

power falls off. The propeller loses some of its efficiency, because of power loss and because blades, being airfoils, will not take as much bite out of the less dense air. Since the propeller is not pulling at maximum force, it takes longer to obtain the necessary forward speed to produce the required lift—thus, a longer takeoff run.

From the above discussion, it is obvious that *a pilot should beware of high, hot, and humid conditions*—high altitudes, hot temperatures, and high moisture content (high relative humidity). A combination of these three conditions could be disastrous (fig. 13), especially when combined with a short runway.

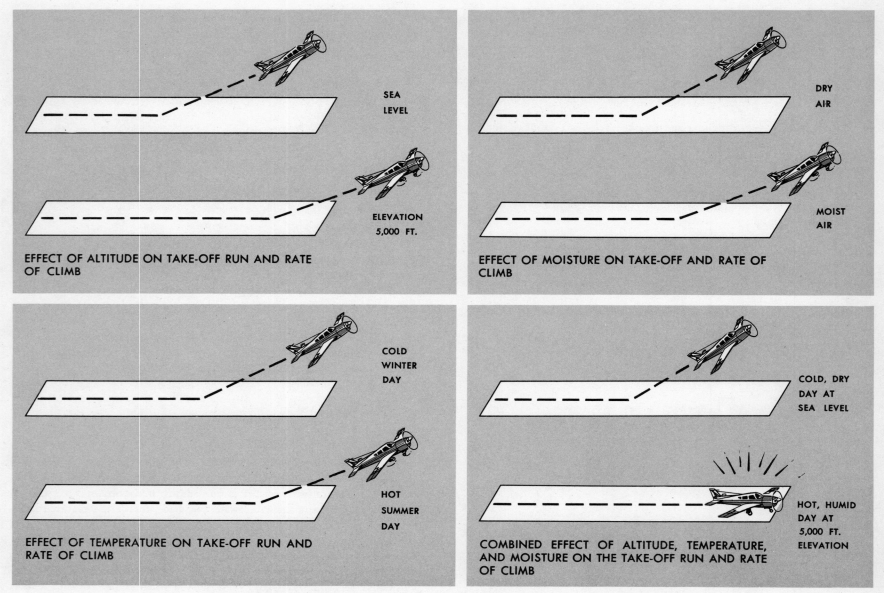

SEA LEVEL

ELEVATION 5,000 FT.

EFFECT OF ALTITUDE ON TAKE-OFF RUN AND RATE OF CLIMB

DRY AIR

MOIST AIR

EFFECT OF MOISTURE ON TAKE-OFF AND RATE OF CLIMB

COLD WINTER DAY

HOT SUMMER DAY

EFFECT OF TEMPERATURE ON TAKE-OFF RUN AND RATE OF CLIMB

COLD, DRY DAY AT SEA LEVEL

HOT, HUMID DAY AT 5,000 FT. ELEVATION

COMBINED EFFECT OF ALTITUDE, TEMPERATURE, AND MOISTURE ON THE TAKE-OFF RUN AND RATE OF CLIMB

Figure 13. *Effect of altitude, temperature, and humidity on takeoff run and rate of climb.*

2. Function of the Controls

Axes of an Airplane in Flight   The airplane may turn about three axes. Whenever the attitude of the airplane changes in flight (with respect to the ground or other fixed object), it will rotate about one or more of these axes.

Think of these axes as imaginary axles around which the airplane turns like a wheel. The three axes intersect at the center of gravity and each one is perpendicular to the other two (fig. 14).

Longitudinal Axis   The imaginary line that extends lengthwise through the fuselage, from nose to tail, is the *longitudinal axis*. Motion about the longitudinal axis is *roll* and is produced by movement of the ailerons located at the trailing edges of the wings.

Lateral Axis   The imaginary line which extends crosswise, wing tip to wing tip, is the *lateral axis*. Motion about the lateral axis is *pitch* and is produced by movement of the elevators at the rear of the horizontal tail assembly.

Vertical Axis   The imaginary line which passes vertically through the center of gravity is the *vertical axis*. Motion about the vertical axis is *yaw* and is produced by movement of the rudder located at the rear of the vertical tail assembly.

Control Surfaces

Figure 15 shows the conventional arrangement of the cockpit controls and the airplane surfaces which respond to these controls.

Ailerons   The two ailerons, one at the outer trailing edge of each wing, are movable surfaces that control movement about the longitudinal axis. The movement is *roll*. Lowering the aileron on one wing raises the aileron on the other. The wing with the lowered aileron goes up because of its increased lift, and the wing with the raised aileron goes down because of its decreased lift (fig. 16). Thus, the effect of moving either aileron is aided by the simultaneous and opposite movement of the aileron on the other wing.

Rods or cables connect the ailerons to each other and to the control wheel (or stick) in the cockpit. When pressure is applied to the right on the control wheel, the left aileron goes down and the right aileron goes up, rolling the airplane to the right. This happens because the down movement of the left aileron increases the wing camber (curvature) and thus increases the angle of attack. The right aileron moves upward and decreases the camber, resulting in a decreased angle of attack. Thus, decreased lift on the right wing and increased lift on the left wing cause a roll and bank to the right.

Elevators   The elevators control the movement of the airplane about its *lateral* axis. This motion is *pitch*. The elevators form the rear part of the horizontal tail assembly and are free to swing up and down. They are hinged to a fixed surface—the horizontal stabilizer. Together, the horizontal stabilizer and the elevators form a single airfoil. A change in position of the elevators modifies the camber of the airfoil, which increases or decreases lift.

Like the ailerons, the elevators are connected to the control wheel (or stick) by control cables. When forward pressure is applied on the wheel, the elevators move downward. This increases the lift produced by the horizontal tail

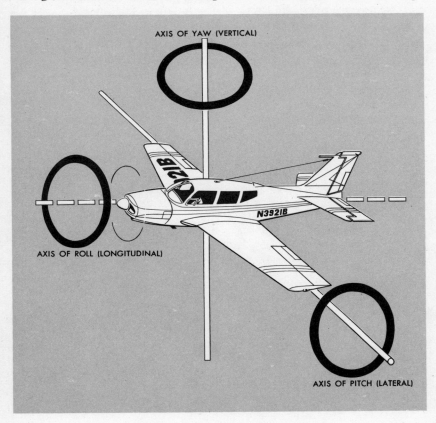

AXIS OF YAW (VERTICAL)

AXIS OF ROLL (LONGITUDINAL)

AXIS OF PITCH (LATERAL)

Figure 14. *Axes of rotation.*

surfaces. The increased lift forces the tail upward, causing the nose to drop (fig. 17). Conversely, when back pressure is applied on the wheel, the elevators move upward, decreasing the lift produced by the horizontal tail surfaces, or maybe even producing a downward force. The tail is forced downward and the nose up.

The elevators control the angle of attack of the wings. When back pressure is applied on the control wheel, the tail lowers and the nose raises, increasing the angle of attack. Conversely, when forward pressure is applied, the tail raises and the nose lowers, decreasing the angle of attack.

Rudder   The rudder controls movement of the airplane about its vertical axis. This motion is *yaw*. Like the other primary control surfaces, the rudder is a movable surface hinged to a fixed surface which, in this case, is the vertical stabilizer, or fin. Its action is very much like that of the elevators, except that it swings in a different plane—from side to side instead of up and down (fig. 19). Control cables connect the rudder to the rudder pedals.

Trim Tabs   A trim tab is a small, adjustable hinged surface on the trailing edge of the aileron, rudder, or elevator control surfaces. Trim tabs are laborsaving devices that enable the pilot to relieve pressure on the controls.

Some airplanes have trim tabs on all three control surfaces that are adjustable from the cockpit; others have them only on the elevator and rudder; and some have them only on the elevator. Some trim tabs are the ground-adjustable type only.

The tab is moved in the direction opposite that of the primary control surface, to relieve pressure on the control wheel (or rudder). For example, consider the situation in which we wish to adjust the elevator trim for level flight. ("Level flight" is the attitude of the airplane that will maintain a constant altitude.) Assume that back pressure is required on the control wheel to maintain level flight and that we wish to adjust the elevator trim tab to relieve this pressure. Since we are holding back pressure, the elevator will be in the "up" position (fig. 20). The trim tab must then be adjusted downward so that the airflow striking the tab will hold the elevators in the desired position. Conversely, if forward pressure is being held, the elevators will be in the down position, so the tab must be moved upward to relieve this pressure. In this example, we are talking about the tab itself and not the cockpit control.

Rudder and aileron trim tabs operate on the same principle as the elevator trim tab to relieve pressure on the rudder pedals and sideward pressure on the control wheel, respectively.

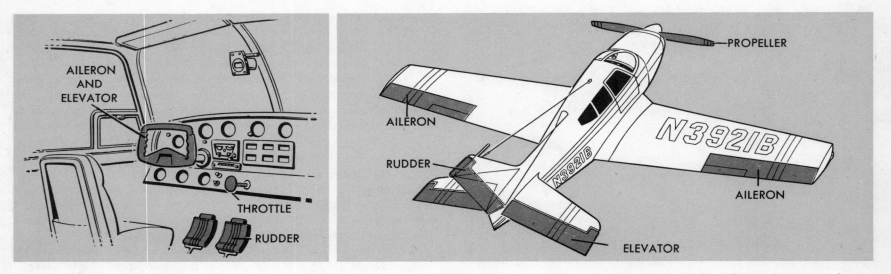

Figure 15. *Conventional arrangement of controls (red) is shown at left. The airplane surfaces that respond to the controls (red) are shown at right.*

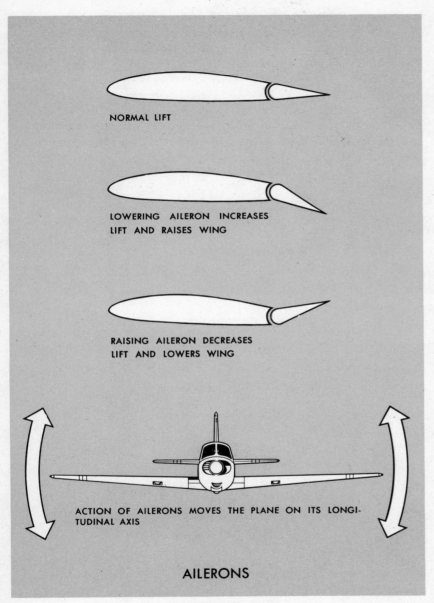

NORMAL LIFT

LOWERING AILERON INCREASES LIFT AND RAISES WING

RAISING AILERON DECREASES LIFT AND LOWERS WING

ACTION OF AILERONS MOVES THE PLANE ON ITS LONGITUDINAL AXIS

AILERONS

Figure 16. *Effect of ailerons.*

3. Loads and Load Factors

Airplane strength is measured basically by the total load the wings are capable of carrying without permanent damage. The load imposed upon the wings depends very largely upon the type of flight. The wings must support not only the weight of the airplane but also the additional loads imposed during maneuvers.

In straight-and-level flight the wings support a weight equal to the airplane and its contents. So long as the airplane is moving at a constant airspeed in a straight line, the load on the wings remains constant. When the airplane assumes a curved flight path—all types of turns, pullouts from dives, and abrupt or excessive back pressure on the elevator control—the actual load on the wings will be much greater because of the centrifugal force produced by the curved flight. This additional load results in the development of much greater stresses in the wing structure.

Load Factor The *load factor* is the actual load on the wings at any time, divided by the normal or basic load (weight of the airplane). A turn is produced by lift pulling the airplane from its straight course while overcoming gravity. Thus, the wings must produce lift equal to the weight of the airplane plus the centrifugal force caused by the turn. The increased lift is normally obtained by increasing the angle of attack (i.e., increasing back pressure on the control wheel). As the bank steepens, this back pressure on the wheel increases, and centrifugal force builds up. Therefore, any time the airplane flies in a curved flight path, the load supported by the wings is greater than the weight of the airplane. The load factor increases. (See fig. 18.)

Each airplane has a maximum permissible load factor (limit load factor) which should not be exceeded. As a pilot, you should have the basic information necessary to fly your airplane safely within its structural limitations. Be familiar with the situations in which the load factor may approach maximum, and avoid them. If you meet such situations inadvertently—in dives and steep descending spirals—you must know the right recovery technique.

One indication the pilot will have of a load increase is the feeling of increased body weight. When load on the wings increases, the effective weight of the pilot also increases. In fact, if you were to sit on a bathroom scale during flight, you would find that although registering your exact weight in straight-and-level flight, the scale would show double your weight in a 60° bank (figs. 18 and 21). This added weight can easily be sensed and is a fairly reliable guide to indicate increases up to twice the normal load. As the load

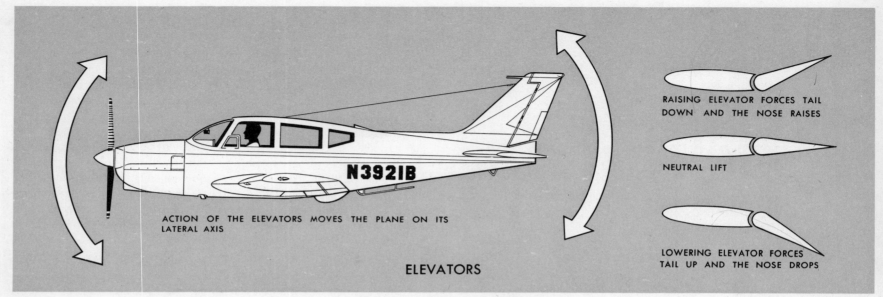

RAISING ELEVATOR FORCES TAIL DOWN AND THE NOSE RAISES

NEUTRAL LIFT

LOWERING ELEVATOR FORCES TAIL UP AND THE NOSE DROPS

ACTION OF THE ELEVATORS MOVES THE PLANE ON ITS LATERAL AXIS

ELEVATORS

Figure 17. *Effect of elevators.*

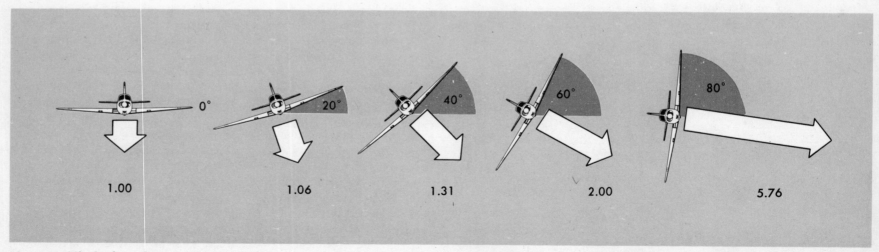

0°   20°   40°   60°   80°

1.00   1.06   1.31   2.00   5.76

Figure 18. *The load on the wings increases when the angle of bank increases. The rate of increase is shown by the length of the white arrows. Figures below the arrows indicate the increase in terms of plane weight. For example, the load during a 60-degree bank is 2.00, twice the weight of the plane in level flight.*

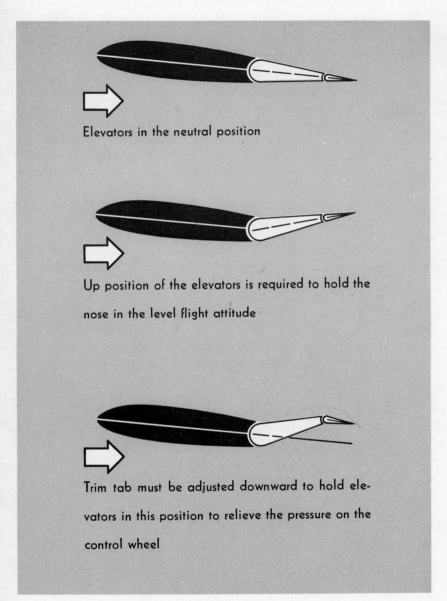

Elevators in the neutral position

Up position of the elevators is required to hold the nose in the level flight attitude

Trim tab must be adjusted downward to hold elevators in this position to relieve the pressure on the control wheel

Figure 20. *Effect of trim tabs.*

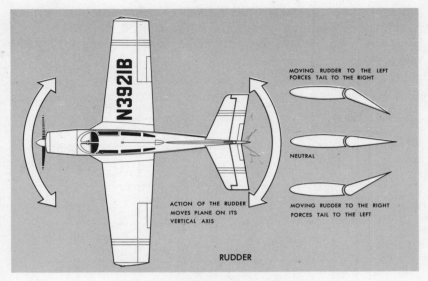

MOVING RUDDER TO THE LEFT FORCES TAIL TO THE RIGHT

NEUTRAL

ACTION OF THE RUDDER MOVES PLANE ON ITS VERTICAL AXIS

MOVING RUDDER TO THE RIGHT FORCES TAIL TO THE LEFT

RUDDER

Figure 19. *Effect of rudder*

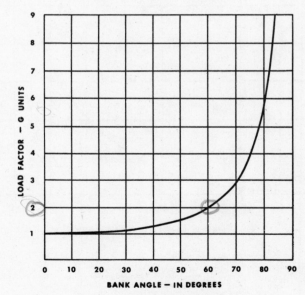

Figure 21. *Load factor chart.*

approaches three times normal, you will notice a sensation ·of blood draining from your head and a tendency of your cheeks to sag. A considerably greater increase in load may cause you to "dim out" or "black out," temporarily losing your vision.

Effect of Turbulence on Load Factors One additional cause of large load factors is severe vertical gusts. These gusts cause a sudden increase in the angle of attack, resulting in large wing loads which are resisted by the inertia of the airplane. If you encounter severe turbulence, immediately slow the airspeed to the *maneuvering speed*, or less (discussed in chapter 19), since the airplane is built to withstand such disturbance at this speed.

Effect of Speed on Load Factor The amount of excess load that can be imposed on the wing depends on how fast the airplane is flying. At slow speeds, the available lifting force of the wing is only slightly greater than the amount necessary to support the weight of the airplane. Consequently, the load factor cannot become excessive even if the controls are moved abruptly or the airplane encounters severe gusts. The reason for this is that the airplane will stall before the load can become excessive. At high speeds, the lifting capacity of the wing is so great that a sudden movement of the controls or a strong gust may increase the load factor beyond safe limits. Because of this relationship between speed and safety, certain "maximum" speeds have been established. Each airplane is restricted in the speed at which it can safely execute maneuvers, withstand abrupt application of the controls, or fly in rough air. This speed is referred to as the maneuvering speed and will be considered in our discussion of the airspeed indicator (Chapter 19).

Summarizing, at speeds below maneuvering speed, the airplane will stall before the load factor can become excessive. At speeds above maneuvering speed, the limit load factor for which an airplane is stressed can be exceeded by abrupt or excessive application of the controls or by strong turbulence.

Effect of Load Factor on Stall Speed As load factor increases, stalling speed increases. We have already stated that load factor increases when an airplane follows a curved flight path—turns, pullouts from dives or sudden or excessive application of back pressure on the control wheel. Consequently, the stalling speed also increases in these same maneuvers.

Figure 22 (and fig. 18) shows that in a 60° bank, the stall speed increases by more than 40 percent. In a 75° bank, the load factor is approximately 4 and the stall speed is doubled (increased by 100 percent).

The minimum limit load factor for normal category airplanes weighing less than 4,000 pounds is 3.8. This value is exceeded in a 75° bank. There are two reasons then why excessively steep banks should be avoided—the airplane will stall at a much higher airspeed and the limit load factor can be exceeded.

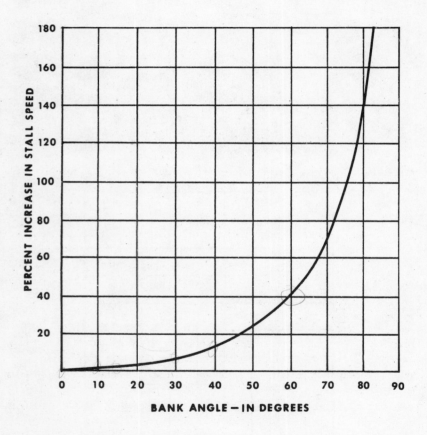

Figure 22. *Stall speed chart.*

SECTION II—WEATHER

4. Weather Information for the Pilot

What does a private pilot need to know about weather? Despite the development of many ingenious devices, improvements in aircraft design, power-plants, radio aids, and navigation techniques, safety in flight is still subject to conditions of limited visibility, turbulence, and icing.

To avoid hazardous flight conditions, private pilots must have a fundamental knowledge of the atmosphere and weather behavior.

The uninitiated may wonder why the pilot needs more than the general information available to him from the predictions of the "weather man." The answer is well known to experienced pilots. Meteorologist's predictions are based upon movements of large air masses and upon local conditions at specific points where weather stations are located. Air masses do not always perform as predicted, and weather stations are sometimes spaced rather widely apart; therefore, the pilot must understand weather conditions occurring between the stations as well as the conditions different from those indicated by the weather reports.

Moreover, the meteorologist can only predict the weather conditions; the pilot must decide whether his particular flight may be hazardous, considering his type of aircraft and equipment, his own flying ability, experience, and physical limitations.

This section is necessarily brief. It is not intended for a meterologist, but is designed to help the private pilot by giving him a general background of weather knowledge plus the following basic information:

1. Aids provided by the Weather Bureau and FAA to give the pilot weather information.
2. Sources of weather information available to the pilot.
3. Special knowledge the pilot needs in order to understand the weather terms commonly used.
4. Interpretation of weather maps, teletypewriter sequences, flying-weather forecasts, and other data.
5. Conditions of clouds, wind, and weather that are merely inconvenient, those that are dangerous, and those that the pilot can use to advantage.
6. Methods for avoiding dangerous conditions.
7. Significance of the cloud formations and precipitation the pilot encounters in flight, and safety procedures advisable.

Although no amount of information will take the place of actual experience, this discussion of weather characteristics will give the pilot practical suggestions for avoiding trouble while he is learning, and will provide a basis upon which he may build sound judgment as he gains experience.

Aids to the Pilot Throughout the United States a network of some 500 airport weather stations determine current weather and report future weather.

At most of these stations, trained personnel are on duty 24 hours a day, making observations and sending hourly reports to central points.

Because weather near the earth's surface often results from conditions at high altitudes, about 160 of the Weather Bureau's stations release and track balloons every 6 hours to determine the wind direction and speed at the upper levels. The Weather Bureau also operates approximately 70 radiosonde stations. From each station a radio transmitting device attached to a balloon ascends every 12 hours to altitudes above 10 miles, providing a complete record of temperature, pressure, and humidity at the higher levels.

Every 6 hours this information is assembled and plotted on weather maps, with other data collected by radio, telephone, and telegraph. The maps provide specific information concerning the weather all over the country and give meteorologists data for making weather predictions.

Four times daily, each flight advisory weather service center issues forecasts especially designed to indicate flying conditions anticipated for the next 12 hours; "area" forecasts for each of the 23 areas into which the United States has been divided for forecast purposes (21 in the 48 conterminous states and 1 each in Alaska and Hawaii); and "terminal" forecasts for more than 380 of the more important air terminals.

This service is available to pilots at airports and weather stations, as well as by radio broadcast. In addition, trained meteorologists are on duty day and night at more than 200 air terminals to chart and analyze weather reports and discuss weather conditions with pilots.

You should visit the Weather Bureau or FAA Flight Service Station (FSS) in person to obtain the weather information appropriate to your flight. However, as a further aid, you can get this preflight weather service by telephone. To take full advantage of the special service, use the following procedure when telephoning for weather information, because it will help the briefer serve you:

1. Identify your self as a pilot (Many callers want information for purposes other than flying.)
2. State your intended route, destination, intended time of takeoff, and approximate time enroute.
3. Advise if you intend to fly only VFR.

A number of the higher aviation activity Weather Bureau offices have available a Pilots' Automatic Telephone Weather Answering Service (PATWAS). This service provides unlisted telephone numbers (i.e. not in the local directory) over which transcribed aviation weather information can be obtained. There also are unlisted telephone numbers that will reach the Weather Bureau office directly, so that you may obtain information directly from the forecaster. These Weather Bureau restricted telephone numbers are listed in the *Airman's Information Manual* and should be used by any pilot wanting the latest weather information and forecasts.

Intelligent use of these aids, and a fundamental knowledge of weather characteristics, will enable the pilot to understand the present weather, be aware of changes likely to occur, and plan and make a safe flight.

5. Nature of the Atmosphere

We live at the bottom of an ocean of air called the atmosphere. This ocean extends upward from the earth's surface for a great many miles, gradually thinning as it nears the top. The exact upper limit has never been determined, but has been estimated to be anywhere from a few hundred miles to a few thousand miles. Near the earth's surface, the air is relatively warm from contact with the earth. (The temperature in the United States averages about 59° F. the year round.) As altitude increases, the temperature decreases by about 3½° F. for every 1,000 feet (normal lapse rate) until air temperature reaches about 67° F. below zero at 7 miles above the earth.

For flight purposes, the atmosphere is divided into two layers: the upper layer, where temperature remains practically constant, is the "stratosphere"; the

16

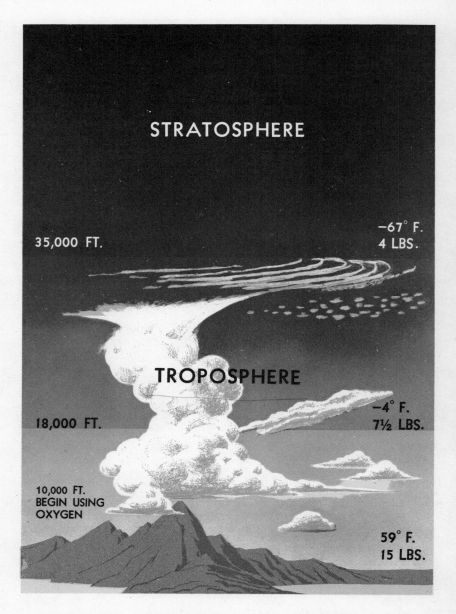

STRATOSPHERE

35,000 FT.   −67° F.
                             4 LBS.

TROPOSPHERE

18,000 FT.   −4° F.
                             7½ LBS.

10,000 FT.
BEGIN USING
OXYGEN

                             59° F.
                             15 LBS.

Figure 23. *The troposphere and stratosphere are the realm of flight.*

PRESSURE AT 5000 FEET = 25 INCHES

WHEN REDUCED TO SEA LEVEL— 25+5 = 30 INCHES

Figure 24. *Barometric pressure at a weather station is expressed as pressure at sea level.*

lower layer, where the temperature changes, is the "troposphere" (see fig. 23). The private pilot has no occasion to go as high as the stratosphere so his interest naturally centers in the lower layer—the troposphere. In this region all weather occurs and practically all our flying is done. The top of the troposphere lies 5 to 10 miles above the earth's surface.

Obviously a body of air as deep as the atmosphere has tremendous weight. It is hard to realize that the normal sea-level pressure upon our bodies is about 15 pounds per square inch, or a total of 20 tons upon the average man. The reason we don't collapse is that this pressure is equalized by an equal pressure within the body. In fact, if the pressure were suddenly released, the human body would explode like a toy balloon. As we fly upward in the atmosphere, we not only become colder (it is usually freezing above 18,000 feet) but we also find that the air is thinner. At first, pressure is rapidly reduced and at 18,000 feet is only half as great as at sea level.

Oxygen and the Human Body   The atmosphere is composed of gases— about four-fifths nitrogen and one-fifth oxygen, with approximately 1 percent of various other gases mixed in. Oxygen is essential to human life. At 18,000 feet, with only half the normal atmospheric pressure, we would be breathing only half the normal amount of oxygen. Our reactions would be definitely below normal, and many of us would become unconscious. In fact, the average person's reactions become subnormal at 10,000 feet.

To overcome these unfavorable conditions at higher altitudes, pilots who fly in this upper atmosphere use oxygen-breathing equipment and wear heavy clothes, often electrically heated; or they fly in sealed cabins in which the temperature, pressure, and oxygen content of the air can be maintained within proper range.

6. Significance of Atmospheric Pressure

In chapter 5 we mentioned that the average pressure exerted by the atmosphere is approximately 15 pounds per square inch at sea level. This means that a column of air 1 inch square extending from sea level to the top of the atmosphere would weigh about 15 pounds. The actual pressure at a given place and time, however, depends upon several factors—altitude, temperature, and density of the air column. These conditions very definitely affect flight.

Measurement of Atmospheric Pressure   How is pressure measured, recorded, and reported by the Weather Bureau? A barometer is generally used which measures the height of a column of mercury in a glass tube, sealed at one end and calibrated in inches. An increase in pressure forces the mercury higher in the tube; a decrease allows some of the mercury to drain out, reducing the height of the column. In this way, changes of pressure register in terms of inches of mercury. The standard sea-level pressure expressed in these terms is 29.92 inches at 59° F.

If all weather stations were at sea level, the barometer readings, when entered on the weather map, would give a correct record of the distribution of atmospheric pressure at a common level. To achieve this result, each station translates its barometer reading into terms of sea-level pressure. A difference of 1,000 feet of elevation makes a difference of about 1 inch in the barometer reading. Thus, if a station located 5,000 feet above sea level found the mercury to be 25 inches high in the barometer tube, it would translate and report this reading as 30 inches (fig. 24). Actually the reduction of pressure to sea level is not so simple, but in this way a uniform measurement can be established which, when entered upon the weather map, will show only the variations in pressure caused by conditions other than altitude.

Since the rate of decrease in atmospheric pressure is fairly constant in the lower layers of the atmosphere, the approximate altitude can be determined by finding the difference between pressure at sea level and pressure at the given altitude.   In fact, this is the principle upon which the airplane altimeter operates. The scale on the altimeter, instead of indicating pressure in terms of inches of mercury, indicates directly in terms of feet of altitude.

Effect of Altitude on Atmospheric Pressure   You have probably concluded that the atmospheric pressure decreases as the altitude increases. This follows from the fact that the pressure at a given point is a measure of the weight of the column of air above that point. As altitude increases, the pressure is diminished by the weight of the air column below. This decrease in pressure, (increase in density altitude) has a pronounced effect on flight.

Effect of Altitude on Flight   For ordinary flights, the most noticeable effect of a decrease in pressure (increase in density altitude) due to an altitude increase becomes evident in take-offs, rates of climb, and landings. An airplane that requires a 1,000-foot run for takeoff at a sea-level airport will require a run almost twice as long to take off at Denver, Colo., which is approximately 5,000 feet above sea level.   The purpose of the takeoff run is to gain enough speed to get lift from the passage of air over the wings. If the air is thin, more speed is required to obtain enough lift for takeoff— hence, a longer ground run. It is also true that the engine is less efficient in thin air, and the thrust of the propeller is less effective. The rate of climb, too, is much slower at Denver, requiring a greater distance to gain the alti-

FEET 250 500 750 1000 1250 1500 1750 2000 2250

SEA LEVEL

Figure 25. *Atmospheric density at sea level enables a plane to take off in a relatively short distance.*

tude to clear any obstructions. In landing, the difference is not so noticeable except that the plane has greater ground speed when it touches the ground (figs. 25 and 26).

Effect of Differences in Density   Differences in density caused by changes in temperature cause changes in pressure which, in turn, create motion in the atmosphere, producing wind, clouds, and precipitation—in fact, all the phenomena called "weather."

These items will be taken up in subsequent chapters. Meanwhile, we are ready to look at a portion of the weather map called a "station model" (fig. 27).

Here the meteorologist records the data received from weather stations, using an abbreviated form the pilot can easily interpret. We shall disregard

some of the items of little importance to the pilot; the others we shall discuss and learn to interpret in succeeding chapters.

At present, we are interested in pressure. The small circle represents the location of the station on the map. To the right, and slightly above, are three digits (203), indicating the pressure at the time of observation.

Pressure Recorded in "Millibars"   The mercury-barometer reading at the individual weather stations is converted to the equivalent sea-level pressure and then translated from terms of inches of mercury to a measure of pressure called millibars. One inch of mercury is equivalent to approximately 34 millibars; hence the normal atmospheric pressure at sea level (29.92), expressed in millibars, is 1,013.2 or roughly 1,000 millibars. For economy of space, the entry is shortened by omitting the initial 9 or 10 and the decimal point. The

19

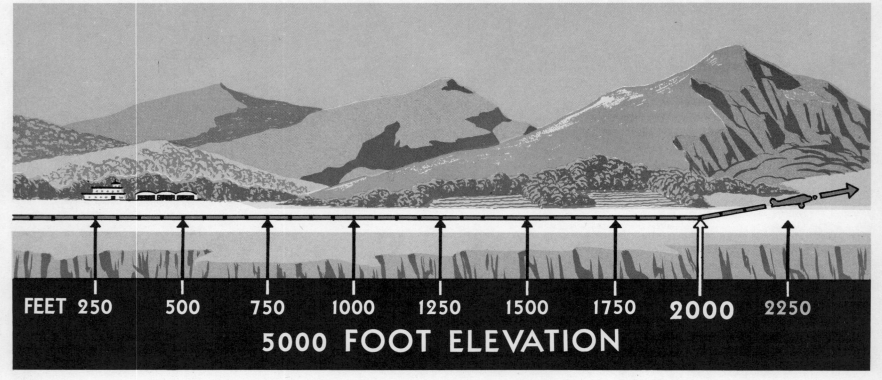

FEET 250 500 750 1000 1250 1500 1750 2000 2250

5000 FOOT ELEVATION

Figure 26. *The distance required for takeoff increases with the altitude of the field.*

usual pressure readings range from 950.0 to 1,040.0. On the station entry, a number beginning with 5 or higher presupposes an initial "9," whereas a number beginning with a 4 or lower presupposes an initial "10." For example: 653 = 965.3; 346 = 1,034.6; 999 = 999.9; 001 = 1,000.1, etc. The reading shown on the present station model is 203, which should be interpreted as 1,020.3 millibars.

Individually these pressure readings are of no particular value to the pilot; but when pressures at different stations are compared or when pressures at the same station show changes in successive readings, it is possible to determine many symptoms indicating the trend of weather conditions. In general, a marked fall indicates the approach of bad weather and a marked rise indicates a clearing of the weather.

The net amount of barometric change within the preceding 3 hours at each station is shown in tenths of millibars directly below the figures for atmospheric pressure. A plus or minus sign is used to show the direction of change. This number is followed by a symbol indicating special characteristics that are of no particular interest to the pilot.

On the present model the figure +4 means that the barometer has risen a total of 4 tenths of a millibar during the preceding 3 hours.

7. Wind

The pressure and temperature changes discussed in the previous chapter produce two kinds of motion in the atmosphere—vertical movement of

20

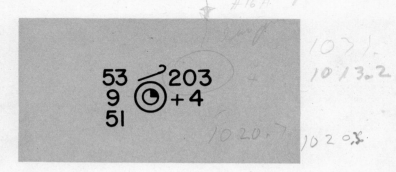

Figure 27. *Station model showing method of recording atmospheric pressure by upper-right group of three digits. The numeral 203 indicates pressure of 1020.3 millibars. Change within preceding 3 hours is shown in tenths-of-millibars immediately below.*

ascending and descending currents, and horizontal flow known as "wind." Both of these motions are of primary interest to the pilot because they affect the flight of aircraft in takeoff, landing, climbing, speed, and direction; and they also bring about changes in weather, which may make the difference between safe flight and disaster.

Conditions of wind and weather occurring at any specific place and time are the result of the general circulation in the atmosphere, which will be discussed briefly in the following pages.

The atmosphere tends to maintain an equal pressure over the entire earth, just as the ocean tends to maintain a constant level. Whenever the equilibrium is disturbed, air begins to flow from areas of higher pressure to areas of lower pressure.

The Cause of Atmospheric Circulation   The factor that upsets the normal equilibrium is the uneven heating of the earth. At the equator, the earth receives more heat than in areas to the north and south. This heat is transferred to the atmosphere, warming the air and causing it to expand and rise. Thus an area of low pressure is produced at the equator, and the heavier, cooler air from the north and south moves along the earth's surface toward the equator to equalize the pressure. This air in turn becomes warm and rises, thereby establishing a constant circulation that might consist of two

circular paths, the air rising at the equator, traveling aloft toward the poles, and returning along the earth's surface to the equator, as shown in figure 28.

This theoretical pattern, however, is greatly modified by many forces, a very important one being the rotation of the earth. In the Northern Hemisphere, this rotation causes air to flow to the right of its normal path. In the Southern Hemisphere, air flows to the left of its normal path. For simplicity we shall confine our discussion to the motion of air in the Northern Hemisphere (fig. 29).

As the air rises and moves northward from the equator, it is deflected toward the east, and by the time it has traveled about a third of the distance to the pole, it is no longer moving northward, but eastward. This causes the air to accumulate in a belt at about latitude 30°, creating an area of high pressure. Some of this air is then forced down to the earth's surface, where part flows southward, returning to the equator, and part flows northward along the surface.

A portion of the air aloft continues its journey northward, being cooled en route, and finally settles down near the pole, where it begins a return trip toward the equator. Before it has progressed very far southward, it comes

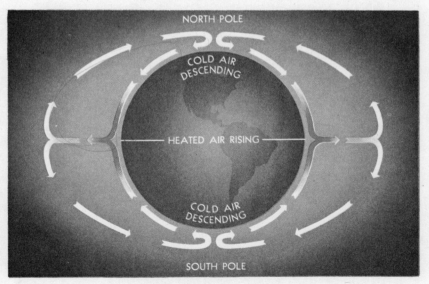

Figure 28. *Heat at the equator would cause the air to circulate uniformly, as shown, if the earth did not rotate.*

21

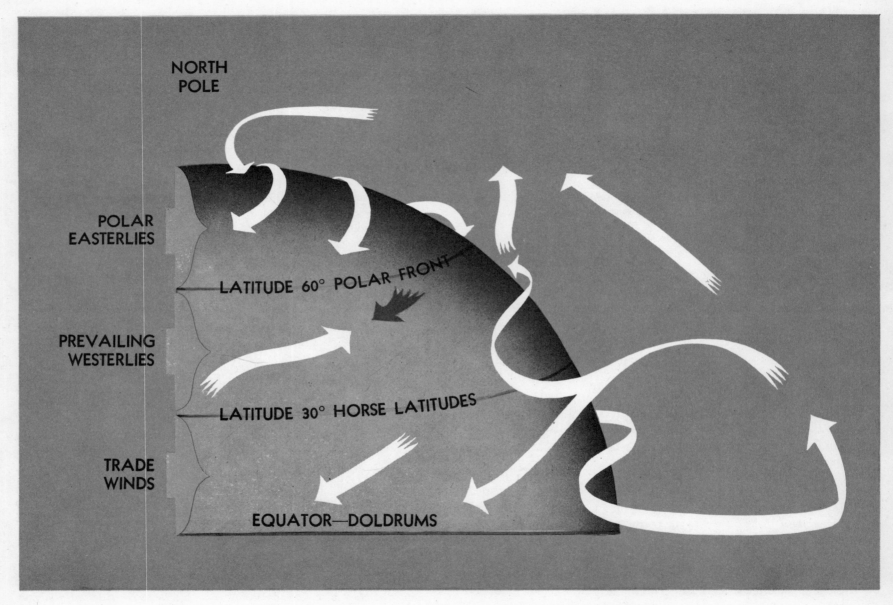

NORTH
POLE

POLAR
EASTERLIES

LATITUDE 60° POLAR FRONT

PREVAILING
WESTERLIES

LATITUDE 30° HORSE LATITUDES

TRADE
WINDS

EQUATOR—DOLDRUMS

Figure 29. *Principal air currents in the Northern Hemisphere.*

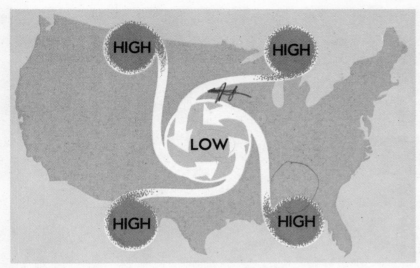

Figure 30. *Circulation of wind within a "low"*.

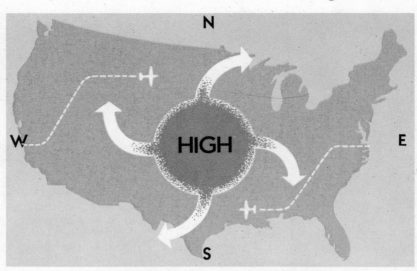

Figure 31. *Use of favorable winds in flight*.

into conflict with the warmer surface air flowing northward from latitude 30°. The warmer air moves up over a wedge of the colder air, and continues northward, producing an accumulation of air in the upper latitudes.

Further complications in the general circulation of the air are brought about by the irregular distribution of oceans and continents, the relative effectiveness of different surfaces in transferring heat to the atmosphere, the daily variation in temperature, the seasonal changes, and many other factors.

Regions of low pressure, called "lows," develop where air lies over land or water surfaces that are warmer than the surrounding areas. In India, for example, a low forms over the hot land during the summer months, but moves out over the warmer ocean when the land cools in winter. Lows of this type are semipermanent, however, and are less significant to the pilot than the "migratory cyclones" or "cyclonic depressions" that form when unlike air masses meet. These lows will be discussed in detail under "occlusions" in chapter 10.

Wind Patterns At present, we are concerned with the wind patterns associated with areas of high and low pressure. In the Northern Hemisphere, wind is deflected to the right of its course. Air moving outward from a "high" flows in a clockwise spiral, and air moving toward a low flows in a counter-

clockwise spiral. A knowledge of these patterns frequently enables a pilot to plan his course to take advantage of favorable winds, particularly during long flights. In flying from east to west, for example, he would find favorable winds to the south of a high, or to the north of a low (figs. 30 and 31).

We have now discussed the theory of general circulation in the atmosphere, and the wind patterns formed within areas of high pressure and low pressure. These concepts account for the large-scale movements of the wind, but do not take into consideration the effects of local conditions that frequently cause drastic modifications in wind direction and speed close to the earth's surface.

Convection Currents Certain kinds of surfaces are more effective than others in heating the air directly above them. Ploughed ground, sand, rocks, and barren land give off a great deal of heat, whereas water and vegetation tend to absorb and retain heat. The uneven heating of the air causes small local circulations called "convection currents," which are similar to the general circulation just described.

This is particularly noticeable over land adjacent to a body of water. During the day, the air over the land becomes heated and rises; the cooler air over the water moves in to replace it in the form of an on-shore wind. At night the land cools, and the water is relatively warmer. The cool air over the land,

WARM AIR
COOLING AND
DESCENDING

AIR HEATED
OVER LAND
AND RISING

COOLER AIR OVER
WATER MOVING
TOWARD LAND

Figure 32. *Convection currents form on-shore winds in daytime.*

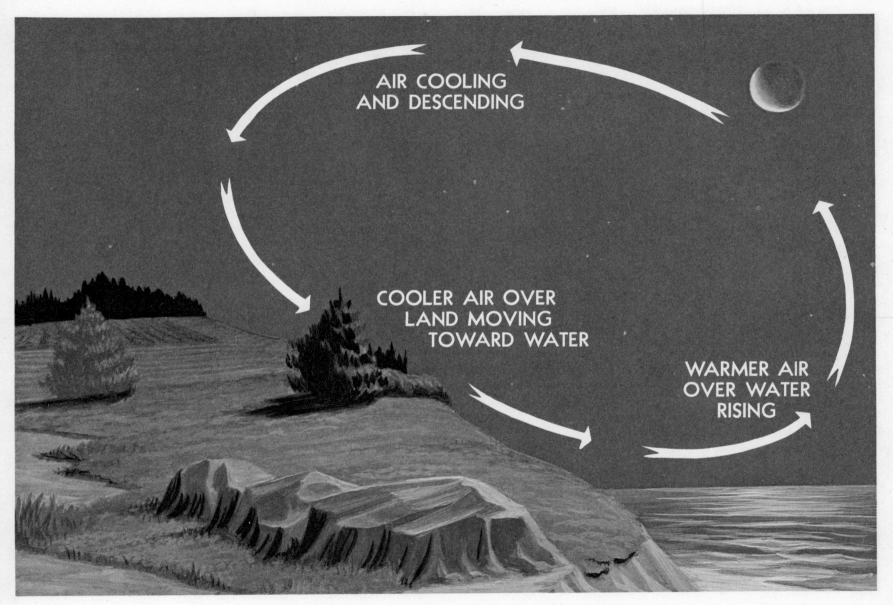

AIR COOLING
AND DESCENDING

COOLER AIR OVER
LAND MOVING
TOWARD WATER

WARMER AIR
OVER WATER
RISING

Figure 33. *Convection currents form off-shore winds at night.*

Figure 34. *Avoiding turbulence caused by convection currents by flying above the cloud level.*

being heavier, then moves toward the water as an off-shore wind, lifting the warmer air and reversing the circulation (figs. 32 and 33).

Convection currents cause the bumpiness experienced by pilots flying at low altitudes in warmer weather. On a low flight over varying surfaces, the pilot will encounter updrafts over pavement or barren places and downdrafts over vegetation or water. Ordinarily, this can be avoided by flight at higher altitudes. When the larger convection currents form cumulus clouds, the pilot will invariably find smooth air above the cloud level (fig. 34).

Convection currents also cause difficulty in making landings, since they affect the rate of descent. For example, a pilot making a constant glide frequently tends to land short of or overshoot his spot, depending upon the presence and severity of convection currents (figs. 35 and 36).

These effects of local convection, however, are less dangerous than the turbulence caused when wind is forced to flow around or over obstructions. The only way for the pilot to avoid this invisible hazard is to be forewarned, and to know where to expect unusual conditions.

Effect of Obstructions on Wind   When the wind flows around an obstruction, it breaks into eddies—gusts with sudden changes in velocity and direction—which may be carried along some distance from the obstruction. A pilot flying through such turbulence should anticipate the bumpy and unsteady flight that may be encountered. This turbulence—the intensity of which depends, of course, upon the size of the obstacle and the velocity of the wind—can present a serious hazard during takeoffs and landings. For example, during landings it can cause a pilot to "drop in"; during takeoffs it could cause the aircraft to fail to gain enough altitude to clear low objects in its path. Any landings or takeoffs attempted under gusty conditions should be made at higher speeds, to maintain adequate control during the periods of low-gust velocity (fig. 37).

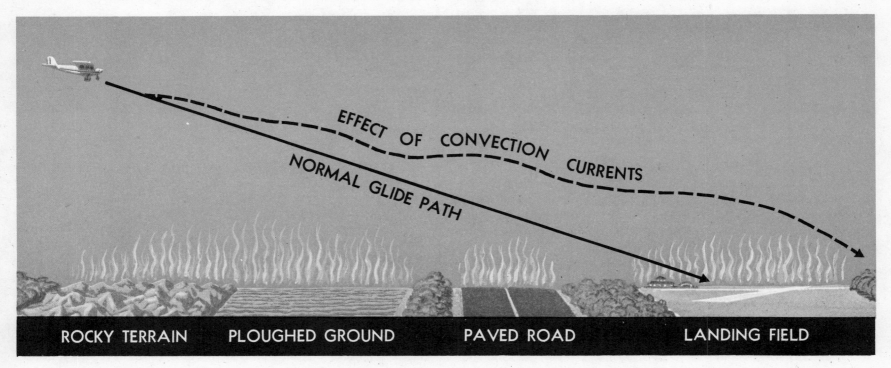

EFFECT OF CONVECTION CURRENTS

NORMAL GLIDE PATH

ROCKY TERRAIN   PLOUGHED GROUND   PAVED ROAD   LANDING FIELD

Figure 35. *Varying surfaces affect the normal glide path. Some surfaces create rising currents which tend to make the pilot overshoot the field.*

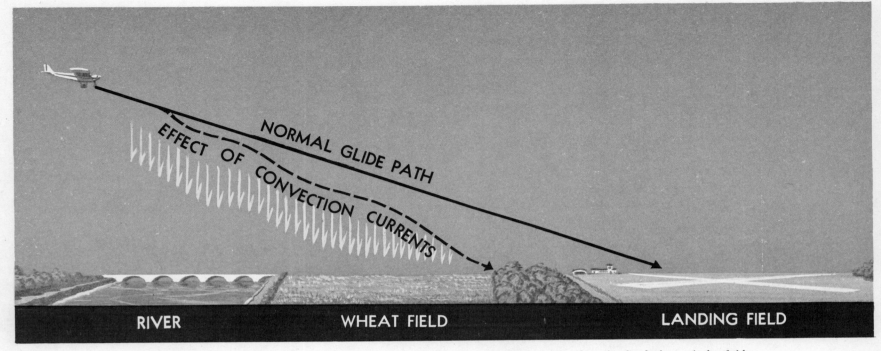

NORMAL GLIDE PATH

EFFECT OF CONVECTION CURRENTS

RIVER   WHEAT FIELD   LANDING FIELD

Figure 36. *Descending currents prevail above some surfaces and tend to make the pilot land short of the field.*

This same condition is more noticeable where larger obstructions such as bluffs or mountains are involved. As shown in figure 38, the wind blowing up the slope on the windward side is relatively smooth and its upward current helps to carry the aircraft over the peak. The wind on the leeward side, following the terrain contour, flows definitely downward with considerable turbulence and tends to force the aircraft into the mountainside. The stronger the wind, the greater the downward pressure and the accompanying turbulence. Consequently, in approaching a hill or mountain from the leeward side, a pilot should gain enough altitude well in advance. *Because of these downdrafts, it is recommended that mountain ridges and peaks be cleared by at least 2,000 feet.* If there is any doubt about having adequate clearance, the pilot should turn away at once and gain more altitude. Between hills or mountains, where there is a canyon or narrow valley, the wind will generally veer from its normal course and flow through the passage with increased velocity and

turbulence. A pilot flying over such terrain needs to be alert for wind shifts, and particularly cautious if he is making a landing.

Wind Representation on Weather Map   The weather map (fig. 39) provides information about winds at the surface. The wind direction at each station is shown by an arrow. The arrowhead is represented by the station circle and points in the direction in which the wind is blowing. Winds are given the name of the direction *from which* they blow; a northwest wind is a wind blowing *from* the northwest.

Wind force is shown by "feathers" or "flags" placed on the end of the arrow. The speed is indicated by the number of half feathers, full feathers, or flags. Each half feather represents approximately 5 knots, each full feather indicates approximately 10 knots, and each flag 50 knots. Thus 2½ feathers indicates a wind speed of approximately 25 knots; a flag and 2½ feathers in-

28

WIND

Figure 37. *Turbulence caused by obstructions to normal flow of air.*

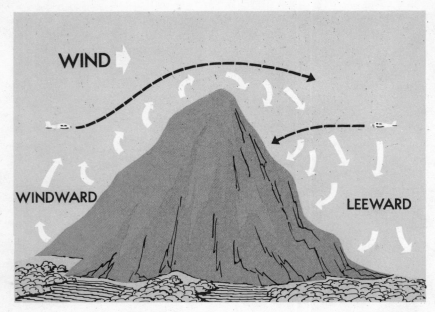

WIND

WINDWARD

LEEWARD

Figure 38. *Planes approaching hills or mountains from windward are helped by rising currents. Those approaching from leeward encounter descending currents.*

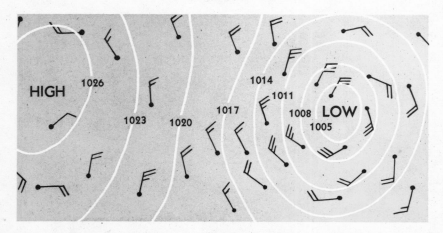

HIGH   1026

1023   1020

1017   1014

1011

1008   **LOW**

1005

Figure 39. *Speed and direction of wind are shown on weather map by wind arrows and isobars.*

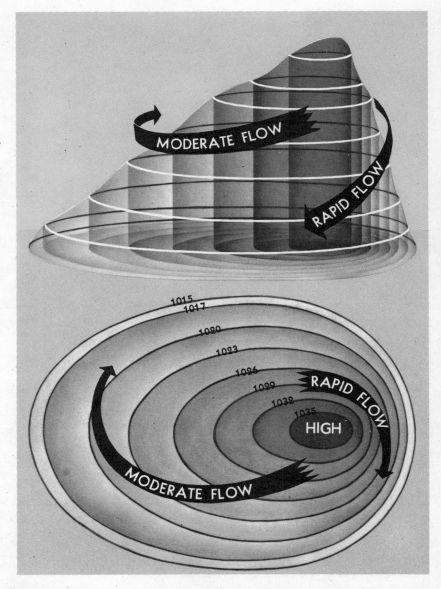

MODERATE FLOW

RAPID FLOW

1015
1017
1020
1023
1026
1029
1032
1035
RAPID FLOW
HIGH
MODERATE FLOW

Figure 40. *Above: Flow of air around a "high." Below: Isobars on a weather map indicate various degrees of pressure within a high.*

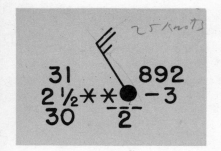
Figure 41. *Station model showing method of indicating wind direction and speed. The wind is shown to be from the northwest, with a speed of 25 knots.*

8. Moisture and Temperature

The atmosphere always contains a certain amount of foreign matter—smoke, dust, salt particles, and particularly moisture in the form of invisible water vapor. The amount of moisture that can be present in the atmosphere depends upon the temperature of the air. For each increase of 20° F. the capacity is about doubled; conversely, for each decrease of 20° F. the capacity becomes only half as much.

Relative Humidity We often speak of "the humidity," by which we mean the apparent dampness in the air. A similar term used by the Weather Bureau is *relative humidity,* a ratio of the amount of moisture present in any given volume of air to the amount of moisture possible in that volume of air at prevailing temperature and pressure. For instance, "relative humidity, 75 percent" means that the air contains three-fourths of its maximum capacity at the existing temperature.

Temperature-Dew point Relationship For the pilot, the relationship discussed under relative humidity is expressed in a slightly different way—as "temperature and dew point." It is apparent from the foregoing discussion that if a mass of air at 80° F. has a relative humidity of 50 percent and temperature is reduced 20°, to 60° F., the air will then be saturated (100 percent relative humidity). In this case, the original relationship will be stated as "temperature 80—dew point 60." In other words, dew point is the temperature to which air must be cooled to become saturated.

Dew point is of tremendous significance to the pilot because it represents a critical condition of the air. When temperature reaches the dew point, water vapor can no longer remain invisible, but is forced to condense, becoming visible on the ground as dew or frost, appearing in the air as fog or clouds, or falling to the earth as rain, snow, or hail. (NOTE: *This is how water can get into the fuel tanks when the tanks are left partially filled overnight.* The temperature cools to the dew point and the water vapor contained in the fuel tank air space condenses. This condensed moisture then sinks to the bottom of the fuel tank, since water is heavier than gasoline. This topic will be discussed in more detail later in this handbook.)

Methods by Which Air Reaches the Saturation Point It is interesting to note the various ways by which air can reach the saturation point. We have already shown how this is brought about by a lowering of temperature such as might occur under the following conditions: when warm air moves over a cold surface; when cold air mixes with warm air; when air is cooled during

dicates a wind speed of approximately 75 knots, etc. The pilot can thus tell at a glance the wind conditions prevailing at map time at any weather station.

Observations of the winds at upper levels are made every 6 hours at about 160 stations. Pilots can obtain this information and forecasts of expected winds through all weather reporting stations.

Isobars The pressure at each station is recorded on the weather map, and lines, _isobars_, are drawn to connect points of equal pressure. Many of the lines make complete circles to surround areas marked H (high) or L (low).

Isobars are quite similar to the contour lines appearing on aeronautical charts. However, instead of indicating altitude of terrain and steepness of slopes, isobars indicate the amount of pressure and steepness of pressure gradients. If the gradient (slope) is steep, the isobars will be close together, and the wind will be strong. If the gradient is gradual, the isobars will be far apart, and the wind gentle (fig. 40).

Isobars furnish valuable information about winds aloft. Close to the earth, wind direction is modified by the contours over which it passes, and wind speed is reduced by friction with the surface. At levels two or three thousand feet above the surface, however, the speed is greater and the direction is usually parallel to the isobars. Thus, while wind arrows on the weather map indicate winds near the surface, isobars indicate winds at slightly higher levels (fig. 39).

In the absence of specific information on upper wind conditions, the pilot can often make a fairly reasonable estimate of the wind conditions in the lower few thousand feet on the basis of the observed surface wind. He generally will find that the wind at an altitude of 2,000 feet above the surface will veer about 45° to the right and almost double in speed. Thus, a north wind of 20 knots at the airport would be likely to change to a northeast wind of 40 knots at 2,000 feet.

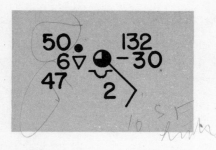

Figure 42. *Station model showing temperature and dew point. The temperature is shown to be 50° F., the dew point, 47° F.*

the night by contact with the cold ground; or when air is forced upward. Only the fourth method needs any special comment.

When air rises, it uses heat energy in expanding and pushing other air out of its path. Consequently, the rising air loses heat rapidly. If the air is unsaturated, the loss will be approximately 5½° F. for every 1,000 feet of altitude.

Air can rise for three reasons: by becoming heated through contact with the earth's surface (convection currents as discussed in chap. 7); by moving up a sloping terrain (as wind blowing up a mountainside); and by being forced to flow over another body of air (when air masses of different temperatures and densities meet). Under the last condition, the warmer, lighter air tends to flow over the cooler, denser air. This will be discussed in "Fronts," chapter 10.

Air can also become saturated if it is subjected to precipitation.

Whatever the cause, the pilot knows that when temperature and dew point at the ground are close together, he must be alert for low clouds and fog.

Station Model Temperature and dew point are indicated in degrees Fahrenheit on the station model, to the left of the center circle, temperature above and dew point below (fig. 42). (NOTE: The chart in figure 43 may be used to convert degrees Fahrenheit to degrees Centigrade, and vice versa. For example 0° C. equals 32° F.)

Effect of Temperature on Air Density Atmospheric pressure not only varies with altitude; it also varies with temperature. When air is heated, it expands and therefore has less density. A cubic foot of warm air is less dense than a cubic foot of cold air. This decrease in air density (increase in density altitude), brought about by an increase in temperature, has a pronounced effect on flight.

Effect of Temperature on Flight Since an increase in temperature makes the air less dense (increases density altitude), the takeoff run will be longer, the rate of climb slower, and the landing speed (ground speed) faster on a hot day than on a cold day. Thus, an increase in temperature has the same effect as an increase in altitude. An airplane which requires a ground run of 1,000 feet on a winter day when the temperature is 0° F. will require a much longer run on a summer day when the temperature is 100° F. An airplane which requires the greater portion of a short runway to take off on a cold winter day may be unable to make it off this runway on a hot summer day (fig. 13).

Effect of High Humidity on Air Density A common misconception of many people is that water vapor weighs more than an equal volume of dry air.

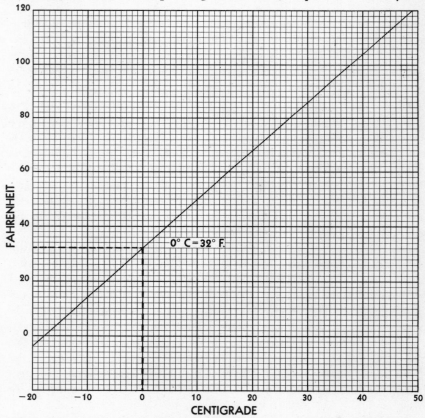

Figure 43. *A chart used for converting degrees Centigrade to degrees Fahrenheit and vice versa.*

CUMULUS

ALTOCUMULUS

CIRROCUMULUS

Figure 44. *Cumulus clouds as they appear at low, intermediate, and high levels.*

This is not true. Water vapor weighs approximately five-eighths as much as an equal volume of perfectly dry air. When the air contains moisture in the form of water vapor, it is not as heavy as dry air and so is less dense.

Assuming that temperature and pressure remain the same, the air density varies inversely with the humidity—that is, as the humidity increases, the air density decreases (density altitude increases); and, as the humidity decreases, the air density increases (density altitude decreases).

The greater the temperature, the greater the moisture-carrying ability of the air. Therefore, air at a temperature of 100° F. and a relative humidity of 80 percent will contain a greater amount of moisture than air at a temperature of 60° F. and a relative humidity of 80 percent.

Effect of High Humidity on Flight As discussed earlier, the thinner (less dense) the air, the longer the takeoff roll, the slower the rate of climb, and the higher the landing speed. Since high humidity makes the air less dense (increases density altitude), the takeoff roll will be longer, rate of climb slower, and landing speed higher (fig. 13).

Combined Effect of High Altitude, High Temperature, and High Humidity on Flight As indicated earlier in this section, each of the foregoing conditions can seriously affect flight characteristics. When all three conditions are present, the conditions are aggravated. Therefore, beware of "high, hot, and humid" conditions (high density altitudes), and take the necessary precautions (by using performance charts) to make sure the runway is long enough for a takeoff (fig. 13). (See Exam-O-Gram No. 11, appendix I.)

9. Results of Condensation

In chapter 8 we noted that when temperature and dew point are close together, the moisture in the air condenses and becomes visible in the form of fog or clouds, and that any further reduction in temperature will cause the moisture to be "squeezed out" in the form of precipitation—dew, frost, rain, snow, hail, etc.

This chapter discusses in more detail the forms of condensation. In connection with each, it is well to learn the basic symbols used by the Weather Bureau to indicate these conditions on the weather maps.

Dew and Frost When the ground cools at night, the temperature of the air immediately adjacent to the ground is frequently lowered to the saturation point, causing condensation. This condensation takes place directly upon objects on the ground as dew if the temperature is above freezing, or as frost below freezing.

Dew is of no importance for aircraft, but a frost deposit creates friction which can interfere with the smooth flow of air over the wing surfaces, preventing takeoff. Therefore, frost should always be wiped off before flight.

Fog When the air near the ground is within a few degrees of the dew point, the water vapor condenses and becomes visible as fog. There are many types of fog, varying in degree of intensity and classified according to the particular phenomena which cause them. One type, "ground fog," which frequently forms at night in low places, is limited to a few feet in height, and is usually dissipated by the heat of the sun shortly after sunrise. Other types, which can form any time conditions are favorable to them, may extend to greater heights and persist for days or even weeks. Along seacoasts, fog often forms over the ocean and is blown inland. All fogs produce low visibilities and therefore constitute a serious hazard to aircraft.

Clouds There are two fundamental types of clouds. First, those formed by vertical currents carrying moist air upward to its condensation point are lumpy or billowy and are called "cumulus" (fig. 44), which means an "accumulation" or a "pile." Second, those which develop horizontally and lie in sheets or formless layers like fog are called "stratus" (fig. 45), which means "spread out."

When clouds are near the earth's surface they are generally designated as "cumulus" or "stratus" unless they are producing precipitation, in which case the word "nimbo" (meaning "rain") is added—as "nimbostratus" or "cumulonimbus" (fig. 46).

If the clouds are ragged and broken, the word "fracto" (meaning "broken") is added—as "fractostratus" or "fractocumulus."

The word "alto" (meaning "high") is generally added to designate clouds at intermediate heights, usually appearing at levels of 5,000 to 20,000 feet—as "altostratus" or "altocumulus."

Clouds formed in the upper levels of the troposphere (commonly between 20,000 and 50,000 feet altitude) are composed of ice crystals and generally have a delicate, curly appearance, somewhat similar to frost on a window pane. For these clouds the word "cirro" (meaning "curly") is added—as "cirrocumulus" or "cirrostratus." At these high altitudes there is also a fibrous type of cloud appearing as curly wisps, bearing the single name "cirrus."

Figure 45. *Stratus-type clouds at various altitudes.*

STRATOCUMULUS   NIMBOSTRATUS   CUMULONIMBUS   FRACTOCUMULUS

Figure 46. *Various types of bad weather clouds.*

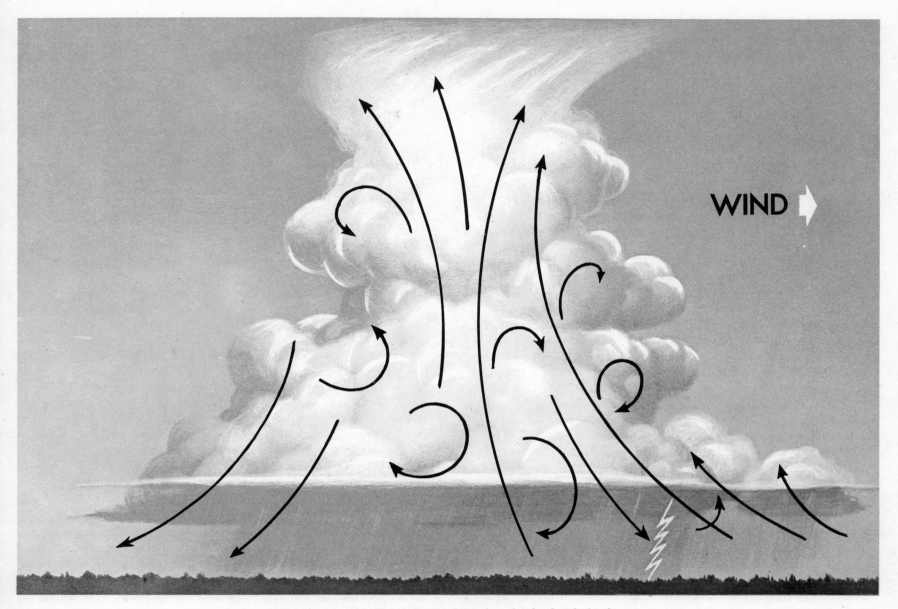

WIND

Figure 47. *Cross-section of a cumulonimbus cloud (thunderhead).*

In chapter 10 the relationship will be shown between the various types of clouds and the kind of weather expected. At present we are chiefly concerned with the flying conditions directly associated with the different cloud formations.

The ice-crystal clouds (cirrus group) are well above ordinary flight levels, and do not concern the pilot except as indications of approaching changes in weather.

The clouds in the "alto" group are not normally encountered in flights of smaller planes, but they sometimes contain icing conditions important for commercial and military planes. Altostratus clouds usually indicate that unfavorable flying weather is near.

The low clouds are of great importance to the pilot because they create low ceilings and low visibilities. They change rapidly, and frequently drop to the ground, forming a complete blanket over landmarks and landing fields. In temperatures near freezing, they are a constant threat because of the probability of icing. The pilot should be constantly alert to any changes in conditions, and be prepared to land before his visibility is suddenly obscured.

Cumulus clouds vary in size from light "scud" or fluffy powder puffs to towering masses rising thousands of feet in the sky. Usually they are somewhat scattered, and the pilot can fly around them without difficulty. Under some conditions, however, particularly in the late afternoon, they are likely to multiply, flatten out, and close in. That leaves the pilot with no alternatives except to reverse his course or find a safe landing field before the clouds close in completely or high winds, squalls, and rain or hail begin.

Cumulonimbus clouds (thunderheads) are very dangerous. When they appear individually or in small groups, they are usually of the type called "air-mass thunderstorms" (caused by heating of the air at the earth's surface) or "orographical thunderstorms" (caused by the upslope motion of air in mountainous regions). On the other hand, when these clouds take the form of a continuous or almost continuous line, they are usually caused by a "front," in which case they are called "frontal thunderstorms." These lines of thunderstorms are often referred to as "squall lines."

Since the cumulonimbus clouds are formed by rising air currents, they are extremely turbulent; moreover, it is possible for an airplane flying near by to be sucked into the cloud. Once inside, it may encounter updrafts and downdrafts with velocities as great as 3,000 feet per minute. Airplanes have been torn apart by the violence of these currents. In addition, the clouds frequently contain large hailstones capable of severely damaging aircraft, lightning, and

great quantities of water at temperatures conducive to heavy icing. Many "unexplained" crashes have probably been caused by the disabling effect of cumulonimbus clouds upon airplanes which have been accidentally or intentionally flown into them. The only practical procedure for a pilot caught within a thunderstorm is to reduce airspeed. This lessens the strain on the aircraft structure, just as slow driving over rough roads lessens the strain on an automobile. A safe speed for an airplane flying through turbulence is an airspeed not greater than the maneuvering speed for the particular airplane (to be discussed in chap. 19).

Figure 47 shows the important characteristics of a typical cumulonimbus cloud. The top of the cloud flattens into an anvil shape, which points in the direction the cloud is moving, generally with the prevailing wind. Near the base, however, the winds blow directly toward the cloud and increase in speed, becoming violent updrafts as they reach the low rolls at the forward edge.

Within the cloud and directly beneath it are updrafts and downdrafts; in the rear portion is a strong downdraft which becomes a wind blowing away from the cloud.

The cloud itself is a storm factory. The updrafts lift the moist air quickly to its saturation point, whereupon it condenses and raindrops begin to fall. Before these have reached the bottom of the cloud, updrafts pick them up and carry them aloft, where they may freeze and again start downward, only to repeat the process many times until they have become heavy enough to break through the updrafts and reach the ground as hail or very large raindrops. As the storm develops, more and more drops fall through the turbulence, until the rain becomes fairly steady. The lightning that accompanies such a storm is probably due to the break-up of raindrops, which produces static electricity that discharges spasmodically as lightning. The lightning causes a sudden expansion of the air in its path, which produces thunder.

It is impossible for a small plane to fly over these clouds (they frequently extend to 50,000 feet). Usually they are too low to fly under. When they are close together the clear space between them is an area of violent turbulence. If the clouds are isolated, indicating local thunderstorms, it usually is possible to fly around them; but they should be given a wide berth since they travel rapidly. If, however, they are "frontal" storms, they may extend for hundreds of miles, and the only safe procedure is to land immediately and wait until the cumulonimbus cloud formation has passed over.

The proportion of sky covered by clouds (sky cover) is shown on the weather map by the extent to which the station circle is filled in (fig. 48).

SKY COVER	NO CLOUDS	1/10 or Less	2/10 or 3/10	4/10	5/10	6/10	7/10 or 8/10	9/10 or overcast with openings	COMPLETELY COVERED	SKY OBSCURED
SYMBOL	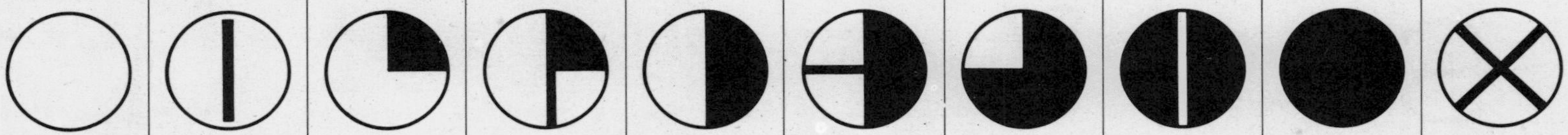									
CODE	0	1	2	3	4	5	6	7	8	9
TERM	CLEAR	SCATTERED				BROKEN			OVERCAST	DUST-STORM, HAZE, SMOKE, ETC.

Figure 48. *Weather map symbols used to indicate sky cover.*

Ceiling The height above ground of the lowest layer of clouds reported as broken or overcast and not classified as "thin" is the ceiling. Clouds are reported as broken when they cover six-tenths to nine-tenths of the sky and as overcast when they cover more than nine-tenths. The ceiling is *unlimited* if the sky is cloudless or less than six-tenths covered as seen from the ground. Height of the lowest cloud layer is shown by a code figure directly below the station circle. Pilots should obtain the latest information on ceilings from the hourly sequence reports. Forecasts of expected changes in ceilings and other conditions also are available at weather stations.

Visibility Closely related to ceiling and cloud cover is "visibility"—the greatest horizontal distance at which prominent objects can be distinguished with the naked eye. Visibility is plotted at the left of the station circle, between the temperature and dew point. On the printed Daily Weather Map, often used for training and with FAA written examinations, visibility is plotted in miles or fractions of miles, e.g. 3 miles or ½ mile, etc. (fig. 50). When visibility is more than 10 miles, it is omitted from the station model on the map.

The Daily Weather Map has abridged plotting. In the official symbolic coded weather station model, visibility is coded in sixteenths of miles (fig. 51).

Precipitation The various forms of precipitation do not require lengthy discussion. In addition to possible damage by hail and the danger of icing, precipitation may be accompanied by low ceilings, and in heavy precipitation, visibilities may suddenly be reduced to zero.

It should be obvious that aircraft which may have accumulated snow while on the ground should never be flown until all traces of snow have been removed, including the hard crust that frequently adheres to the surfaces. An aircraft which has been exposed to rain followed by freezing temperatures

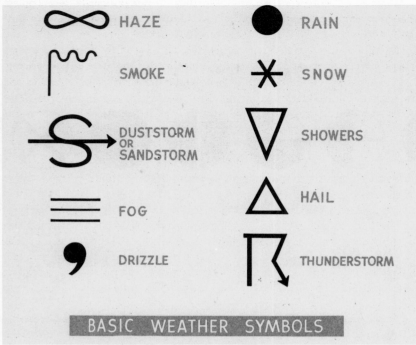

Figure 49. *Basic weather symbols used on weather maps.*

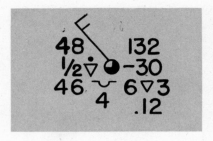

Figure 50. *Typical station model report on printed daily weather map.*

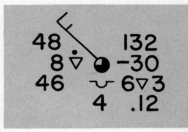

Figure 51. *Sample plotted station model using official weather code.*

should be carefully checked before takeoff to ascertain that the controls operate freely.

More than 100 symbols are used on weather maps to indicate "state of weather." The basic symbols are given in figure 49. (The complete key is posted at airport weather stations and also is listed on the reverse side of the Sunday edition of the Daily Weather Map.)

These symbols may be used in combination, e.g., ≡• rain and fog, or •* rain and snow mixed; or may be multiplied to indicate greater intensity, e.g., •• means continuous light rain; •• means continuous moderate rain; •• means continuous heavy rain. A bracket (]) indicates that the weather represented has occurred within the last hour, but not at the time of observation.

On the weather map, areas of precipitation are shown by green or gray shading.

10. Air Masses and Fronts

The various air masses assimilate the temperature and moisture characteristics of the areas in which they originate—the coldness of polar regions, the heat of the tropics, the moisture of oceans, the dryness of continents.

As they move away from their source regions and pass over land and sea, the air masses are constantly being modified through heating or cooling from below, lifting or subsiding, absorbing or losing moisture. In general, however, they retain some of their original characteristics and can be recognized and identified.

Classification of Air Masses The source of an air mass is indicated on weather maps by use of the following symbols:

A = artic   m = maritime (formed over
                          oceans)
P = polar
                   c = continental (formed over
T = tropical   land).

Two additional symbols (k = cold, w = warm) are based on temperature. However, the actual temperature of the mass is less important than its temperature in relation to the land or water surface over which it is passing. Temperature classification is, therefore, based upon this relationship. For example, an air mass moving from the polar regions usually will be colder than the land and sea areas over which it passes. It will, therefore, be classified as cold (k). On the other hand, an air mass moving from the Gulf of Mexico in winter usually will be warmer than the territory over which it passes and will therefore be classified as warm (w). As an air mass moves from one surface to another, its temperature classification may be changed to indicate whether it is warmer or colder than the surface below. A polar air mass, originally classified as cold (cPk), might prove to be warmer than the ground in the Rocky Mountains over which it passes. Consequently, it would be reclassified as warm (cPw).

If the air is colder than the surface (k), it will be warmed from below and convection currents will be set up, causing turbulence. Dust, smoke, and atmospheric pollution near the ground will be carried upward by these currents and dissipated at high levels, improving surface visibility. Such air is called "unstable."

Conversely, if the air is warmer than the surface (w), there is no tendency for convection currents to form, and the air is smooth. Smoke, dust, etc., are concentrated in lower levels with resulting poor visibility. Such air is called "stable."

From the combination of the source characteristics and the temperature relationship just described, we can predict with a fair degree of accuracy the flying conditions likely to be found within a given air mass.

Characteristics of a Cold Air Mass

Type of clouds .... cumulus and cumulonimbus
Ceilings .... generally unlimited (except during precipitation)
Visibilities .... excellent (except during precipitation)
Unstable air .... pronounced turbulence in lower levels (because of convection currents)
Type of precipitation ...... occasional local thunderstorms or showers — hail, sleet, snow flurries

Characteristics of a Warm Air Mass

Type of clouds .... stratus and stratocumulus (fog, haze)
Ceilings .... generally low
Visibilities .... poor (smoke and dust held in lower levels)
Stable air .... smooth, with little or no turbulence
Type of precipitation ...... drizzle

Movement of Air Masses Since the general motion of the atmosphere in the United States is toward the east, the polar and arctic air masses generally move toward the southeast and the tropical and equatorial air masses move toward the northeast. The speed varies according to the season and the type of air mass, but it generally averages 500 to 700 miles a day. Cold air masses move somewhat more rapidly than warm.

When two different air masses meet, they do not ordinarily mix (unless their temperatures, pressures, and relative humidities happen to be very similar). Instead, they set up boundaries called frontal zones, or "fronts," the colder air mass projecting under the warmer air mass in the form of a wedge. This condition is termed a "stationary front" if the boundary is not moving.

Usually, however, the boundary moves along the earth's surface, and as one air mass withdraws from a given area, it is replaced by another air mass. This action creates a moving front. If warmer air is replacing colder air, the front is called "warm"; if colder air is replacing warmer air, the front is called "cold."

Warm Front

When a warm front moves forward, the warm air slides up over the wedge of colder air lying ahead of it.

Warm air usually has high humidity. As this warm air is lifted, its temperature is lowered. As the lifting process continues, condensation occurs, low nimbostratus and stratus clouds form and drizzle and rain develop. The rain falls through the colder air below, increasing its moisture content so that it also becomes saturated. Any reduction of temperature in the colder air, which might be caused by upslope motion or cooling of the ground after sunset, may result in extensive fog.

As the warm air progresses up the slope, with constantly falling temperature, clouds appear at increasing heights in the form of altostratus and cirrostratus, if the warm air is stable. (If the warm air is unstable, cumulonimbus clouds and altocumulus clouds will form and frequently produce thunderstorms.) Finally, the air is forced up near the stratosphere, and in the freezing temperatures at that level, the condensation appears as thin wisps of cirrus clouds. The upslope movement is very gradual, rising about 1,000 feet every 20 miles. Thus, the cirrus clouds, forming at perhaps 25,000 feet altitude, may appear as far as 500 miles in advance of the point on the ground which marks the position of the front (fig. 52.)

Flight Toward an Approaching Warm Front Although no two fronts are exactly alike, we may gain a clearer understanding of the general pattern if we consider the atmospheric conditions which might exist when a warm front is moving eastward from St. Louis, Mo. (Refer to fig. 52 during this discussion.)

At St. Louis, the weather would be very unpleasant, with drizzle and probably fog.

At Indianapolis, Ind., 200 miles in advance of the warm front, the sky

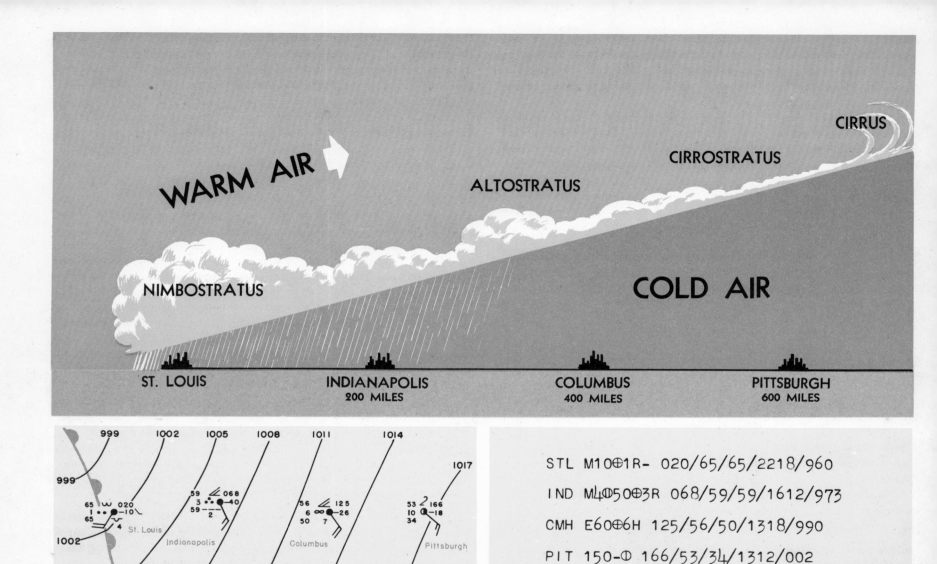

WARM AIR

CIRRUS

CIRROSTRATUS

ALTOSTRATUS

NIMBOSTRATUS

COLD AIR

ST. LOUIS

INDIANAPOLIS
200 MILES

COLUMBUS
400 MILES

PITTSBURGH
600 MILES

STL M10⊕1R- 020/65/65/2218/960

IND M4Ⓞ50⊕3R 068/59/59/1612/973

CMH E60⊕6H 125/56/50/1318/990

PIT 150-Ⓞ 166/53/34/1312/002

Figure 52. *A warm front: (upper) cross-section; (lower left) as shown on weather map; (lower right) as reported by teletype sequences.*

would be overcast with nimbostratus clouds, and continuous rain.

At Columbus, Ohio, 400 miles in advance, the sky would be broken, stratus and altostratus clouds predominating. A steady rain would be about to begin.

At Pittsburgh, Pa., 600 miles ahead of the front, there would probably be high cirrus and cirrostratus clouds.

If we flew from Pittsburgh to St. Louis, ceiling and visibility would decrease steadily. Starting under bright skies, with unlimited ceilings and visibilities, we would note lowering stratus-type clouds as we neared Columbus and soon afterward we would encounter precipitation. After arriving at Indianapolis, we would find the ceiling too low for further flight. Precipitation would reduce visibilities to practically zero.

Thus, we would be forced to remain in Indianapolis until the warm front had passed, which might require a day or two.

If we wished to return to Pittsburgh, we would have to wait until the front had passed beyond Pittsburgh, which might require 3 or 4 days. Warm fronts generally move at the rate of 10 to 25 miles an hour.

On our trip to Indianapolis we probably would have noticed a gradual increase in temperature and a much faster increase in dew point, until the two coincided.

We would also have found the atmospheric pressure gradually lessening because the warmer air aloft would have less weight than the colder air it was replacing. This condition illustrates the general principle that a falling barometer indicates the approach of stormy weather.

Cold Front

Consider now the weather conditions accompanying a cold front. When the cold front moves forward, it acts like a snow plow, sliding under the warmer air and tossing it aloft. This causes sudden cooling of the warm air and forms cloud types that depend on the stability of the warm air.

Fast-Moving Cold Fronts In fast-moving cold fronts, friction retards the front near the ground, which brings about a steeper frontal surface. This steep frontal surface results in a narrower band of weather concentrated along the forward edge of the front. If the warm air is stable, an overcast sky may occur for some distance ahead of the front, accompanied by general rain. If the warm air is conditionally unstable, scattered thunderstorms and showers may form in the warm air. In some cases, an almost continuous line of thunderstorms may form along the front or ahead of it. These lines of thunder-storms, "squall lines," contain some of the most turbulent weather experienced by pilots.

Behind the fast-moving cold front there is usually rapid clearing, with gusty and turbulent surface winds, and colder temperatures.

Comparison of Cold Fronts With Warm Fronts The slope of a cold front is much steeper than that of a warm front and the progress is generally more rapid—usually from 20 to 35 miles per hour, although, in extreme cases, cold fronts have been known to move at 60 miles per hour. Weather activity is more violent and usually takes place directly at the front instead of in advance of the front. However, especially in late afternoon during the warm season, a squall line will frequently develop as much as 50 to 200 miles in advance of the actual cold front. Whereas warm front dangers lie in low ceilings and visibilities, cold front dangers lie chiefly in sudden storms, high and gusty winds, and turbulence.

Unlike the warm front, the cold front rushes in almost unannounced, makes a complete change in the weather within the space of a few hours, and passes on. The squall line is ordinarily quite narrow—50 to 100 miles in width—but is likely to extend for hundreds of miles in length, frequently lying across the entire United States in a line running from northeast to southwest. Altostratus clouds sometimes form slightly ahead of the front, but these are seldom more than 100 miles in advance. After the front has passed, the weather clears rapidly and we have cooler, drier air and usually unlimited ceilings and visibilities—almost perfect flying conditions.

Flight Toward an Approaching Cold Front If we were to make the flight from Pittsburgh toward St. Louis (fig. 53) when a cold front was approaching from St. Louis, we would experience conditions quite different from those associated with a warm front. The sky in Pittsburgh would probably be somewhat overcast with stratocumulus clouds typical of a warm air mass, the air smooth, and the ceilings and visibilities relatively low although suitable for flight.

As the flight proceeded, these conditions would prevail until we reached Indianapolis. If we were wise, we would at this point check the position of the cold front by consulting a recent weather map and teletype sequences, or the meteorologist. We should probably find that the front was now about 75 miles west of Indianapolis. A pilot with sound judgment based on knowledge of frontal conditions, would remain in Indianapolis until the front had passed —a matter of a few hours—and then continue to his destination under near perfect flying conditions.

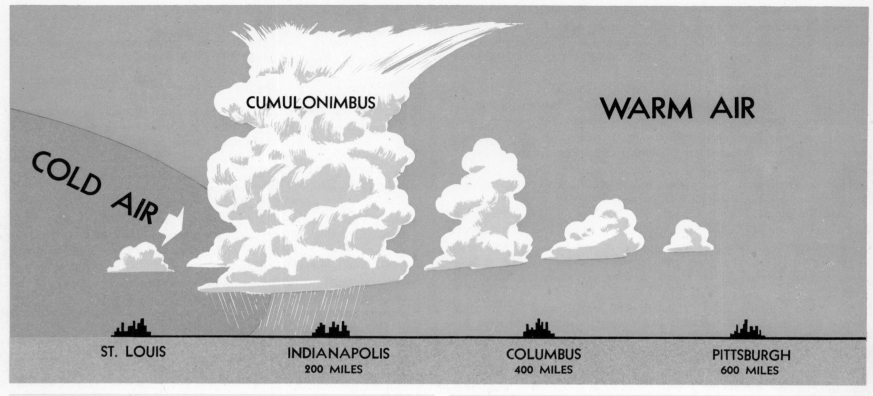

CUMULONIMBUS

WARM AIR

COLD AIR

ST. LOUIS

INDIANAPOLIS
200 MILES

COLUMBUS
400 MILES

PITTSBURGH
600 MILES

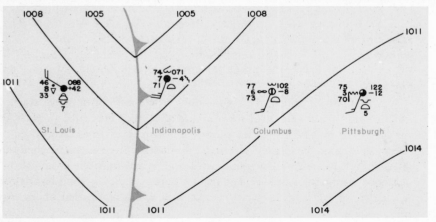

STL E50⊕120⊕8RW− 088/46/33/2918/979

IND 20⊕E100⊕7 071/74/71/2024/974

CMH 15⊕100⊕6H 102/77/73/2012/983

PIT 15⊕M20⊕3K 122/75/70/2012/989

Figure 53. *A cold front: (upper) cross-section; (lower left) as shown on a weather map; (lower right) as reported by teletype sequences.*

44

If, however, we were foolhardy enough to continue our flight toward the approaching cold front, we would soon notice a few altostratus clouds and a dark layer of nimbostratus lying low on the horizon, with perhaps cumulonimbus in the background. Two courses would now be open to us: either to turn around and outdistance the storm, or to make an immediate landing which might be extremely dangerous because of gustiness and sudden wind shifts.

If we were to continue farther, we would be trapped in a line of squalls and cumulonimbus clouds, the dangers of which have already been described. It may be diastrous to fly beneath these clouds; impossible, in a small plane, to fly above them. At low altitudes, there are no safe passages through them. Usually there is no possibility of flying around them because they often extend in a line for 300 to 500 miles.

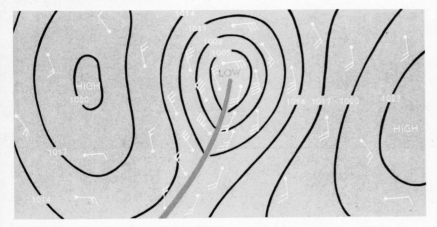

Figure 54. *Weather map indication of wind shift line (center line leading to low)*

Wind Shifts   Wind shifts perhaps require further explanation. The wind in a "high" blows in a clockwise spiral. When two highs are adjacent, the winds are in almost direct opposition at the point of contact as illustrated in figure 54. Since fronts normally lie between two areas of higher pressure, wind shifts occur in all types of fronts, but they usually are more pronounced in cold fronts.

Occluded Front

One other form of front with which the pilot should become familiar is the "occlusion" or "occluded front." This is a condition in which an air mass is trapped between two colder air masses and forced aloft to higher and higher levels until it finally spreads out and loses its identity.

Meterologists subdivide occlusions into two types, but so far as the pilot is concerned, the weather in any occlusion is a combination of warm front and cold front conditions. As the occlusion approaches, the usual warm front indications prevail—lowering ceilings, lowering visibilities, and precipitation. Generally, the warm front weather is then followed almost immediately by the cold front type, with squalls, turbulence, and thunderstorms.

Figure 55 is a vertical cross section of an occlusion. Figure 56 shows the various stages as they might occur during development of a typical occlusion. Usually the development requires 3 or 4 days, during which the air masses may progress as indicated on the map.

The first stage (A) represents a boundary between two air masses, the cold and warm air moving in opposite directions along a front. Soon, however, the cooler air, being more aggressive, thrusts a wedge under the warm air, breaking the continuity of the boundary, as shown in (B). Once begun, the process continues rapidly to the complete occlusion as shown in (C). As the warmer air is forced aloft, it cools quickly and its moisture condenses, causing severe precipitation. The air becomes extremely turbulent, with sudden changes in pressure and temperature.

Figure 57 shows the development of the occluded front in greater detail.

Figure 58 is an enlarged view of (C) in figure 56, showing the cloud formations and the areas of precipitation.

In figures 52, 53, and 55 a panel representing a daily weather map is placed below each cross-sectional view. These panels represent a bird's-eye or plan view, and show how the weather conditions are recorded. A warm front is indicated by a red line, a cold front by a blue line, an occluded front by a purple line, and a stationary front by alternating red and blue dashes. The rounded and pointed projections are generally omitted from the manuscript maps, but are placed on printed or duplicated maps to distinguish the different fronts.

Remember that the frontal lines on the weather map represent the points on the earth's surface where the fronts are located. A pilot flying west at an altitude of 5,000 feet would pass through the frontal boundary about 100 miles in advance of the point where the warm front is shown, or about 25 to 50 miles to the rear of the line on the map representing the cold front.

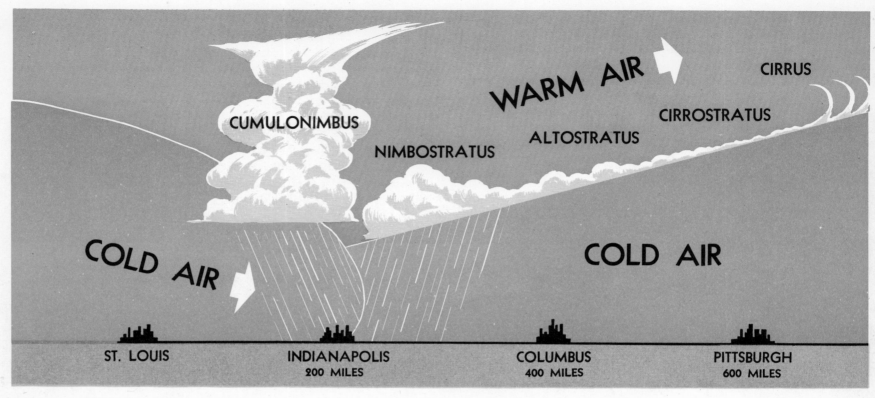

WARM AIR

CIRRUS

CIRROSTRATUS

ALTOSTRATUS

CUMULONIMBUS

NIMBOSTRATUS

COLD AIR

COLD AIR

ST. LOUIS

INDIANAPOLIS
200 MILES

COLUMBUS
400 MILES

PITTSBURGH
600 MILES

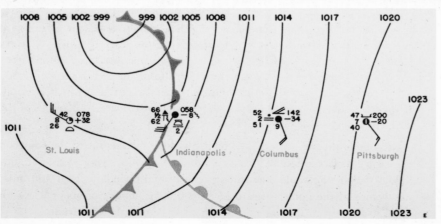

STL 35⊕8 078/42/26/2923G40/976

IND E5⊕1/2TA-RW 058/66/62/2228G45/970

CMH B80⊕2R-F 142/52/51/1617/995

PIT E130⊕7 200/47/40/1312/012

Figure 55. *An occluded front: (upper) cross-section; (lower left) as shown on a weather map; (lower right) as reported by teletype sequences.*

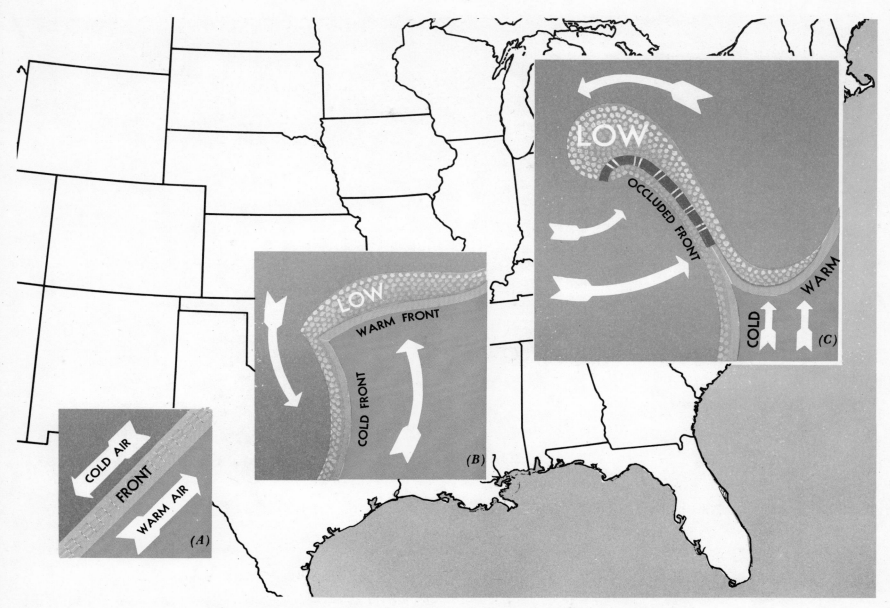

Figure 56. *Three stages in the development of a typical occlusion moving northeastward.*

(A) Air flowing along a front in equilibrium.

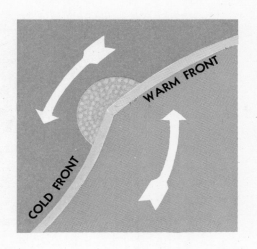

(B) Increased cold-air pressure causes "bend."

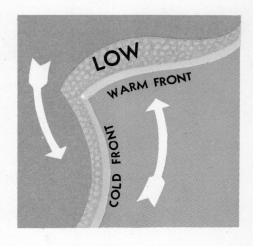

(C) Cold air begins to surround warm air.

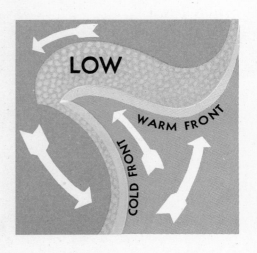

(D) Precipitation becomes heavier.

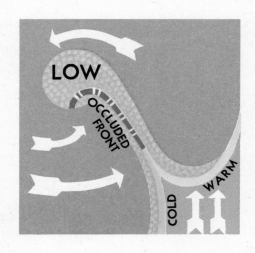

(E) Warm air completely surrounded.

(F) Warm-air sector ends in mild whirl.

Figure 57. *Development of an occlusion. If warm air were red and cold air were blue, this is how various stages of an occlusion would appear to a person aloft looking toward the earth. (Precipitation is green.)*

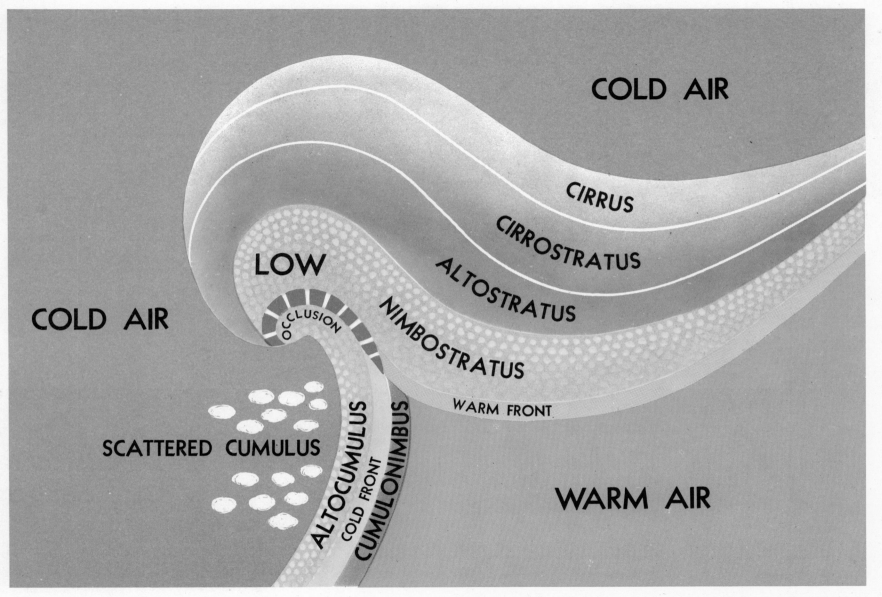

COLD AIR

COLD AIR

WARM AIR

LOW

CIRRUS

CIRROSTRATUS

ALTOSTRATUS

NIMBOSTRATUS

OCCLUSION

WARM FRONT

SCATTERED CUMULUS

ALTOCUMULUS

COLD FRONT

CUMULONIMBUS

Figure 58. *Cloud formations and precipitation accompanying a typical occlusion. (Details of the third stage of development series shown in figure 56.)*

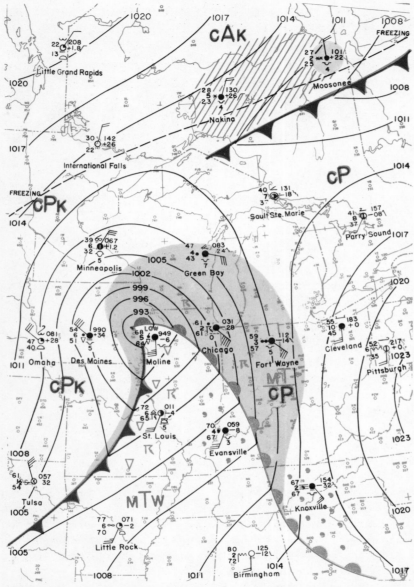

Figure 59. *Section of typical weather map showing methods indicating weather facts important to pilots.*

All the foregoing information about air masses and fronts is available to the pilot in abbreviated form on weather maps. For the pilot who understands the meaning of the symbols, a brief study of the current map will provide a fairly complete picture of the weather conditions he is likely to encounter in flight. He must realize that the facsimile synoptic map may be as much as 8 hours old, and that the fronts will have moved during that time. The meteorologist on duty will be able to supplement the weather map information with the latest data arriving hourly on the teletype sequences. He should invariably be consulted before flights which involve long distances or traverse areas in which frontal activity is taking place. Figure 59 represents a portion of a typical weather map showing the symbols usually used.

The surface weather maps available to the pilot at an airport weather bureau station vary in certain respects from the printed Daily Weather Map shown in figure 59. The surface weather maps to be found at airport stations are:

1. The facsimile synoptic surface weather map. This map is issued each 6-hour period and weather data is plotted according to the official station model. However, visibility and cloud heights are not shown since these are readily available from the hourly sequence reports.

2. The 3-hourly surface weather map plotted at many local Airport Weather Bureau Stations.

11. Aviation Weather Forecasts and Reports

Several forecasts and reports, issued by the Weather Bureau and available to pilots, were discussed briefly in chapter 4. These forecasts and reports, with others, will be discussed in greater detail in this chapter. Those of greatest interest to the private pilot are: weather maps, area forecasts, terminal forecasts, SIGMETS and advisories for light aircraft (AIRMETS), sequence reports, and winds-aloft forecasts.

These aviation weather reports and forecasts, among others, are displayed at each Weather Bureau station. Also, the greater part of these reports and forecasts are available at the Flight Service Stations (FSS). FSS personnel have received special training in weather briefing and help VFR pilots with the weather aspects of their flights. Pilots should take advantage of all this aviation weather information and ask for the assistance of a weather briefer. There is also every advantage in going personally to obtain the weather rather than doing it by telephone. The pilot who goes in person can see the information first-hand, especially the weather map, and get a bird's-eye view of the general situation. However, if a personal visit is not practical, always remember that phone calls are welcome. This procedure has been covered in chapter 4.

Area Forecasts

These reports, issued every 6 hours, forecast the weather for a 12-hour period for each of the 23 areas of the United States; the reports also give the outlook for the following 12 hours. They describe such conditions as the location of areas of low clouds, heights of cloud bases and cloud tops, surface visibilities, and the movement of major weather disturbances such as thunderstorms and squall lines. They also contain information on the height of the freezing level and zones of expected icing and turbulence (See fig. 60).

Example of an Area Forecast

FA MKC Ø41852

13C SUN-Ø1C MON

NEB EXCP PHNDL IA KANS NWRN MO

CLDS AND WX. STM CNTRD EXTRM NE COLO MOVG NEWD TO SE SDKT AND INTSFYG BY Ø1C MON.

NEB EXCP PHNDL. CSDRBL LOW CLDNS AND FOG AND SCTD RAIN OR DRZL WITH CIGS MOSTLY 8-15 ⊕ VSBYS OCNLY 2 TO 4

MIS IN FOG. SCTD AREAS CIGS BLO 5 HND AND VSBYS BLO 1 MIS MOSTLY OVR SW PTN. STG NLY WNDS 3Ø TO 4Ø KTS WITH VSBYS 1 TO 3 MIS IN SNW SPRDG OVR WRN AND CNTRL PTNS FLWG STM CNTR BY MIDN.

KANS. CIGS 1Ø-15 ⓌV⊕ SCTD R- OCNL CIGS 8 ⊕ 3R-F OVR ERN PTN TO 15-2Ø ⓌVⓌWRN PTN. CNDS BCMG MOSTLY 1Ø-2Ø ⊕ OCNL R- EXTRM WRN PTN BY LATE AFTN CHNG TO SNW ERLY EVE BCMG 5-1Ø⊕ AGL VSBYS 1 TO 3 MIS IN SNW OCNLY BLO 1 MI. STG NLY WNDS 3Ø-4Ø KTS BY ERLY EVE. FEW WDLY SCTD TSTMS

OVR ERN PTN DRG AFTN AND ERLY EVE HRS. STG NLY WNDS AND SNW SPRDG THRU MOST OF EXTRM WRN AND NW PTNS BY MIDN. SLY WNDS 25-35 KTS ERN KANS.

NWRN MO AND IA. 1Ø-15 Ⓦ OCNL R- WRN PTN THIS RGN TO 2Ø-3Ø ⓌV⊕AGL ERN PTN. CNDS LWRG TO CIGS 5-1Ø ⊕ 3R-F OVR MOST WRN IA AND NWRN MO BY MIDN. FEW WDLY SCTD TSTMS AFTN AND EVE OVR NWRN MO.

ICG. OCNL MDT ICGIC. FRZG LVL 8Ø-1ØØ LWRG TO NEAR SFC BHND LO CNTR.

TURBC. OCNL MDT TURBC BLO 5Ø-6Ø.

OTLK Ø1C-13C MON. SNW WITH LOW CIGS AND VSBYS SPRDG THRU RMNDR OF NEB AND IA BY MRNG AND LGT SNW THRU KANS AND NWRN MO BY MID MRNG. STG SFC WNDS OVR RGN AND CSDRBL LOW CLDNS.

Plain Language Interpretation In the first line of the area forecast, FA indicates it is an area forecast, MKC identifies the originating station, and "Ø4" indicates it was made on the fourth day of the month with "1852" being the time of the report in Greenwich Mean Time. The forecast covers the period from 1300 central standard time (1 p.m.) Sunday to 0100 central standard time (1 a.m.) Monday.

The plain language interpretation of this area forecast is as follows:

Area forecast for period 1 p.m. Sunday to 1 a.m. Monday Central Standard Time for Nebraska (except Panhandle), Iowa, Kansas, and northwestern Missouri.

Clouds and weather.—A storm centered in extreme northeast Colorado will move northeastward to southeast South Dakota and intensify by 1 a.m. Monday.

In Nebraska (except Panhandle), there will be considerable low cloudiness, fog, and scattered rain or drizzle with ceilings mostly 800 to 1,500 feet overcast and visibilities occasionally 2 to 4 miles in fog. In scattered areas, the ceilings will be below 500 feet and visibility below 1 mile, mostly over the southwestern portion. By midnight, strong northerly winds of 30 to 40 knots and visibilities of 1 to 3 miles in snow will spread over western and central portions following the storm center.

In Kansas, ceilings will be 1,000 to 1,500 feet broken variable overcast with scattered light rain and occasional overcast ceilings of 800 feet with

KEY TO AVIATION WEATHER REPORTS.......

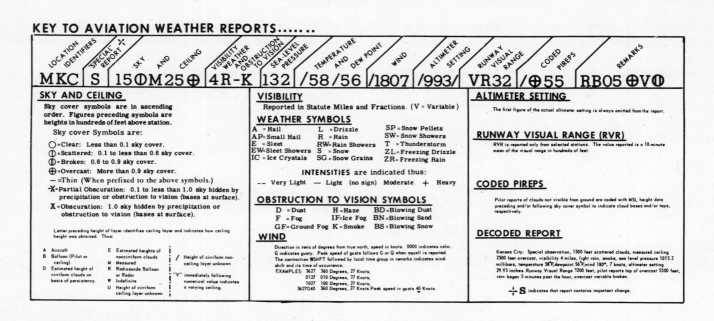

LOCATION IDENTIFIERS	SPECIAL REPORT ⊕	SKY AND CEILING	VISIBILITY WEATHER AND OBSTRUCTION TO VISION	SEA LEVEL PRESSURE	TEMPERATURE AND DEW POINT	WIND	ALTIMETER SETTING	RUNWAY VISUAL RANGE	CODED PIREPS	REMARKS
MKC	S	15①M25⊕	4R-K	132	/58/56	/1807	/993/	VR32	/⊕55	RB05⊕V①

SKY AND CEILING

Sky cover symbols are in ascending order. Figures preceding symbols are heights in hundreds of feet above station.

Sky cover Symbols are:

○ = Clear: Less than 0.1 sky cover.
① = Scattered: 0.1 to less than 0.6 sky cover.
① = Broken: 0.6 to 0.9 sky cover.
⊕ = Overcast: More than 0.9 sky cover.
− = Thin (When prefixed to the above symbols.)
X = Partial Obscuration: 0.1 to less than 1.0 sky hidden by precipitation or obstruction to vision (bases at surface).
X = Obscuration: 1.0 sky hidden by precipitation or obstruction to vision (bases at surface).

Letter preceding height of layer identifies ceiling layer and indicates how ceiling height was obtained. Thus:

A Aircraft
B Balloon (Pilot or ceiling)
D Estimated height of cirriform clouds on basis of persistency.
E Estimated heights of noncirriform clouds
M Measured
R Radiosonde Balloon or Radar
W Indefinite
U Height of cirriform ceiling layer unknown
/ Height of cirriform non-ceiling layer unknown
"V" immediately following numerical value indicates a varying ceiling.

VISIBILITY

Reported in Statute Miles and Fractions. (V = Variable)

WEATHER SYMBOLS

A = Hail   L = Drizzle   SP = Snow Pellets
AP = Small Hail   R = Rain   SW = Snow Showers
E = Sleet   RW = Rain Showers   T = Thunderstorm
EW = Sleet Showers   S = Snow   ZL = Freezing Drizzle
IC = Ice Crystals   SG = Snow Grains   ZR = Freezing Rain

INTENSITIES are indicated thus:

−− Very Light   − Light (no sign)   Moderate   + Heavy

OBSTRUCTION TO VISION SYMBOLS

D = Dust   H = Haze   BD = Blowing Dust
F = Fog   IF = Ice Fog   BN = Blowing Sand
GF = Ground Fog   K = Smoke   BS = Blowing Snow

WIND

Direction in tens of degrees from true north, speed in knots. 0000 indicates calm. G indicates gusty. Peak speed of gusts follows G or Q when squall is reported. The contraction WSHFT followed by local time group in remarks indicates wind-shift and its time of occurrence.
EXAMPLES: 3627 360 Degrees, 27 Knots;
0127 010 Degrees, 27 Knots;
1027 100 Degrees, 27 Knots;
3627G40 360 Degrees, 27 Knots Peak speed in gusts 40 Knots.

ALTIMETER SETTING

The first figure of the actual altimeter setting is always omitted from the report.

RUNWAY VISUAL RANGE (RVR)

RVR is reported only from selected stations. The value reported is a 10-minute mean of the visual range in hundreds of feet.

CODED PIREPS

Pilot reports of clouds not visible from ground are coded with MSL height data preceding and/or following sky cover symbol to indicate cloud bases and/or tops, respectively.

DECODED REPORT

Kansas City: Special observation, 1500 feet scattered clouds, measured ceiling 2500 feet overcast, visibility 4 miles, light rain, smoke, sea level pressure 1013.2 millibars, temperature 58°F, dewpoint 56°F, wind 180°, 7 knots, altimeter setting 29.93 inches. Runway Visual Range 3200 feet, pilot reports top of overcast 5500 feet, rain began 5 minutes past the hour, overcast variable broken.

∻S indicates that report contains important change.

TERMINAL FORECASTS contain information for specific airports on ceiling, cloud heights, cloud amounts, visibility, weather condition and surface wind. They are written in a form similar to the AVIATION WEATHER REPORT.

CEILING: Identified by the letter "C"
CLOUD HEIGHTS: In hundreds of feet above the station
CLOUD LAYERS: Stated in ascending order of height
VISIBILITY: In statute miles, but omitted if over 8 miles.
SURFACE WIND: In tens of degrees and knots; omitted when less than 10.

Examples of TERMINAL FORECASTS:

C15①   Ceiling 1500', broken clouds.

C15⊕6K   Ceiling 1500' overcast, visibility 6 miles, smoke.

20①C70⊕3230G   Scattered clouds at 2000' ceiling 7000' overcast, surface wind 320 degrees 30 knots, gusty.

○11/2GF   Clear, visibility one and one-half miles, ground fog.

C5X1/4S   Sky obscured, vertical visibility 500', visibility one-fourth mile, moderate snow.

AREA FORECASTS are 12-hour forecasts of cloud and weather conditions, cloud tops, fronts, icing and turbulence for an area the size of several states. A 12-hour OUTLOOK is added. Heights of cloud tops, icing, and turbulence are above SEA LEVEL.

SIGMET advisories include weather phenomena potentially hazardous to all aircraft.

AIRMETs include weather phenomena of less severity than that covered by **SIGMETs** which are potentially hazardous to aircraft having limited capability due to lack of equipment or instrumentation or pilot qualifications and are at least of operational interest to all aircraft.

WINDS ALOFT FORECASTS provide a 12-hour forecast of wind conditions at selected flight levels. Temperatures will be included to all levels above 3000, except 5000 feet when this is the lowest level forecast and 7000.

EXAMPLE:

LVL	3000	5000FT	7000	10000FT	15000FT	20000FT	25000FT
MKC	2222	2220+19	2220	2414+10	2713+01	2815−09	2815−17

3000FT (MSL) 220° 22KT

10000FT (MSL) 240° 14KT TEMP +10°C.

PILOTS report in-flight weather to nearest FSS.

Figure 60. *Key to aviation weather reports and forecasts.*

visibility 3 miles in light rain and fog over eastern portion becoming 1,500 to 2,000 feet scattered variable broken in the western portion. Conditions will become mostly overcast with ceilings of 1,000 to 2,000 feet with occasional light rain in extreme western portion by late afternoon changing to snow in early evening becoming 500 to 1,000 feet overcast with visibilities 1 to 3 miles in snow and occasionally below 1 mile. There will be strong northerly winds of 30 to 40 knots by early evening. There will be a few widely scattered thunderstorms over the eastern portion during the afternoon and early evening hours. Strong northerly winds and snow will spread through most of extreme western and northwestern portions by midnight. In eastern Kansas winds will be southerly at 25 to 35 knots.

In northwestern Missouri and Iowa, ceilings will be 1,000 to 1,500 feet broken with occasional light rain in the western portion of this region, becoming 2,000 to 3,000 feet broken variable overcast in the eastern portion. Conditions will lower to ceilings of 500 to 1,000 feet overcast and visibility of 3 miles in light rain and fog over most of western Iowa and northwestern Missouri by midnight. There will be a few widely scattered thunderstorms in the afternoon and evening over northwestern Missouri.

Icing.—Occasional moderate icing in clouds. Freezing level height 8,000 to 10,000 feet above sea level lowering to near the surface behind the low pressure center.

Turbulence.—Occasional moderate turbulence below 5,000 to 6,000 feet (above sea level).

Outlook 1 a.m. to 1 p.m. Monday. Snow with low ceilings and visibilities will spread through the remainder of Nebraska and Iowa by morning and light snow will spread through Kansas and northwestern Missouri by mid-morning. There will be strong surface winds over the region and considerable low cloudiness.

Terminal Forecasts

These reports, issued every 6 hours generally for a 12-hour period, give detailed forecasts for approximately 380 of the more important air terminals in the United States. They state specifically the expected ceiling, visibility, and wind conditions for this 12-hour period at each particular location. If a change is expected during the forecast period, this change, and the expected time of the change, will be given. If the surface wind is expected to be less than 10 knots, it will be omitted from the forecast. If the visibility is expected to be greater than 8 miles, it also will be omitted.

The terminal forecasts are very similar in form to the surface weather observations contained in the aviation weather (hourly sequence) reports. Pilots who are able to read and interpret sequence reports should experience no difficulty with terminal forecasts (see fig. 60).

Examples of Terminal Forecasts

FT   042252
17C SUN-05C MON

SPI C40⊕ 1820. 2200C C30⊕ 1820 OCNL RW−. 0400C C20⊕3RW− 1820G.

UIN C60⊕ 1815G. 2200C C30⊕
1820 OCNL RW−. 0400C C15⊕3RW−F 1818G.

CBI 30⊕C60⊕ 1620 OCNLY C30⊕. 2200C C30⊕ 1615G OCNL RW−. 0400C C15⊕3RW−F 1615G.

STL 40⊕C80⊕ 1815 OCNLY C40⊕. 2300C C30⊕ 1815 OCNL RW−. 0400C C20⊕ 1815G OCNL RW− or TRW−.

JLN C10⊕30⊕3RW− 1620G OCNLY C6⊕20⊕2TRW 2235G. 0200C COLD FROPA C30⊕ 2520G OCNLY 30⊕C100⊕

SGF 12⊕C25⊕RW− 1620G OCNLY C12⊕20⊕2TRW 2230G. 2300C C15⊕RW− 1620G OCNLY C10X1TRW+ 2240G.

Plain Language Interpretation In this terminal forecast, "FT" indicates terminal forecast, "04" that it is the fourth day of the month, and "2252" the time of the report in Greenwich Mean Time. The period of the forecast is from 1700 Central Standard Time (5 p.m.) Sunday to 0500 Central Standard Time (5 a.m.) Monday.

> NOTE: In actual practice, you may find three different ways in which zero is represented in aviation weather reports. It may be represented in the normal way (0), or as a normal zero with a slash through it (0) or as a normal zero with another zero inside.

The plain language interpretation of the terminal forecast for SPI (Springfield, Ill.) is: Ceiling 4,000 feet, broken clouds, surface wind from 180° at 20 knots. By 10 p.m. (Central Standard Time): ceiling 3,000 feet, broken clouds, surface wind from 180° at 20 knots; occasional light rain showers. By 4 a.m.: ceiling 2,000 feet overcast, visibility 3 miles in light rain showers, surface wind from 180° at 20 knots and gusty.

The plain language interpretation of the terminal forecast for STL (St. Louis, Mo.) is: 4,000 feet, scattered clouds, ceiling 8,000 feet, broken clouds, surface wind from 180° at 15 knots, occasionally ceiling 4,000 feet, broken clouds. By 11 p.m. (Central Standard Time) ceiling 3,000 feet, broken clouds, surface wind from 180° at 15 knots, occasional light rain showers. By 4 a.m. ceiling 2,000 feet, broken clouds, surface wind from 180° at 15 knots and gusty, occasional light rain showers or thunderstorms with light rain showers.

Note that the visibility is not given throughout the St. Louis terminal forecast. This would indicate that the visibility is expected to be greater than 8 miles during the entire forecast period.

Note also that a "C" appears in two different ways in the terminal forecasts. In one case, it indicates Central Standard Time and in the other, ceiling. The "C" does not mean "clear."

Severe Weather Advisories

Before June 1, 1961, the Weather Bureau issued warnings of potentially hazardous or severe weather in the form of FLASH ADVISORIES. Now these warnings are issued in two categories—SIGMETS and AIRMETS.

SIGMET A SIGMET identifies weather phenomena of particular significance to the safety of transport category (multiengine aircraft over 12,500 pounds) and other aircraft. This advisory covers tornadoes, lines of thunderstorms (squall lines), hail of three-fourths inch or more, severe and extreme turbulence, heavy icing, and widespread duststorms or sandstorms lowering visibilities to less than 2 miles. Flight Service Stations will broadcast SIGMETs on navigation aid voice channels upon receipt and also at quarter-hour intervals during the valid period. Of course, at 15 and 45 minutes past the hour, it will fall during the regularly scheduled weather broadcasts. FSS stations and control towers will make announcement on enroute voice frequencies when a SIGMET is to be issued by advising pilots to monitor a VOR voice frequency. Remember, a SIGMET may be important for all aircraft.

AIRMET An AIRMET (formerly advisory for light aircraft) identifies weather phenomena less severe than those covered by a SIGMET but still important to light aircraft safety. This advisory covers moderate icing, moderate turbulence, the initial onset of phenomena producing extensive areas of visibilities less than 2 miles or ceilings less than 1,000 feet, including mountain ridges and passes, and winds of 40 knots or more within 2,000 feet of the surface.

Flight Service Stations will broadcast AIRMETs upon receipt and during the regularly scheduled weather broadcasts at 15 and 45 minutes past the hour. FSS stations will also announce over regular FSS frequencies when such an advisory is issued which pertains to an area within 200 miles of the particular station. Pilots of light aircraft hearing this announcement should monitor a VOR voice frequency.

During preflight briefings by FSS and Weather Bureau stations, pilots will be advised of both SIGMETs and AIRMETs that may be valid at that time. Pilots will also be advised of these advisories during in-flight radio contacts with FSS stations.

Example of a SIGMET

FL DEN 1Ø2115
1415M–1815M SAT
SIGMET NR1. LINE OF TSTMS LARAMIE TO ABT 2ØSW DOUGLAS WYO MOVG E AND NEWD 25 KTS TO EXTRM WRN NEB PNHDL BY 18M. FEW SVR TSTMS LKLY WITH HAIL AND EXTRM TURBC. WDLY SCTD TSTMS ALSO OVR RMNDR NEB PNHDL AND ERN COLO WITH ISLTD SML HAIL. SFC WND GUSTS TO 4Ø KTS.

Plain Language Interpretation

The SIGMET is valid from 1415 to 1815 Mountain Standard Time (2:15 P.M. to 6:15 P.M.).

SIGMET #1. Line of thunderstorms extending from Laramie to about 20 nautical miles southwest of Douglas, Wyo., moving eastward and northeastward 25 knots to extreme western Nebraska Panhandle by 6 p.m. Mountain Standard Time. A few severe thunderstorms are likely with hail and extreme turbulence. Widely scattered thunderstorms will also occur over the remainder of the Nebraska Panhandle and eastern Colorado with isolated small hail. Surface wind gusts will reach 40 knots.

Examples of AIRMETs

FL ELP 1Ø171Ø
1Ø1ØM–141ØM SAT
AIRMET NR 1. IN SRN ARIZ SRN NM AND EXTRM SWRN TEX MDT TURBC OCNLY SVR FOR LGT ACFT BLO 13Ø MSL AFT 11M
FL CHI 100720
0120C–0520C SAT

AIRMET NR 1. OVR NRN THIRD IND GND FOG IS FRMG RPDLY AND EXPCTD TO COVER MOST OF NRN IND WITH CIGS BLO 5 HND FEET AND VSBYS BLO 1 MILE AND WITH CNDS FRQNTLY NEAR ZERO ZERO BY 02C.

Plain Language Interpretation

The first AIRMET is valid from 1010 to 1410 Mountain Standard Time (10:10 A.M. to 2:10 P.M.). The second one is valid from 0120 to 0520 Central Standard Time (1:20 A.M. to 5:20 A.M.).

AIRMET #1. In southern Arizona, southern New Mexico, and extreme southwest Texas, moderate turbulence will occur and occasionally become severe below 13,000 feet Mean Sea Level for light aircraft after 11 a.m. Mountain Standard Time.

AIRMET #1. Over the northern third of Indiana, ground fog is forming rapidly, and is expected to cover most of northern Indiana, producing ceilings below 500 feet and visibilities below 1 mile with conditions frequently near zero zero by 2 a.m. Central Standard Time.

Aviation Weather (Sequence) Reports

Changes in weather frequently are so rapid that conditions at the time of flight are likely to be quite different from those shown on a weather map issued several hours previously. The very latest information is available in the hourly aviation weather teletype sequence reports transmitted by weather stations. The information is substantially the same as on the weather map, but the pilot must become familiar with a few symbols and abbreviations in order to read the sequences. Facility in reading these reports can be acquired in a surprisingly short time, and the reward is well worth the effort. Teletype sequence reports are given below the panels in figures 52, 53, and 55.

The table on pages 56 and 57 present a typical sequence report, with an explanation for interpreting all sequences (also, see fig. 60). It will be noted that the information is in three groups, which might be broadly classified as:
1. Identification.
2. Visual observations.
3. Instrumental observations.

Winds-Aloft Forecasts

There are two types of winds-aloft reports. One report is based on observed data. This report will not normally interest the private pilot, since it does not necessarily represent the wind that will be encountered on subsequent flights. The private pilot is most interested in the *winds-aloft forecast*, which forecasts the winds at selected altitudes for a 12-hour period and is issued every 6 hours. Winds are normally forecast for Mean Sea Level (MSL) altitudes of 3,000 feet, 5,000 feet, 7,000 feet, 10,000 feet; and thereafter for each 5,000-foot interval. Because of terrain effect, no forecasts will be made for levels within 1,000 feet of station elevation. For example, if station elevation is between 2,000 and 3,000 feet, no forecast will be given for the 3,000-foot level. If station elevation is between 4,000 and 5,000 feet, no forecast will be given for the 5,000-foot level and so on.

The winds-aloft forecasts also contain temperature forecasts for all wind-reporting levels except for 7,000 feet and the initial level when this initial level is below 10,000 feet. If 3,000 feet is the initial reported level, 5,000 feet will be the first level that will have a temperature forecast; if 5,000 feet is the initial reported level, 10,000 feet will have the first temperature forecast, and so on. The 10,000-foot level will always have the temperature forecast even though it is the initial reported level. The 3,000-foot and 7,000-foot levels will not have a forecast temperature.

Examples of Winds-Aloft Forecasts

FD 2 WBC 041150
12 — 18Z SUN

LVL	3000	5000 FT	7000	10000 FT	15000 FT
MKC	2045	2250+09	2150	2055+04	1960−09
DDC		1950	2050	2055−02	2070−11
GLD		1815	1825	1835−02	2045−12
ICT	2045	2250+11	2245	2140−02	2060−09

20000 FT	25000 FT
2250−21	2155−31
2070−22	2175−33
1960−24	1970−35
1960−20	1870−30

Interpretation of Winds-Aloft Forecast

In the first line "FD 2 WBC 041150," "FD" indicates a winds-aloft forecast and the "2" indicates that it is the forecast for reporting stations located in the central section of the United States. "WBC" (Weather Bureau Computer) indicates that the winds-aloft forecast is prepared at the National Me-

Interpretation of Weather Reports Sent by Teletype

DCA 212100Z 15 ① E30 ⊕ 11/2VTRW—BD 152/68/60/2918G30/996/DRK NW VSBY 1V2

SYMBOL	ITEM	INTERPRETATION	TRANSLATION
		GROUP I. — DCA 212100Z	
DCA	Station identification.	Indicated by call letters. Call letters and all abbreviations are available at weather offices.	Washington, D. C.
212100Z	Date and Greenwich time	The first two digits indicate the day of the month; the next four digits give the time (on the 24-hour clock) in Greenwich time. To convert to local time *subtract* 5 hours for eastern standard time, 6 hours for central, 7 hours for mountain, and 8 hours for Pacific. Regular sequences are sent each hour on the hour. When crucial changes occur between reporting times, a special report may be sent. In this case the date-time data will follow the station identification symbol, and the letter "S", followed by a numeral, will be added.	21st day of the month, 4:00 p. m., eastern standard time.
		GROUP II.— 15 ① E30 ⊕ 11/2VTRW—BD	
15①	Sky cover	Figures represent hundreds of feet (15 = 1,500 feet). Symbol indicates amount of cover: O = clear; ① = scattered; ⓪ = broken; ⊕ = overcast. The letter "X" will be used instead of these symbols whenever fog, dust, smoke, or precipitation obscure the sky. If clouds are at varying levels, two or more sets of figures and symbols are entered in ascending order of height.	Scattered clouds at 1,500 feet.
E30⊕	Ceiling	The ceiling figure will always be preceded by one of the following letters: E = estimated; M = measured; W = indefinite; B = balloon; P = precipitation; A = reported by aircraft. If the ceiling is below 3,000 feet and is variable, the ceiling symbol will be followed by the letter "V", and in the remarks the range of height will be indicated.	Ceiling estimated 3,000 feet.
11/2V	Visibility	Figures represent miles and fractions of miles. Followed by "V" if less than 3 miles and variable. If the visibility is 6 miles or less, the reason is always given under "Precipitation" or "Obstruction."	Visibility 1½ miles, variable.
TRW—	Precipitation, thunderstorm, or tornado.	R = Rain; L = drizzLe; E = slEet; A = hAil; S = Snow; W = shoWers; T = Thunderstorm; Z = freeZing. Sometimes followed by + meaning heavy, or by − meaning light. Item omitted if there is no precipitation. Tornado is spelled out.	Thunderstorm; light rain shower.

SYMBOL	ITEM	INTERPRETATION	TRANSLATION
BD........................	Obstructions to vision.	F = Fog; H = Haze; D = Dust; N = saNd; K = smoKe (sometimes the above letters are preceded by G = ground; I = ice; B = blowing).	Blowing dust.

GROUP III. — 152/68/60/2918G30/996/DRK
NW VSBY 1V2

Most of .the items in this group are separated by diagonal lines (/).

SYMBOL	ITEM	INTERPRETATION	TRANSLATION
152/........................	Pressure	Stated in millibars using same system as on the weather map (omitting initial "9" or "10").	Pressure 1015.2 millibars.
68/........................	Temperature	In degrees Fahrenheit................	Temperature 68° F.
60/........................	Dew point	In degrees Fahrenheit................	Dew point 60° F.
2918G30/....................	Wind	The wind group consists of at least 4 digits. These 4 digits are interpreted in the same way as in winds-aloft forecasts. The first pair of digits shows the wind direction to the nearest 10 degrees in relation to true north. The second pair of digits represents the wind speed in knots. The symbol "G" following the wind speed indicates gusts. The peak speed of gusts (in knots) follows the "G" symbol, or follows a "Q" symbol when squalls are reported. A calm wind is indicated by 0000. Wind shifts are indicated in remarks by the contraction "WSHFT" followed by the local time of the wind shift.	Wind 290° True, 18 knots; gusts to 30 knots.
996/........................	Altimeter setting.	Barometric pressure in inches for the setting of altimeters on aircraft. Given in three figures with the initial 2 or 3 omitted. A number beginning with 5 or higher presupposes an initial 2; a number beginning with 4 or lower presupposes an initial 3. (993 = 29.93; 002 = 30.02, etc.).	Altimeter setting at 29.96 inches.
DRK NW VSBY 1V2............	Remarks	Any additional remarks are given in teletype symbols and in abbreviations of English words. Any items which are normally sent, but for some reason are missing from the transmission, are represented by the letter "M."	Dark overcast to the northwest. Visibility variable 1 to 2 miles.

teorological Center through the use of digital computers. (Since all winds-aloft forecasts are now prepared by computers in the National Meteorological Center, the coding WBC will appear on all FD reports.) In "041150" the first two digits (04) mean the fourth day of the month. "1150" indicates the time (24-hour clock) of the report in Greenwich Mean Time (Z). The second line, "12 - 18Z SUN" indicates that the forecast is for Sunday from 12 o'clock noon to 6 o'clock in the afternoon Greenwich Mean Time. This would be from 7 o'clock in the morning (7:00 a.m.) to 1 o'clock in the afternoon (1:00 p.m.) Eastern Standard Time (EST), 6 o'clock in the morning to 12 o'clock noon Central Standard Time (CST), and so on.

In the third line of the report "LVL 3000, 5000 FT . . . ," LVL represents Mean Sea Level; "3000, 5000, etc." represent the Mean-Sea-Level altitudes at which winds are forecast; and the "FT" following all levels except the 3000 and 7000 levels (and 5,000 feet where it is the first reported level) means "forecast temperature." The temperature is never forecast for the 3000-foot and 7000-foot levels. The wind forecast for each station at 3,000 feet MSL appears in the column below "3000"; the wind and temperature (if applicable) at 5,000 feet MSL appear in the column below "5000 FT" and so on.

The first reporting station is Kansas City, Mo. (MKC). The group of figures "2045" appear in the "3000" column opposite MKC. The first pair of digits of this group when multiplied by 10 represents the true wind direction (the same result is obtained by adding a zero to these two digits). The second pair of digits represents the wind speed in knots. Applying these rules on the group of figures, the wind direction at 3,000 feet above sea level (MSL) at Kansas City, Mo. is forecast to be from 200° (true) and the wind speed is forecast to be 45 knots. The figure group "2250+09" is in the column headed by "5000 FT" for Kansas City. Applying the rules to this grouping, the wind direction at 5,000 feet above sea level at Kansas City is forecast to be from 220° (true), wind speed is forecast to be 50 knots, and the temperature is forecast to be +09 degrees Centigrade. The temperature at 15,000 feet at Kansas City is forecast to be −09 degrees Centigrade.

The first reported level for Dodge City (DDC), Kansas, and Goodland (GLD), Kansas, is 5,000 feet. The elevation at these two locations is be-tween 2,000 and 4,000 feet MSL so the first reported level would be 5,000. Note that on all of the reports that the first reported level and the 7,000-foot level do not include a temperature forecast.

When the wind speed reaches 100 knots or more, a special rule must be applied to the four-digit grouping to find wind direction and speed. Since a private pilot will not normally fly at altitudes where such wind speeds will be encountered, the rule will not be covered in this text. The group of figures "9900" indicates a light and variable wind.

Interpolation for Intermediate Winds

To obtain the wind direction and speed at an altitude intermediate to those given in the winds-aloft forecast, you must interpolate. For example, the forecast wind direction, wind speed, and temperature at 8,500 feet at Kansas City are 205° (true), 52.5 knots, and 5.5°C. We find these values by first finding the value of the wind direction and speed at 7,000 and 10,000 feet, and the forecast temperature at 5,000 and 10,000 feet.

Level	Wind Direction	Wind Speed	Temperature
5,000	—	—	+09
7,000	210°	50	—
8,500	?	?	?
10,000	200°	55	+04

Since 8,500 feet is half-way between 7,000 feet and 10,000 feet, we assume that the wind direction and wind speed are halfway between the respective values at 7,000 feet and 10,000 feet. 205° is halfway between 210° and 200° and 52.5 knots is half-way between 50 and 55 knots.

8,500 feet is at seven-tenths of the interval from 5,000 feet to 10,000 feet. We assume the temperature to fall at this same interval from +9° to +4°. 5.5° is the forecast temperature at 8,500 feet. By a similar reasoning, the values could be found at any intermediate altitude.

SECTION III—NAVIGATION

12. Navigation Aids

Every pilot takes pride in his ability to navigate with precision. It is a source of real satisfaction to plan and execute a flight which proceeds directly to the destination, arriving safely according to a predetermined plan with no worry or loss of time because of poor navigating technique.

Lack of skill in navigation may lead to unpleasant and sometimes dangerous situations in which changes of weather, approaching darkness, or shortage of fuel may force the pilot to attempt a landing under hazardous conditions.

Navigation used to be considered a difficult art shrouded in the mysteries of higher mathematics and requiring a combination of skill, intuition, and luck. To a certain extent that was true, but many improvements in instruments, aeronautical charts, pilot techniques, and navigation aids have enabled pilots in recent years to plan their flights with confidence and to reach their destinations according to plan. The prime requirement for success in navigation is a knowledge of a few simple facts and the ability to exercise good judgment based upon those facts.

Our discussion of navigation is limited to the needs of the private pilot without instrument rating. As he gains more experience in flying, he will wish to study the subject in greater detail, but our primary purpose here is to furnish information of practical value in flying under visual flight rules (VFR).

To navigate successfully, a pilot must know his approximate position at all times or be able to determine it whenever he wishes. Position may be determined by:

1. Pilotage (by reference to visible landmarks).
2. Dead reckoning (by computing direction and distance from a known position).
3. Radio navigation (by use of radio aids).
4. Celestial navigation (by reference to the sun, moon, and other celestial bodies).

The basic form of navigation for the inexperienced pilot is pilotage, and it should be mastered first. An understanding of the principles of dead reckoning, however, will enable him to make necessary calculations of flight time and fuel consumption. The ever-increasing use of radio equipment in private planes makes it highly desirable for the pilot to have a thorough knowledge of the use of radio for navigation and communications. Celestial navigation is of little value to the private pilot and is not explained in this handbook.

Airways A significant part of the work of the Federal Aviation Agency is the development and operation of Federal Airways—a vast network of thousands of miles of air highways covering the entire United States, connecting all the principal cities and rapidly being extended. While a pilot on a VFR flight is not required to follow the airways, he frequently will find them convenient because they are equipped with various aids and have been established specifically to promote his convenience and safety.

Airway Aids Along the airways, radio navigation aids are appropriately spaced to provide navigation guidance and air-ground communications facilities. Weather reporting service is available through twice-hourly weather broadcasts, or by the pilot's request. Beacon lights and intermediate landing fields are located at many points along the airways. The Federal Aviation Agency operates many additional facilities and services to assist pilots and to direct the flow of traffic along the airways—such as air route traffic control centers. Flight Service Stations (FSS), airport traffic control towers, radar facilities and instrument approach and landing systems. Some of these facilities and services are discussed more fully in later chapters.

Aeronautical Charts Aeronautical charts for use in the United States are published by the U.S. Coast and Geodetic Survey. The types of charts of greatest interest to private pilots are:

1. Sectional Aeronautical Charts (scale: about 8 statute miles per inch)— fairly complete detail, primarily for use in pilotage, most widely used by private pilots. These charts are identified by the names of principal cities or geographical features (fig. 61), such as the Dallas Sectional, which accompanies this handbook. Complete set of charts consists of 87 sheets. Price 30 cents per sheet.

2. Local Aeronautical Charts (scale: about 4 statute miles per inch)—

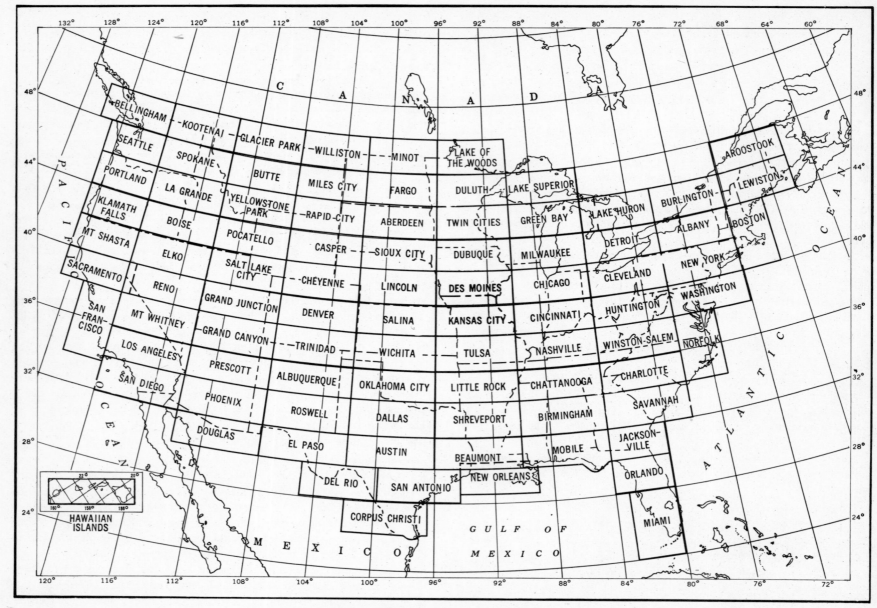

Figure 61. *Index of sectional charts.*

large scale, primarily for use on VFR flights in highly congested areas, more topographical detail than any other chart. The charts are identified by the names of cities, such as Atlanta Local. Price: 30 cents per chart.

3. Aeronautical Planning Chart (scale: about 80 statute miles per inch)—designed for planning long flights, selected key points may be transferred to more detailed local charts for actual flight use. Price: Planning Chart of the United States (AP-9)—40 cents.

4. World Aeronautical Charts (scale: about 16 statute miles per inch)—Omit many topographic details, designed for experienced pilots flying relatively fast airplanes on long trips, *difficult for inexperienced pilots when navigating by pilotage.* Complete set consists of 43 sheets, each identified by a number, such as WAC 407. Price: 25 cents per sheet.

A free index of these and other charts, listing their prices with instructions for ordering, is available upon request from:

Director
Coast and Geodetic Survey
U. S. Department of Commerce
Washington, D. C. 20230

Figure 61 shows a map of the United States upon which is superimposed a key identifying the Sectional Charts and indicating the area covered by each.

It is vitally important that pilots check the publication date on each aeronautical chart to be used on any flight. *Obsolete charts should be discarded and replaced by new editions, ordinarily published every 6 months.* (The Airman's Information Manual contains a list of the dates of the latest edition of each chart.) This is extremely important because critical revisions in aeronautical information are occurring constantly. These include changes in radio frequencies, construction of new obstructions, temporary closing of certain runways and airports, and other temporary and permanent hazards to flight. To make sure your sectional aeronautical chart is up to date, refer to the Sectional Chart Bulletin in the *Airman's Information Manual* (AIM), Section III. This Bulletin provides the VFR pilot with the essential information necessary to update and maintain his chart current. It lists the major changes in aeronautical information that have occurred since the last publication date of each sectional chart. Specifically, it contains the following:

1. Changes to controlled airspace and special use airspace that present hazardous conditions or impose restrictions on the pilot.

2. Major changes to airports and radio navigational facilities.

When a sectional chart is republished, the corrections will be removed from AIM and begin again for the new chart. See Chapter 24 for further information.

To help make sure that the latest charts are used, regularly revised lists entitled "Dates of Latest Prints" are published and are available from the same source as the charts.

13. Chart Reading

Sectional Aeronautical Charts While studying this chapter use the Dallas Sectional chart folded inside the back cover of this booklet. This is one of the new-type sectional charts the U.S. Coast and Geodetic Survey now issues. All of the 87 sectional charts eventually will be converted to the new type, and therefore pilots should be familiar with both old and revised types. Discussions here deal with the new series.

The pilot should have little difficulty in reading aeronautical charts. They are like automobile road maps. By referring to the reverse side of the sheet, he may identify aeronautical and topographical symbols, including those used to represent highways, railroads, cities, and rivers, together with landmarks easily recognizable from the air such as racetracks, surface structures of mines, open-air theaters, and obstructions (such as radio and television towers). Landmarks not classified are identified by brief descriptions beside small black squares marking their exact locations. When drawn on the chart, many of the items are exaggerated in order to be seen easily.

Valuable information is printed on the reverse side of each sectional chart. It includes: airports in the particular area covered by the chart; prohibited, restricted, caution, and warning areas; and information concerning various types of charts. When space permits, additional material is shown, relating to such items as flight plans, search and rescue procedures, and weather minimums for VFR flights.

Remember, however, that the information on aeronautical charts may be as many as 6 months old depending on the date published. Check the *Airman's Information Manual* for latest aeronautical data.

Relief The elevation of land surface, *relief,* is shown on aeronautical charts by brown contour lines drawn at 1,000-foot intervals. These are emphasized by various tints, as indicated in the color legend appearing on each chart.

The manner in which contours express elevation, form, and degree of slope is shown in figure 62. The sketch in the upper part of the figure represents a

Figure 62. *Altitude, form and slope of terrain as indicated by contour lines and numerals (U.S. Geological Survey).*

river valley lying between two hills. In the foreground is the sea, with a bay that is partly enclosed by a hooked sandbar. On each side of the valley is a terrace into which small streams have cut narrow gullies. The hill on the right has a rounded summit and gently sloping spurs separated by ravines. The spurs are cut off sharply at their lower ends by a sea cliff. The hill at the left terminates abruptly at the valley in a steep and almost vertical bluff, from which it slopes gradually away and forms an inclined tableland traversed by a few shallow gullies. Each of these features is represented directly beneath its position in the sketch by contour lines. In figure 62 the contours represent successive differences in elevation of 20 feet—that is, the contour interval is 20 feet. A small interval was used to illustrate better the terrain features that may be visualized through contours.

Aeronautical Data The aeronautical information on new-type sectional charts is for the most part self-explanatory. Information concerning very high frequency (VHF) radio facilities such as tower frequencies, omnidirectional radio ranges (VOR), and other VHF communications frequencies is shown in blue. Likewise, a narrow band of blue tint is used to indicate the center lines of Victor Airways (VOR civil airways between omnirange stations). Low frequency—medium frequency (LF/MF) radio facilities are shown in magenta (purplish shade of red), and a narrow band of magenta tint is used to indicate LF/MF airways.

In most instances, FAA radio range stations identify themselves by broadcasting their call signs in International Morse Code. VOR stations use three-letter identifiers, whereas LF/MF range stations may use three-letter identifiers or two-letter identifiers. The two-letter identification is normally used only in areas where there are a VOR facility and an LF/MF range facility using the same name. For example, the Lubbock, Tex., VOR facility is identified by the letters LBB (.–.. –... –...) and the Lubbock LF/MF range facility is identified by the letters LX (.–.. –..–). Therefore, both identifiers (two-letter for the LF/MF; three-letter for the VOR) and both codes appear on the aeronautical charts; LF/MF in magenta (purplish shade of red) and VOR in blue.

All airports having permanent-type hard-surfaced runways are shown by runway patterns for more positive identification and to enhance their value as landmarks. Information pertaining to airports with a control tower or flight service station is given in blue figures in a blue box adjacent to the airport symbol which is also in blue. Information pertaining to other airports is given in magenta adjacent to the airport symbol which is also in magenta. Abandoned airports may be indicated by small black squares which are labeled, abandoned airports.

The symbol for obstructions is another important feature. The elevation of the top of obstructions above sea level is given in blue figures beside the obstruction symbol. Specific elevations of certain high points in terrain are shown on charts by dots accompanied by black figures indicating the number of feet above sea level.

An explanation for all symbols used on aeronautical charts appears either on the back of the chart or around the margin on the front of the chart.

Airway Lighting Aids On sectional charts, lighting aids are shown by a blue star along with certain other coded information. For those more experienced private pilots who plan to do cross-country flying at night, lighted airways are the primary visual aid in rough or sparsely populated areas.

The lighted airways consist of a line of rotating lights regularly spaced between cities, and are supplemented by nonrotating lights for identification and hazard marking. Beacon lights usually are numbered and may be easily identified by a number which is flashed in code. Rotating lights with various color combinations are used to indicate the locations of airports and intermediate landing fields. For a more complete description of airway lighting aids, consult the current *Airman's Information Manual*.

14. Measurement of Direction

The equator is an imaginary circle equidistant from the poles of the earth. Circles parallel to the equator (lines running east and west), *parallels of*

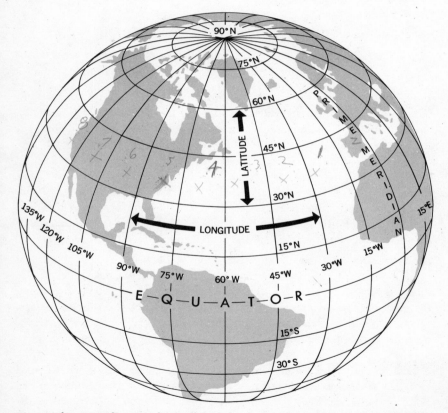

Figure 63. *Meridians and parallels—the basis of measuring time, distance and direction.*

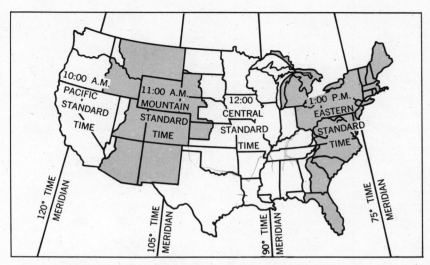

Figure 64. *When the sun is directly above the meridian, the time at points on that meridian is noon. This is the basis on which time zones are established.*

latitude, enable us to measure distance in degrees of latitude north or south of the equator. Consequently, the angular distance from the equator to the pole (one-fourth of a circle) is 90°. The 48 conterminous states of the United States lie between 25° and 49° N. latitude.

Meridians of longitude are drawn from the North Pole to the South Pole and are at right angles to the equator. The meridian passing through Greenwich, England, the "Prime Meridian," is used generally as the zero line from which measurements are made in degrees east and west to 180°. The 48 conterminous states of the United States lie between 67° and 125° W. longitude.

Any specific geographical point can thus be located by reference to its longitude and latitude. Washington, D.C., is approximately 39° N. latitude, 77° W. longitude. Chicago is approximately 42° N. latitude, 88° W. longitude (fig. 63).

The meridians are also useful for designating time belts. A day is defined as the time required for the earth to make 1 complete revolution of 360°. Since the day is divided into 24 hours, the earth revolves at the rate of 15° an hour. Noon is the time when the sun lies directly above a meridian; to the west of that meridian is forenoon, to the east is afternoon.

The standard practice is to establish a time belt for each 15° of longitude, which makes a difference of exactly 1 hour between each belt. In the United States are four such belts—Eastern (75°), Central (90°), Mountain (105°), and Pacific (120°). The dividing lines are somewhat irregular because communities near the boundaries often find it more convenient to use time designations of neighboring communities or trade centers.

Figure 64 shows the time zones in the United States. When the sun is directly above the 90th meridian, it is noon Central Standard Time. At the same time it will be 1 p.m. Eastern Standard Time, 11 a.m. Mountain Standard Time, and 10 a.m. Pacific Standard Time.

This time zone difference must be taken into account during a long flight east—especially one that must be completed before dark. Remember, you may be losing an hour when flying from one time zone to another, or, for that matter, when flying from the western edge to the eastern edge of the same time

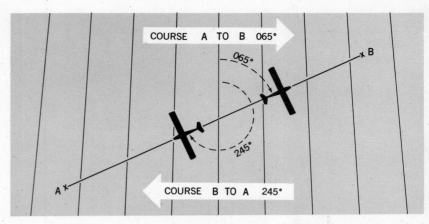

Figure 66. *Courses are determined by reference to meridians on aeronautical charts.*

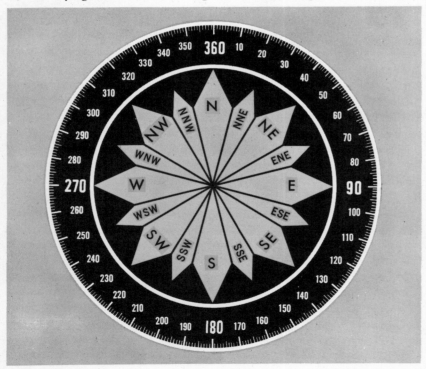

Figure 65. *The compass rose enables the pilot to determine direction in terms of points of the compass and degrees of arc.*

zone. Check the time of sunset at your point of destination and take this into account when you plan an eastbound flight, if the flight must be completed during daylight. Times of sunset can normally be obtained from a Flight Service Station (FSS) or Weather Bureau Station.

In most aviation operations, time is expressed in terms of the 24-hour clock. Air traffic control instructions, weather reports and broadcasts, and estimated times of arrival are all based on this system. For example: 9 a.m. Central Standard Time is expressed as 0900C; 1 p.m. Mountain Standard Time is 1300M; 10 p.m. Eastern Standard Time 2200E. These times will often be abbreviated as 09C, 13M, and 22E, respectively.

Measurement of Courses By using the meridians, direction from one point to another can be indicated in terms of degrees measured in a clockwise direction from true north. Thus, to indicate a course to be followed in flight, the pilot will draw a line on the chart from the point of departure to the destination and measure the angle which this line makes with a meridian. Direction is expressed in terms of degrees, as shown by the compass rose in figure 65.

Because meridians converge toward the poles, course measurement should be taken at a *meridian near the midpoint* of the course rather than at the point of departure. The course thus measured on the chart is known as the *true course,* because it represents a direction measured by reference to a meridian or true north. As shown in figure 66, the direction from A to B would

Figure 67. *Magnetic meridians are in black, geographic meridians and parallels in blue; variation is the angle between a magnetic and geographic meridian.*

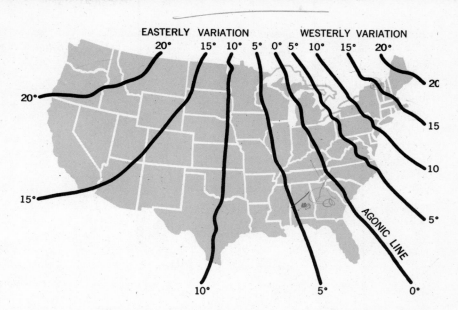

Figure 68. *A typical isogonic chart. The black lines are isogonic lines which connect geographical points with identical magnetic variation.*

be a true course of 065°, whereas the return trip (sometimes called the reciprocal) would be a true course of 245°.

The direction in which the nose of the airplane points during a flight is the *true heading*. Usually it is necessary to head the plane in a direction slightly different from the true course to offset the effect of wind; consequently, the true heading generally does not correspond with the true course. This will be discussed more fully in subsequent chapters; *in this chapter we shall assume no-wind conditions, under which heading and course would coincide.* Thus, for a true course of 065° the true heading would be 065°. However, if we wished to fly by the compass, we should have to make corrections for magnetic variation and for compass deviation.

Variation Variation is the angle between true north and magnetic north at any given place. It is expressed as *east variation* or *west variation* depending upon whether magnetic north (MN) is to the east or west of true north (TN), respectively.

The north magnetic pole is located close to latitude 71° N., longitude 96° W.—about 1,300 miles from the geographic or true north pole, as indicated

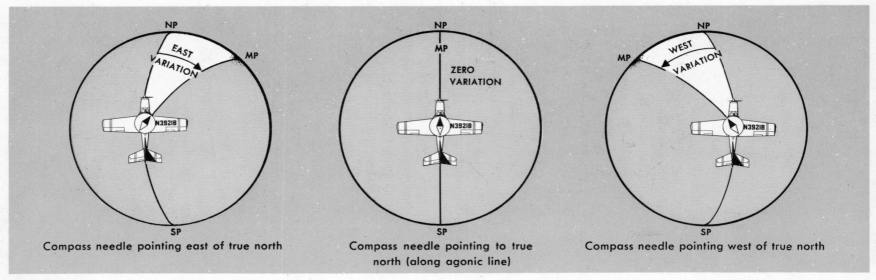

Figure 69. *In an area of west variation a compass needle points west of true north; in an area of zero variation it points to true north; in an area of east variation it points east of true north.*

in figure 67. If the earth were uniformly magnetized, the compass needle would point toward the magnetic pole, in which case the variation between true north (as shown by the geographical meridians) and magnetic north (as shown by the magnetic meridians) could be measured at any intersection of the meridians.

Actually, the earth is not uniformly magnetized. In the United States the needle usually points in the general direction of the magnetic pole but it may vary in certain geographical localities by many degrees. Consequently, the exact amount of variation at thousands of selected locations in the United States has been carefully determined by the U.S. Coast and Geodetic Survey. The amount and the direction of variation, which change slightly from time to time, are shown on most aeronautical charts as broken red lines, *called isogonic lines,* which connect points of equal magnetic variation. (The line connecting points at which there is no variation between true north and magnetic north is the *agonic line.*) An isogonic chart is shown in figure 68. Minor bends and turns in the isogonic and agonic lines probably are caused by unusual geological conditions that affect the magnetic forces in certain areas.

From this it can be readily seen that on the west coast of the United States the compass needle will point to the east of true north, on the east coast it will point to the west of true north. On a line running roughly through Lake Michigan, the Appalachian Mountains and off the coast of Florida, magnetic north and true north coincide (fig. 68).

Because courses are measured by geographical meridians which point toward true north, and are flown by reference to the compass which points along the magnetic meridian (in the general direction of magnetic north), the true direction must be converted into magnetic direction for the purpose of flight. This conversion is made by adding or subtracting the variation indicated by the nearest isogonic line on the chart. The true heading, when corrected for variation, is known as *magnetic heading.*

At Providence, R. I., the variation is shown as "14° W." This means that magnetic north is 14° west of true north. If we wished to fly a true heading of north, we would have to add these 14° and fly a magnetic heading of 014°. The same correction for variation must be applied to the true heading to obtain any magnetic heading at Providence, or at any point close to the isogonic line "14° W." Thus, to fly east, we would use a magnetic heading of 090° +

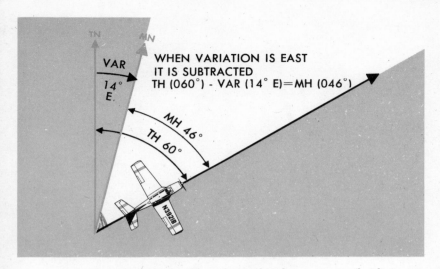

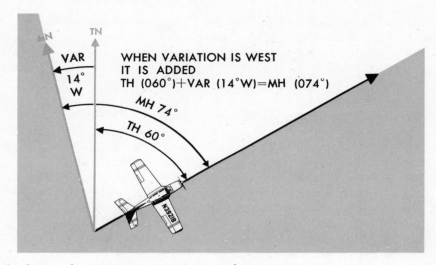

Figure 70. *The relationship between true heading, magnetic heading, and variation in areas of east and west variation.*

14° = 104°. To fly south, the magnetic heading would be 180° + 14° = 194°. To fly west, it would be 270° + 14° = 284°. To fly a true heading of 060°, we would use a magnetic heading of 060° + 14° = 074° (fig. 70).

Now suppose we are in Denver, Colo., where the isogonic line shows the variation to be "14° E." This means that magnetic north is 14° to the east of true north. Therefore, to fly a true heading of north, we would have to subtract these 14° and fly a magnetic heading of 346° (360° minus 14°). Again the 14° would be subtracted from the appropriate true heading to obtain the magnetic heading at any point close to the isogonic line "14° E." Thus, to fly east we would use a magnetic heading of 076° (090° minus 14°). To fly south the magnetic heading would be 166° (180° minus 14°). To fly west it would be 256° (270° minus 14°). To fly a true heading of 060°, we would use a magnetic heading of 060° — 14° = 046° (fig. 70).

To summarize: To convert TRUE (measured from the meridians on the chart) to MAGNETIC, note the variation shown by the nearest isogonic line. If variation is west, add; if east, subtract.

Many methods have been devised for remembering whether to add or subtract variation. The following jingle has proved helpful: *West is best* (add) — *East is least* (subtract).

Deviation The magnetic heading is of no particular value to the pilot ex-

cept as an intermediate step necessary to obtain the correct compass reading for the flight. The remaining step is the correction for deviation. Because of magnetic influences within the airplane itself (electrical circuits, radio, lights, tools, engine, magnetized metal parts, etc.), the compass needle is frequently deflected from its normal reading. This deflection is *deviation*. The deviation is different for each airplane; it also varies for different headings of the same airplane. For instance, if magnetism in the engine attracts the north end of

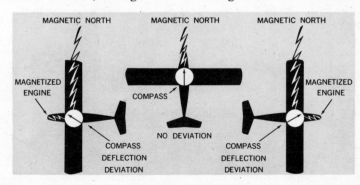

Figure 71. *Magnetized portions of the plane cause the compass to deviate from its normal indication.*

the compass, the effect is nil when the plane is heading toward magnetic north. On easterly or westerly headings, the compass indications are in error, as shown in figure 71. Magnetic attraction may lie in many other parts of the airplane; the assumption of attraction in the engine is merely used for purpose of illustration.

Some adjustment of the compass, *compensation*, can be made to reduce this error, but the remaining correction must be applied by the pilot.

Proper compensating of the compass requires special skill and technique, and is best performed by a competent technician. Since the magnetic forces within the plane frequently change, owing to landing shocks, vibration, mechanical work, or changes in equipment, the pilot should have his deviation card checked occasionally, particularly before any flight which might depend upon the use of the compass. The procedure used to check the deviation card (called "swinging the compass") is briefly outlined.

The airplane is placed on a magnetic compass rose, the engine started, and electrical devices normally used (such as radio) are turned on. (Tailwheel-types of airplanes will first have to be jacked up into flying position.) The plane is aligned with magnetic north indicated on the compass rose and the reading shown on the compass is recorded. The plane is rotated through each 30° and each reading is recorded. If the airplane is to be flown at night, the lights are turned on and any significant changes in the readings are noted. If so, additional entries are made for use at night.

As a practical method of roughly checking the accuracy of the compass, the pilot may compare the compass reading with known runway headings.

On the compass card the letters, N, E, S, and W, are used for north, east, south, and west. The final zero is omitted from the degree markings so that figures may be larger and more easily seen.

A deviation card, similar to figure 72, is mounted near the compass, showing the addition or subtraction required to correct for deviation on various headings, usually at intervals of 30°. For intermediate readings, the pilot can interpolate mentally with sufficient accuracy. For example, if the pilot wanted

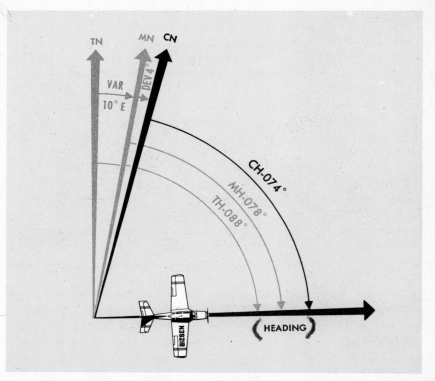

Figure 73. *Relationship between true, magnetic, and compass heading for a particular instance.*

the correction for 195° and noted the correction for 180° to be 0 and for 210° to be +2, he would assume that the correction for 195° would be +1. *The magnetic heading, when corrected for deviation, is known as compass heading.*

To illustrate the application of the compass corrections, assume that we wish to make a flight from Winston Airport southwest of Snyder, Texas (32° 42′ N. Latitude; 100° 57′ W. Longitude), direct to Mineral Wells Airport southwest of Mineral Wells, Texas (32° 47′ N. Latitude; 98° 03′ W. Longitude). *A line should be drawn on the Dallas chart from the center of the Winston Airport to the center of the Mineral Wells Airport.* The midmeridian is at 99° 30′ longitude. Measuring the direction of the course line at this meridian with a protractor gives us a true course (TC) of 088°. If there were no wind, our true heading (TH) would be the same as our true course, or

FOR (MAGNETIC)	N	30	60	E	120	150
STEER (COMPASS)	0	28	57	86	117	148
FOR (MAGNETIC)	S	210	240	W	300	330
STEER (COMPASS)	180	212	243	274	303	332

Figure 72. *Compass deviation card.*

088°. Variation (V) is shown by the mid-isogonic line as 10° E. Subtracting 10° from 088° gives us a magnetic heading (MH) of 078°. Checking the deviation card for our airplane, we find the instructions "for E (090°) steer 086°," which tell us to subtract 4° from the magnetic heading, making our compass heading (CH) read 078° − 4°, or 074°. We should now be able to take off from Winston Airport and fly direct to Mineral Wells Airport (assuming no wind) with our magnetic compass reading 074°. Figure 73 shows the relationship between true heading, magnetic heading, and compass heading in this particular problem. Of course, the lines depicting true north (TN), magnetic north (MN), and compass north (CN) might fall in any order depending upon the direction of variation and deviation.

The compass is a thoroughly reliable instrument upon which the pilot may depend if he is aware of its idiosyncrasies (see Exam-O-Gram No. 12, appendix I). When the airplane is banked in a turn, the compass is tilted from the horizontal plane and will give an incorrect reading. This is often called the northerly turning error. When the speed of the airplane is increasing or decreasing the compass is subject to an acceleration error. But when the airplane is in steady level flight, the pilot may be quite sure that if his judgment disagrees with the compass reading, the error lies in judgment and not in the compass. Frequently, a pilot suffers the illusion that the compass is stuck. This, of course, is possible, but not probable. A simple test is to make a 90° turn using some line on the ground as a point of reference and resume level flight. If the compass then shows a change of 90° in the reading, the pilot may return to his original course with the assurance that his compass is not seriously in error. The magnetic compass will be more fully covered in the section on instruments.

15. Basic Calculations

In chapter 14 we determined how to measure the true course on the aeronautical chart and how to make corrections for variation and deviation, but one important factor has not been considered—wind effect.

Effect of Wind   As we learned in our study of the atmosphere, wind is a term used to indicate that a body of air is moving over the surface of the earth in a definite direction. When we say that the wind is blowing from the north at 25 mph, we simply mean that air is moving southward over the earth's surface at the rate of 25 miles in 1 hour.

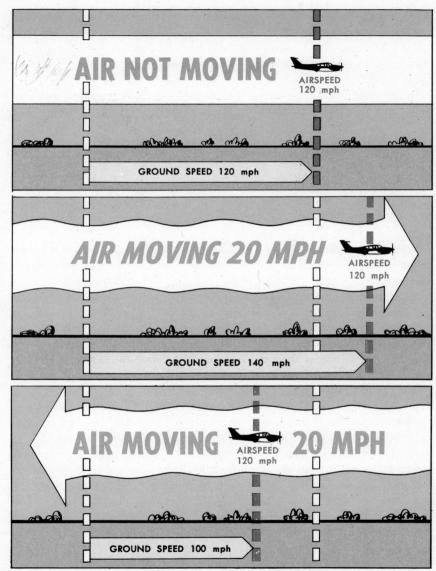

Figure 74. *Motion of the air affects the speed with which airplanes move over the earth's surface. Airspeed, the rate at which a plane moves through the air, is not affected by air motion.*

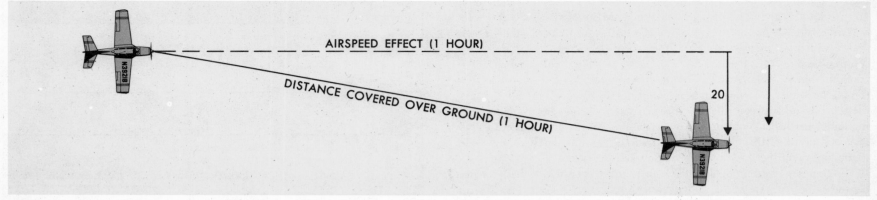

AIRSPEED EFFECT (1 HOUR)

DISTANCE COVERED OVER GROUND (1 HOUR)

20

Figure 75. *Airplane flight path resulting from its airspeed and direction, and the wind speed and direction.*

Under these conditions, any inert object wholly free from contact with the earth will be carried 25 miles southward in 1 hour. This effect becomes apparent when we observe clouds, dust, toy balloons, etc., blown along by the wind. Obviously, an airplane flying within the moving mass of air will be affected in exactly the same way. However, the airplane moves through the air at the same time that the air is moving over the ground. Consequently, at the end of 1 hour of flight, the airplane will be in a position which results from a combination of these two motions: the movement of the air mass in reference to the ground, and the forward movement of the airplane through the air mass.

Actually, these two motions are independent. So far as the airplane's flight through the air is concerned, it makes no difference whether the air is moving or is stationary. A pilot flying in a 70-mile gale would be totally unaware of any wind (except for possible turbulence) unless he looked at the ground. In reference to the ground, however, the airplane would appear to fly faster with a tailwind or slower with a headwind, or to drift right or left with a sidewind.

As shown in figure 74, an airplane flying eastward at an airspeed of 120 mph in still air, will have a ground speed exactly the same—120 mph. If the mass of air is moving eastward at 20 mph, the speed of the airplane (airspeed) will not be affected, but the progress of the plane as measured over the ground will be 120 plus 20, or a ground speed of 140 mph. On the other hand, if the mass of air is moving westward at 20 mph, the speed of the airplane still remains the same, but ground speed becomes 120 minus 20 or 100 mph.

If the plane is heading eastward at 120 mph, and the air mass moving southward at 20 mph, the plane at the end of 1 hour will be 120 miles east of its point of departure (due to its progress through the air) and 20 miles south (due to the motion of the air) (fig. 75). Under these circumstances the airspeed remains 120 mph, but the ground speed is determined by combining the movement of the airplane with the movement of the air mass. Ground speed can be measured as the distance from the point of departure to the position of the airplane at the end of 1 hour. The ground speed can be computed in flight by noting the time required to fly between two points a known distance apart (such as two checkpoints on the course). It also can be determined before flight by constructing a wind triangle, which will be explained in chapter 16.

The direction in which the plane is pointing as it flies is *heading*. Its actual path over the ground, a combination of the motion of the airplane and the motion of the air, is *track*. The angle between the heading and the track is *drift angle*. If the airplane is headed down the course line with the wind blowing from the left, the track will not coincide with the desired course. The wind will drift the airplane to the right, so the track will fall to the right of the desired course (fig. 76).

By anticipating the amount of drift, the pilot can counteract the effect of the wind, thereby making the track of the airplane coincide with the desired course. If the mass of air is moving across the course from the left, the airplane will drift to the right, and a correction must be made by heading the airplane sufficiently to the left to offset this drift. To state it another way, if

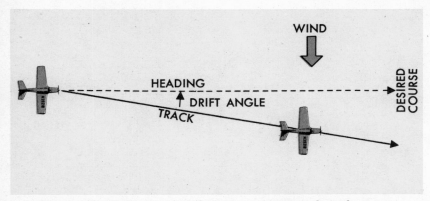

Figure 76. *Effects of wind drift on maintaining desired course.*

the wind is from the left the correction will be made by turning the airplane to the left—correct into the wind. This is the wind correction angle and is expressed in terms of degrees right or left of the true course (fig. 77).

To summarize:

COURSE is the direction toward the destination, as measured on the chart.

HEADING is the direction in which the nose of the airplane points during flight.

TRACK is the actual path made over the ground in flight. (If proper correction has been made for the wind, track and course will be identical.)

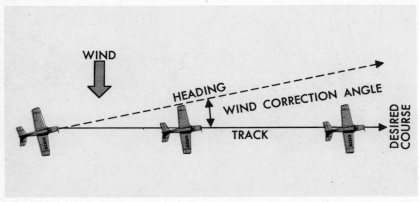

Figure 77. *Establishing a wind correction angle that will counteract wind drift and maintain the desired course.*

DRIFT ANGLE is the angle between heading and track.

WIND CORRECTION ANGLE is correction applied to the course to establish a heading that will make track coincide with course.

AIRSPEED is the rate of the plane's progress through the air.

GROUND SPEED is the rate of the plane's progress over the ground.

Calculating Time, Speed, Distance, and Fuel Consumption Before attempting a cross-country flight, a pilot will need to know how to make common calculations for time, speed, and distance, and the amount of fuel required. These are all matters of simple arithmetic, which should present no difficulty.

Converting Minutes to Equivalent in Hours Because speed is expressed in miles per hour, it frequently is necessary to convert minutes into equivalent hours when solving speed, time, and distance problems. To convert minutes to hours, divide by 60 (60 minutes = 1 hour). Thus, 30 minutes equals $\frac{30}{60} =$ 0.5 hour. To convert hours to minutes, multiply by 60. Thus, 0.75 hour equals $0.75 \times 60 = 45$ minutes.

Time — $T = \dfrac{D}{GS}$ To find the time (T) in flight, divide the distance (D) by the ground speed (GS). The time to fly 210 miles at a ground speed of 140 mph is 210 divided by 140, or 1.5 hours. (The 0.5 hour multiplied by 60 minutes equals 30 minutes.) Answer: 1:30.

Distance — $D = GS \times T$ To find the distance flown in a given time, multiply ground speed by time. The distance flown in 1 hour and 45 minutes at a ground speed of 120 mph is 120×1.75, or 210 miles.

Ground Speed — $GS = \dfrac{D}{T}$ To find the ground speed, divide the distance flown by the time required. If an airplane flies 270 miles in 3 hours, the ground speed is 270 divided by 3 = 90 mph.

Converting Knots to Miles Per Hour Another important conversion is changing knots to miles per hour. Air carriers and the military services use knots rather than miles per hour when reporting speeds. The Weather Bureau reports both surface winds and winds aloft in knots. However, airspeed indicators in personal-type airplanes are normally calibrated in miles per hour (although many are now calibrated in both miles per hour and knots). Private pilots, therefore, should learn to convert wind speeds in knots to miles per hour.

A knot is 1 nautical mile per hour. Because there are 6,076.1 feet in a nautical mile and 5,280 feet in a statute mile, the conversion factor is 1.15. To convert knots to miles per hour, simply multiply knots by 1.15. For example: a wind speed of 20 knots is equivalent to 23 mph.

Most computers used in navigation have a means of making this conversion simply by reading the scale. Another quick method of conversion is to use the scales of nautical miles and statute miles at the bottom of aeronautical charts.

Fuel Consumption   Airplane fuel consumption rate is computed in gallons per hour.

Consequently, to determine the fuel required for a given flight, you must know the time required. Time in flight multiplied by rate of consumption gives the quantity of fuel required. For example, a flight of 400 miles at a ground speed of 100 mph requires 4 hours. If the plane consumes 5 gallons an hour, the total fuel consumption will be 4 × 5, or 20 gallons.

The rate of fuel consumption depends on many factors: the condition of the engine, the pitch and speed of propeller rotation, the richness of the mixture, and particularly the percentage of horsepower used for flight at cruising speed. Ordinarily, the pilot will know the approximate rate from cruise performance charts, from his own experience, or from the experience of someone familiar with the plane. In addition to the amount of fuel required for his trip, he should always allow enough reserve for *at least* an additional 45 minutes of flight.

16. The Wind Triangle

The wind triangle is a simple graphic explanation of the effect of wind upon flight. It gives the pilot essential information about ground speed, heading, and time for any flight. It is used by all pilots, from the novice to the most experienced navigator, and applies to the simplest kind of cross-country flight as well as the most complicated instrument flight. The seasoned pilot becomes so familiar with the fundamental principles that he usually can make rough estimates adequate for visual flight without actually drawing the diagrams. *The beginning student, however, needs to develop skill in constructing the diagrams as an aid to his complete understanding of the wind effect.* Either consciously or unconsciously, every good pilot thinks of his flight in terms of the wind triangle.

Figures 78 and 79 show how to construct the wind triangle with a protractor or ruler.

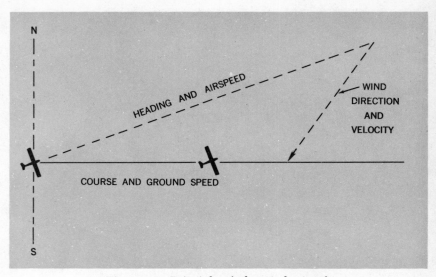

Figure 78. *Principle of the wind triangle.*

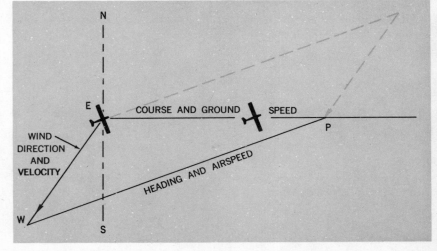

Figure 79. *The wind triangle as it is drawn in navigation practice. Blue lines show the triangle as drawn in figure 78.*

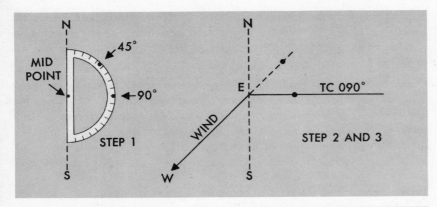

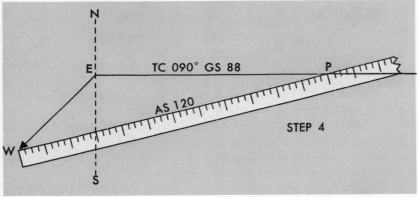

Figure 80. *Steps in drawing the wind triangle.*

Take a typical problem. Suppose we wish to fly from E to P. We draw a line on the chart connecting the two points, measure its direction (see chapter 14) with a protractor, and find the true course to be due east (090°). We learn from the Weather Bureau that the weather is favorable and the wind at the altitude we intend to fly is 35 knots from the northeast (045°). Since the Weather Bureau reports the windspeed in knots, we convert that speed to approximately 40 mph. We know that our normal airspeed is 120 mph.

Now on a plain sheet of paper we draw a vertical line representing north and south. (The various steps are shown in fig. 80).

We then place the protractor with the base resting on this line and the curved edge facing east. At the center point of the base we make a dot which we label "E" (point of departure) and at the curved edge we make a dot at 90° (indicating the direction of our course) and another at 45° (indicating wind direction).

Now with the ruler we draw the true course line from E extending it somewhat beyond the dot at 90°, and labeling it "TC 090°."

Next we align the ruler with E and the dot at 45°, and draw the wind arrow from E, not toward 045°, but in the direction the wind is blowing, making it 40 units long, to correspond with the wind velocity of 40 mph. This line we identify as the wind line by placing the letter "W" at the end to show the wind direction. Finally, we measure 120 units on the ruler to represent the airspeed, making a dot on the ruler at this point. We then place

If we wish to fly a course to the east, with a wind blowing from northeast, we know we must head the plane somewhat to the north of east to counteract drift. This we can represent by a diagram as shown in figure 78. Each line represents direction and speed. The long dotted line shows the direction the plane is heading, and its length represents the airspeed for 1 hour. The short dotted line at the right shows the wind direction, and its length represents the wind velocity for 1 hour. The solid line shows the direction of the track, or the path of the airplane as measured over the ground, and its length represents the distance traveled in 1 hour, or the ground speed.

In actual practice, we do not draw the triangle illustrated in figure 78; instead we construct a similar triangle as shown by the black lines in figure 79.

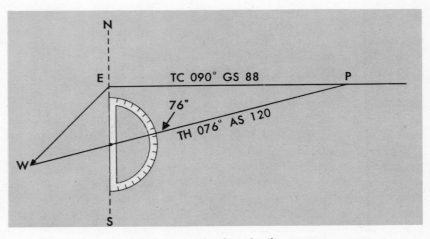

Figure 81. *Finding true heading by direct measurement.*

the ruler so that the end is on the arrowhead (W) and the 120-mile dot intercepts the true course line. We draw the line and label it "AS 120." The point "P," placed at the intersection, represents the position of the plane at the end of 1 hour.

The diagram is now complete.

The distance flown in 1 hour (ground speed) is measured as the number of units on the true course line (88 mph.).

The true heading necessary to offset drift is indicated by the direction of the airspeed line which can be determined in two ways:

1. By placing the straight side of the protractor along the north-south line, with its center point at the intersection of the airspeed line and north-south line, we can read the true heading directly in degrees (076°) (fig. 81).

2. By placing the straight side of the protractor along the true course line, with its center at P, we can read the angle between the true course and the airspeed line. This is the wind correction angle (WCA) which must be applied to the true course to obtain the true heading. If the wind blows from the right, the angle will be added; if from the left, it will be subtracted. In the example given, the WCA is 14° and the wind is from the left; therefore, we subtract 14° from true course of 090°, making the true heading 076° (fig. 82).

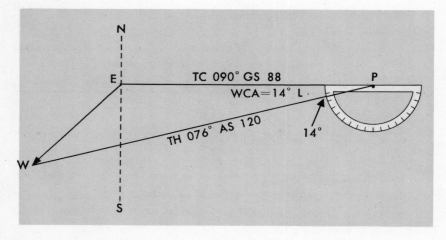

Figure 82. *Finding true heading by the wind correction angle.*

After obtaining the true heading, we can apply the correction for magnetic variation to obtain magnetic heading, and the correction for compass deviation to obtain a compass heading which enables us to fly directly to our destination by dead reckoning.

Distance, Time, and Fuel We find the distance to our destination by measuring the length of the course line drawn on the aeronautical chart (*using the appropriate scale at the bottom of the chart*). This scale is approximately 8 miles to an inch for sectional charts. If the distance measures 220 miles we divide by our ground speed of 88 mph, which gives us 2.5 hours (or 2:30) as the time required. If our fuel consumption is 8 gallons an hour we shall use 8 × 2.5 or about 20 gallons.

Briefly summarized, the steps in obtaining flight information are as follows:

TRUE COURSE.—Direction of the line connecting two desired points, drawn on the chart and measured clockwise in degrees from true north on the midmeridian.

WIND CORRECTION ANGLE.—Determined from wind triangle. (Added to TC if the wind is from the right; subtracted if wind is from the left.)

TRUE HEADING.—The direction in which the nose of the plane should point to make good the desired course.

VARIATION.—Obtained from the isogonic line on the chart. (Added to TH if west; subtracted if east.)

MAGNETIC HEADING.—An intermediate step in the conversion. (Obtained by applying variation to true heading.)

DEVIATION.—Obtained from the deviation card on the airplane. (Added to MH or subtracted; as indicated.)

COMPASS HEADING.—The reading on the compass (found by applying deviation to MH) which will be followed to make good the desired course.

TOTAL DISTANCE.—Obtained by measuring the length of the TC line on the chart (using the scale at the bottom of the chart.)

GROUND SPEED.—Obtained by measuring the length of the TC line on the wind triangle (using the scale employed for drawing the diagram.)

TIME FOR FLIGHT.—Total distance divided by ground speed.

FUEL RATE.—Predetermined gallons per hour used at cruising speed.

FUEL CONSUMPTION.—Fuel rate multiplied by time required.

NOTE: Additional fuel for 45 minutes of flight should be added as a safety measure.

A useful combination Planning Sheet and Flight Log form is shown in figure 83.

Plane Identification

PILOT'S PLANNING SHEET

Date

CRUISING AIRSPEED	TC	WIND		WCA	TH	VAR	MH	DEV	CH	TOTAL MILES	GS	TOTAL TIME	FUEL RATE	TOTAL FUEL
		MPH	FROM	R+ L−		W+ E−								
From:														
To:														
From:														
To:														

VISUAL FLIGHT LOG

TIME OF DEPARTURE	RADIO FREQUENCIES		DISTANCE		ELAPSED TIME		CLOCK TIME		GS		CH		REMARKS
POINT OF DEPARTURE	TOWER	RANGE	POINT TO POINT	CUMULATIVE	ESTIMATED	ACTUAL	ESTIMATED	ACTUAL	ESTIMATED	ACTUAL	ESTIMATED	ACTUAL	BRACKETS, WEATHER, ETC.
CHECKPOINTS 1.													
2.													
3.													
4.													
5.													
DESTINATION 6.													

The Pilot's Planning Sheet provides space for entering dead-reckoning data.

The Visual Flight Log may be prepared in advance by entering the selected checkpoints, together with the following data: Distance between checkpoints, and cumulative distance; estimated time between checkpoints; clock or cumulative time; groundspeed and Compass Heading.

As the flight progresses, the actual time, groundspeed and Compass Heading should be filled in, thus completing the log.

Figure 83. *Pilot's planning sheet and visual flight log.*

Data for Return Trip The true course for the return trip will be the reciprocal of the outbound course. This can be measured on the chart, or found more easily by adding 180° to the outbound course (090° + 180° = 270°), if the outbound course is less than 180°. If the outbound course is greater than 180°, the 180° should be subtracted instead of added. For example, if the outbound course is 200°, the reciprocal will be 200° − 180° = 020°. The wind correction angle will be the same number of degrees as for the outbound course, but since the wind will be on the opposite side (right) of the plane, in the above example, the correction will have to be added to the true course instead of subtracted (270° + 14° = 284°). Thus, the true heading for the return trip will be 284°.

To find the ground speed, construct a new wind triangle. Instead of drawing another complete diagram, however, consider the point E on the previous diagram as the starting point for the return trip and extend the true course line in the direction opposite to the outbound course. The wind line is then in the proper relationship and does not need to be redrawn. The airspeed line (120 units long) can be drawn from the point of the wind arrow (W) to intersect the return-trip true course line, as indicated in figure 84. The distance measured on this course line from the north-south line to the intersection gives the ground speed for the return trip (147 mph).

Figure 85 shows the various steps for constructing the wind triangle and

measuring the true heading and the wind correction angle for the problem in which the true course is 110°, the wind is 20 mph from the southwest (225°), and the airspeed is 100 mph. Notice that the true heading line has to be extended to intersect the north-south line to measure the true heading directly.

Before attempting to use a computer, you should understand the relationships involved by constructing other wind triangles for various airspeeds, winds, and true courses. Practice on the following problems:

Exercise No. 1 By constructing a wind triangle, find the wind correction angle (WCA), true heading (TH), and ground speed (GS) for each of the following conditions:

		WIND		*True Course degrees*	*True Airspeed (mph)*
		Direction degrees	*Speed (mph)*		
1.	....	135	30	240	120
2.	....	215	20	260	130
3.	....	050	33	260	150
4.	....	330	45	350	150
5.	....	300	45	100	150
6.	....	220	30	130	150

NOTE: See appendix II for correct answers.

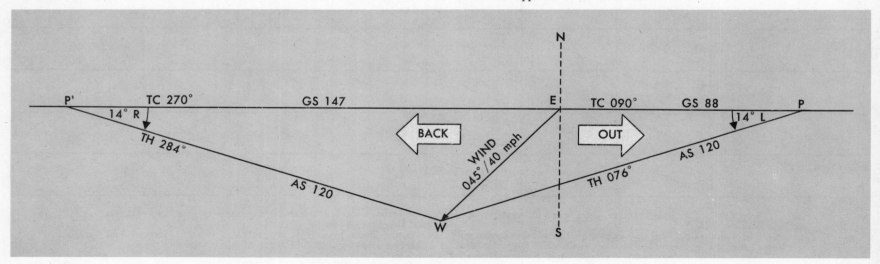

Figure 84. *Computations for a round-trip flight.*

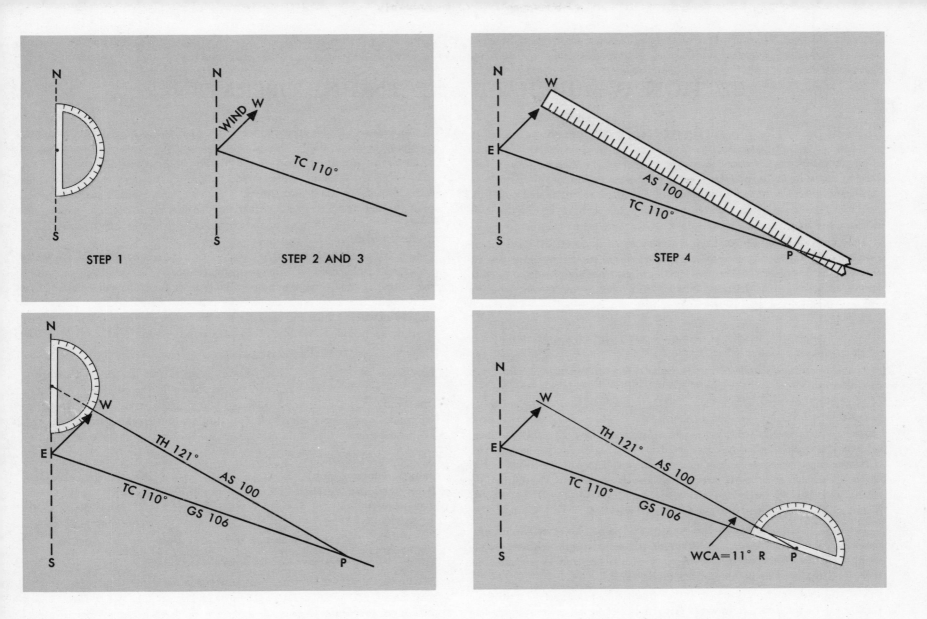

Figure 85. *Steps in constructing the wind triangle and the various measurements for a true course of 110°; wind 20 mph from 225°; airspeed of 100 mph.*

SECTION IV—AIRCRAFT AND ENGINE OPERATION

17. Airplane Structure

Of the many activities conducted by the Federal Aviation Agency in promoting safety in flight, perhaps none is of greater importance to pilots than certificates of airworthiness for airplanes. Every airplane certificated under the Standard classification has been manufactured under rigid specifications of design, materials, workmanship, construction, and performance.

Thousands of wing designs have been developed in an effort to determine the best types for specific purposes. Basically, all are similar to those used by the Wrights and other pioneers, but modifications have been made to increase lifting capacity, reduce friction, increase structural strength, and generally improve flight characteristics. Airfoils of new design are subjected to painstaking analysis before they are approved for use on certificated airplanes. Strength tests are conducted to determine the effect of strains and stresses which might be encountered in flight.

The most minute details of the entire structure of the airplane are given careful consideration—the strength and durability of each part, the method of assembling, the weight and balance. Maximums and minimums are established for performance—takeoff distance, rate of climb, landing speed, spin recovery characteristics, etc. Before delivery, every new airplane has been subjected to a thorough inspection and has been flight-tested. The Standard classification gives adequate assurance that the airplane will not be subject to structural failure *if* properly maintained and flown within the limitations clearly specified. However the airplane is not safe if abused, improperly maintained, or flown without regard to its limitations.

The goal of airplane design and construction is to obtain maximum efficiency, combined with adequate strength. Excess strength requires excess weight and therefore lowers the efficiency of the airplane by reducing its speed and the amount of useful load it can carry.

The required structural strength is based on the airplane's use. An airplane which is to be used only for normal flying is not expected to be subjected to the excessive strains of acrobatic maneuvers and therefore will not need to be as strong as an airplane intended for acrobatic flight or other special purposes involving severe in-flight stresses.

To permit utmost efficiency of construction without sacrificing safety, FAA has established several categories, with minimum strength requirements for each. Information about limitations of each airplane is made available to the pilot through markings on instruments, placards on instrument panels, operating limitations attached to airworthiness certificates, or airplane flight manuals carried in the airplane.

Airplane strength is measured basically by the total load which the wings are capable of carrying without permanent damage. The load imposed upon the wings depends very largely upon the type of flight in which the airplane is engaged. The wing must support not only the weight of the airplane but also the additional loads imposed during maneuvers such as turns and pullouts from dives. Rough air (turbulence) also imposes additional loads. This has been discussed in chapter 3.

Categories of Airplanes   Airplanes in categories of interest to the private pilot will withstand the limit-load factors shown in the table which follows. The limit loads should not be exceeded in actual operation even though a safety factor of 50 percent above limit loads is incorporated in the strength of the airplane.

Category	*Positive limit load*
Normal (nonacrobatic)	3.8 times gross weight
Utility (normal operations and limited acrobatic maneuvers)	4.4 times gross weight
Acrobatic	6.0 times gross weight

> NOTE: The negative limit load factors shall not be less than —0.4 times the positive load factor for the N and U categories, and shall not be less than —0.5 times the positive load factor for the A category.

Maintenance   If an airplane is to remain safe for flight, it must be properly maintained. FAA regulations require that an aircraft shall not be flown unless within the preceding 12 calendar months it has been given an annual inspection conducted by authorized personnel. (NOTE: A period of 12 calendar

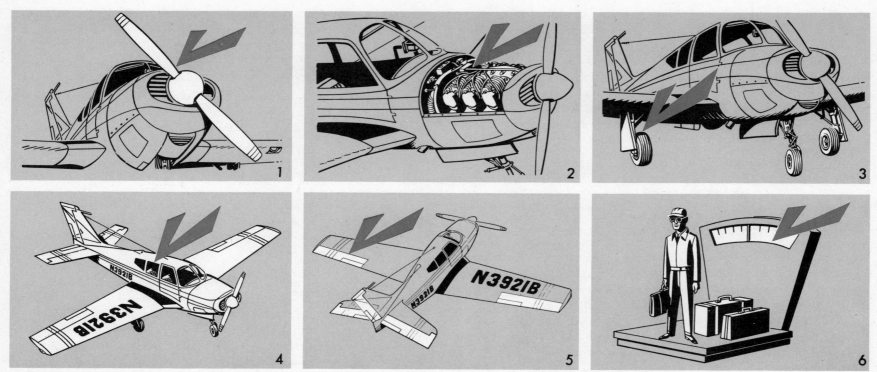

Figure 86. *Preflight inspection should include at least: (1) propeller; (2) engine; (3) landing gear; (4) wings and fuselage; (5) control surfaces and controls; (6) weight of baggage and passengers.*

months extends from any day within any month to the end of the last day of the same month of the following year.) When an airplane is to be used to carry passengers for hire or for flight instruction for hire, it must also have had a 100-hour inspection (that is, inspected in accordance with FAA regulations, within each 100 hours). The private pilot is prohibited by the regulations from carrying passengers for hire (except in certain special cases) or giving flight instruction for hire.

Any unusual conditions, such as excessive strain incurred in flight, hard landings, or abuse in the hangar, make additional inspections advisable. Frequent additional inspections give the pilot assurance that his airplane is thoroughly airworthy and reveal malfunctions which may be remedied quickly before developing into serious defects calling for major repairs.

Preflight Inspection

A careful pilot will always conduct a routine inspection before flight. By always beginning at a certain point and using an orderly procedure, the check can be made systematically and quickly. It should include at least the following items, all of which are not shown in figure 86.

Cockpit Battery (or master) and ignition switches should be checked in the OFF position. The landing gear handle (if retractable-gear type) should be checked in the DOWN position.

Powerplant

Propeller.—Check for nicks and cracks, tightness of hub, safetying of nuts.

Engine.—Check for tightness and safetying of all parts (including cowling). Check for security of all fuel lines and oil lines and look for fuel and oil leaks. Check exhaust manifolds for tightness and absence of cracks or holes (a cracked or broken exhaust manifold is a fire and carbon monoxide hazard).

Fuel and Oil.—Check supply visually—do not rely on gauges. Drain into a container a substantial amount of fuel from the fuel strainer (gascolator) and fuel tank, and check for contamination. See that fuel and oil caps are fastened securely to avoid fuel or oil syphonage, which may result in fire or fuel or oil starvation. Be sure fuel and oil vents are open and properly aligned; this will insure proper pressure in the fuel or oil tanks, maintaining steady fuel and oil flow.

Landing Gear Check tires for cuts, cracks, and proper inflation. Check struts and fittings for safetying and evidence of cracks, bends, or wear. Lubrication should be adequate but not excessive. Check brake assemblies and look for possible hydraulic leaks.

Wing, Fuselage, and Tail Surfaces Check covering for holes, wrinkles, wear and rot. Wrinkles may indicate internal damage. Check control cables for tension. Check fittings and cables for wear and safetying. Check ailerons, rudder, and elevator for tightness and freedom of movement. Check to see that all surfaces are free from mud, snow, ice, and frost.

Pitot-Static System.—Check to see that the static vents are open and that the pitot tube is unobstructed. Obstructions will result in unreliable readings on the airspeed indicator and other pitot-static instruments.

Controls Check controls for proper movement. Set stabilizer or elevator trim tab for takeoff position.

Check the loading to be sure it does not exceed limitations as given in the FAA-approved Airplane Flight Manual. Be sure that the maximum weight allowance in the baggage compartment is NOT exceeded. This may produce a tail-heavy airplane that has very undesirable flight characteristics and is dangerous.

NOTE: The Airplane Flight Manual should be checked for further items of importance to be considered during the preflight inspection.

18. Engine Operation

Knowing a few general principles of engine operation will help you obtain dependable and efficient service and avoid engine failure. In this short chapter, it is impractical to discuss in detail the various types of engines and the finer points of operation which you, as a pilot, will learn only through experience. You will have access to the manufacturer's instruction manual, you will be familiar with the operating limitations for the airplane, and you will be able to get specific advice from your flight instructor.

How an Engine Operates

Most airplane engines operate upon the same principle as automobile engines. As shown in figure 87, the mechanism consists of a cylinder, a piston, a connecting rod, and a crankshaft. One end of the connecting rod is attached to the piston and the other to a crankshaft which converts the straight-line motion of the piston to a rotary motion which turns the propeller. At the closed end of the cylinder there are normally two spark plugs, to ignite the fuel, and two openings, controlled by valves—one to admit the mixture of fuel and air, and the other to permit the burned gases to escape. Operation of the engine requires four strokes of the piston:

Diagram A of figure 87 shows the piston moving away from the cylinder head. The intake valve is opened and the fuel-air mixture is sucked into the cylinder.

Diagram B shows the piston returning to the top of the cylinder. Both valves are closed, and the fuel-air mixture compressed.

When the piston is approximately at the top of the cylinder head, a spark from the plugs ignites the mixture, which burns very rapidly. Expansion of the burning gas exerts pressure on the piston, forcing it downward in the power stroke, shown in diagram C.

Just before the piston completes the power stroke, the exhaust valve starts to open, and the burned gases are forced out as the piston returns to the top of the cylinder. The cycle is ready to begin again (diagram D).

From this description notice that a 1-cylinder engine delivers power only once in every four strokes of the piston or every two revolutions of the crankshaft. The momentum of the crankshaft carries the piston through the other three strokes. To increase power and gain smoothness of operation, other cylinders are added and the power strokes are timed to occur at successive intervals during the revolution of the crankshaft.

Cooling of the Engine

The burning of fuel within the cylinders produces intense heat, most of which is expelled through the exhaust. Much of the remaining heat, however, must be removed to prevent the engine from overheating. In practically all automobile engines, excess heat is carried away by water circulating around

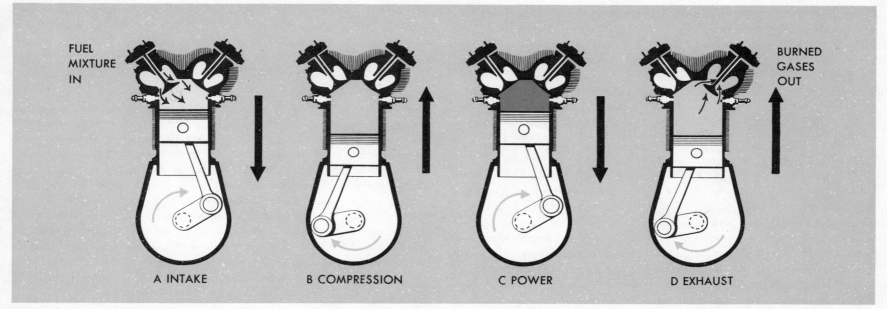

FUEL MIXTURE IN

BURNED GASES OUT

A INTAKE   B COMPRESSION   C POWER   D EXHAUST

Figure 87. *Four strokes of the piston produce power: (A) Fuel mixture (light blue) is drawn into cylinder by downward stroke. (B) Mixture (darker blue) is compressed by upward stroke. (C) Spark ignites mixture (red), forcing piston downward and producing power that turns propeller. (D) Burned gases (light red) pushed out of cylinder by upward stroke.*

the cylinder walls. Most airplane engines are air-cooled. They are built with fins projecting from the cylinder walls so that heat will be carried away by air flowing past the fins.

When an engine is operating on the ground, very little air flows past the cylinders (particularly if the engine is closely cowled) and overheating is likely to occur. Overheating may also occur during a prolonged climb, because the engine is usually developing high power at relatively slow air speed.

Operating the engine at a higher temperature than it was designed for will cause loss of power, excessive oil consumption, and detonation. It will also lead to serious permanent injury, scoring the cylinder walls, damaging the pistons and rings, burning and warping the valves.

For engines with a cylinder-head temperature gauge, the proper operating temperature can readily be determined. Many light engines, however, do not have such a gauge, and the pilot must rely on the oil-temperature gauge to indicate engine temperature.

Oil, used primarily to lubricate the moving parts of the engine, also helps reduce engine temperature by removing some of the heat from the cylinders. The pilot should keep a constant check on oil gauges because a variation beyond normal limits indicates engine trouble which calls for an immediate adjustment or landing to prevent serious damage. Using the kind of oil specified by the engine manufacturer will prevent the expensive repairs that inevitably result from improper lubrication.

Proper Fuel Essential

The engine must have the proper fuel to operate satisfactorily. Automobile gasoline should not be used because gums and other harmful substances may form in the engine. In addition, automobile gasoline has a much higher vapor pressure than aviation fuel and may produce *vapor-lock*, a vaporization of gasoline in the fuel lines which prevents the flow of fuel to the carburetor.

81

Aviation gasoline is classified by *octane ratings* and *performance number* power ratings. The proper fuel rating for the engine, as specified by the manufacturer, is always found in the operating limitations and is usually placarded at the fuel filler opening. Using aviation gasoline of a rating higher than specified does not improve engine operation and may sometimes be harmful. *Using aviation gasoline of a lower rating is* definitely *harmful under any circumstances* because it may cause loss of power, excessive heat, burned spark plugs, burned and stuck valves, high oil consumption, and detonation.

Use of Mixture Control The fuel-air mixture in most engines can be changed by adjusting the *mixture control* in the cockpit. The mixture control will normally have a red knob (an indication to use caution). This control enables the pilot to adjust the ratio of the fuel-to-air mixture that goes into the cylinders. This ratio of fuel to air is the most important single factor affecting the power output of an engine.

If the fuel-air mixture is too lean (too little fuel for the amount of air—in terms of weight), rough engine operation, sudden "cutting out" or "backfiring," detonation, overheating, or an appreciable loss of engine power may occur. Lean mixtures must be especially avoided when an engine is operating near its maximum output (such as on takeoffs, climbs, and go-arounds). At altitudes of less than 5,000 feet an excessively lean mixture may cause serious overheating and loss of power.

If the fuel-air mixture is too rich (too much fuel for the amount of air—in terms of weight), rough engine operation and an appreciable loss of engine power may also occur.

Carburetors are normally calibrated for sea-level operation, which means that the correct mixture of fuel and air will be obtained at sea level with the mixture control in the "full rich" position. As altitude increases, we have already learned, the air density decreases, which means that a cubic foot of air will not weigh as much as it would at a lower altitude. This means that as the flight altitude increases, the weight of air entering the carburetor will decrease, although the volume remains the same. The amount of fuel entering the carburetor depends on the volume of air and not the weight of air. Therefore, as the flight altitude increases, the amount of fuel entering the carburetor will remain approximately the same for any given throttle setting if the position of the mixture control remains unchanged. Since the same amount (weight) of fuel is entering the carburetor, but a lesser amount (weight) of air, the fuel-air mixture becomes richer as altitude increases.

We have already discussed the effects of too rich a mixture. To maintain the correct fuel-air ratio, the pilot must be able to adjust the amount of fuel mixed with the incoming air as his altitude increases. To do this the pilot uses the mixture control in the cockpit, which is connected to the carburetor by mechanical linkage.

Follow the manufacturer's recommendations on leaning the fuel mixture for the particular airplane.

Detonation Detonation, which is easily detected in an automobile engine by a "pinging" sound, may not be heard in an airplane engine because of other noises. When the engine is operating normally, the spark plug ignites the fuel at the proper instant, and the fuel burns and expands rapidly, exerting an even pressure on the piston. Detonation occurs if the fuel explodes instead of burning evenly. The resulting shock causes loss of power and frequently leads to serious engine trouble. As already stated, detonation may be produced by overheating, low grade fuel, or too lean a mixture. It may also be caused by opening the throttle abruptly when the engine is running at slow speed. To prevent detonation, therefore, the pilot should use the correct grade of fuel, maintain a sufficiently rich mixture, open the throttle smoothly, and keep the temperature of the engine within recommended operating limits.

Refueling Procedure Static electricity, formed by the friction of air passing over the surfaces of an airplane in flight and by the flow of fuel through the hose and nozzle, creates a fire hazard during refueling. To guard against the possibility of a spark igniting fuel fumes, a ground wire should be attached to the aircraft before the cap is removed from the tank. The refueling nozzle should be grounded to the aircraft before refueling is begun and throughout the refueling process. The fuel truck should also be grounded to the aircraft and the ground.

Fuel Contamination

Water and dirt contamination of fuel systems is potentially dangerous; the pilot must prevent contamination or eliminate contamination that has occurred. Of the many accidents attributed to powerplant failure from fuel contamination, most have been traced directly to:

1. Inadequate preflight inspection by the pilot.
2. Servicing of aircraft with improperly filtered fuel from small tanks or drums.
3. Storing aircraft with partially filled fuel tanks.
4. Lack of proper maintenance.

Each of these factors may result in fuel contamination. (See Exam-O-Gram No. 10, appendix I.)

Preventive Measures for Contaminated Fuel   What can the pilot do to help prevent water from contaminating the fuel? As one preventive measure, he should have the fuel tanks completely filled after each flight, or at least after the last flight of the day. This will prevent moisture condensation within the tank since no air space will be left. Suppose the pilot knows that on his next flight, to be made the next day, he will not be able to carry a full fuel load because of the weight of his passengers and baggage. If this situation arises and he chooses to refuel with only the amount he can carry on his next flight, he must realize that he is adding to the risk of having his fuel contaminated by moisture condensation within the tank. If his flight is cancelled the next day for some reason, then each additional day may add to the amount of moisture condensation within the tanks.

A second preventive measure the pilot can take is *not* to refuel from cans and drums. This practice introduces a major likelihood of fuel contamination. Should a pilot have to use this method, the fuel should be strained through a good chamois skin to prevent any water and dirt in the can from entering the fuel tanks.

Elimination Measures for Contaminated Fuel   What can the pilot do to eliminate water present in the fuel system of his aircraft? First of all, he should always assume that his fuel *is* contaminated with water, and take the necessary steps to eliminate it during his preflight inspection. He should drain a substantial amount of fuel from the fuel strainer (gascolator) quick drain and from each fuel tank sump into a transparent container and check for dirt and water. Water will sink to the bottom of the sample. Water, being heavier than gasoline, seeks the lowest levels in the fuel system. However, experiments have shown that when the fuel strainer is being drained, water in the tank may not appear until all the fuel has been drained from the lines leading to the tank. This would indicate that the water is staying in the tank itself and not forcing the fuel out of the fuel lines leading to the fuel strainer. Therefore, drain enough fuel from the fuel strainer to be sure that fuel is being obtained from the tank itself. This amount will depend on the length of fuel line from the tank to the drain. If water is found in the first sample, drain further samples until no trace appears.

Experiments have also shown that water still remained in the fuel tanks after the drainage from the fuel strainer had ceased to show any trace of water. This residual water could be removed only by draining the fuel tank sumps. Aircraft owners should have quick-drain valves installed in aircraft fuel tanks if not already installed.

Ignition System

The function of the ignition system is to provide a spark to ignite the fuel-air mixture in the cylinder. The magneto ignition system is used on most modern aircraft engines. Magnetos are self-contained units supplying ignition current without using an external current supply. However, the magneto has to be actuated and the engine started. The aircraft battery furnishes electrical power to operate the starter system; the starter system actuates the rotating element of the magneto; and the magneto then furnishes the spark to each cylinder to start the engine. After the engine starts, the starter system is disengaged, and the battery no longer has any part in the actual operation of the engine. If the battery (or master) switch were turned OFF, the engine would continue to run. However, this should not be done, since battery power is necessary at low engine rpm to operate other electrical equipment (radio, lights, etc.) and, when the generator is operating, the battery will be storing up a charge.

Most modern engines have a dual ignition system—that is, two magnetos to supply the electric current to the dual spark plugs contained in each combustion chamber. One magneto system supplies the current to one set of plugs; the second magneto system supplies the current to the other set of plugs. That is why the ignition switch has four positions: OFF, L, R, and BOTH. With the switch in the "L" or "R" position, only one magneto is supplying current and only one set of spark plugs is firing. With the switch in the BOTH position, both magnetos are supplying current and both sets of spark plugs are firing. The main advantages of the dual system are:

1. Increased safety. In case one system fails, the engine may be operated on the other until a landing is safely made.

NOTE: That is why it is extremely important for each magneto to be checked for proper operation during the preflight check. This should be done in accordance with the manufacturer's recommendations in the *Airplane Flight Manual.*

2. Improved burning and combustion of the mixture, and consequently improved performance.

Carburetor Icing

Carburetor icing is a frequent cause of engine failure. The vaporization of fuel, combined with the expansion of air as it passes through the carburetor, causes a sudden cooling of the mixture. The temperature of the air passing through the carburetor may drop as much as 60° F. within a fraction of a second. Water vapor in the air is "squeezed out" by this cooling, and, if the temperature in the carburetor reaches 32° F. or below, the moisture will be deposited as frost or ice inside the carburetor passages. Even a slight accumulation of this deposit will reduce power and may lead to complete engine failure, particularly when the throttle is partly or fully closed (fig. 88).

Conditions Favorable for Carburetor Icing   On dry days, or when the temperature is well below freezing, the moisture in the air is not generally enough to cause trouble. But if the temperature is between 20° F. and 70° F., with visible moisture or high humidity, the pilot should be constantly on the alert for carburetor ice. During low or closed throttle settings, an engine is particularly susceptible to carburetor icing.

Indications of Carburetor Icing   For airplanes with fixed-pitch propellers, the first indication of carburetor icing is loss of rpm. For airplanes with controllable pitch (constant-speed) propellers, the first indication is usually a drop in manifold pressure. In both cases, a roughness in engine operation may develop later. There will be no reduction in rpm in airplanes with constant-speed propellers since propeller pitch is automatically adjusted to compensate for the loss of power, thus maintaining constant rpm.

Use of Carburetor Heat   The carburetor heater is an anti-icing device that preheats the air before it reaches the carburetor. This preheating can be used to melt any ice or snow entering the intake, to melt ice that forms in the carburetor passages (provided the accumulation is not too great), and to keep the fuel mixture above the freezing point to prevent formation of carburetor ice.

When conditions are favorable for carburetor icing, the pilot should make the proper checks to see if any is present. When he notes indications of icing, he should immediately apply carburetor heat. In either case the procedure is the same. When initially applying carburetor heat, use the full-on position. It should be left in this position until the pilot is certain no ice is present or, if ice was present, that it has all been removed. If ice is present, applying partial heat or leaving heat on for an insufficient time may aggravate the situation.

When heat is first applied there will be a drop in rpm in airplanes equipped with fixed-pitch propellers and a drop in manifold pressure in airplanes equipped with controllable-pitch propellers. If there is no carburetor ice, there will be no further change in rpm or manifold pressure until the carburetor heat is turned off, when the rpm or manifold pressure will return to the reading before heat was applied. If carburetor ice is present, there will normally

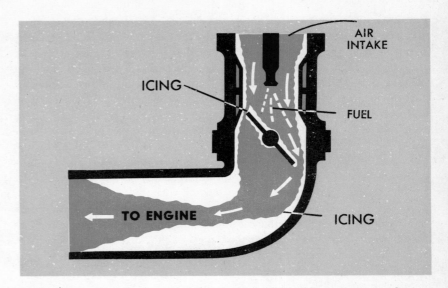

Figure 88. *Formation of ice (white) in the fuel intake system may reduce or block fuel flow (red) to the engine.*

be an immediate rise in rpm or manifold pressure (often accompanied by intermittent engine roughness); and then, when the carburetor heat is removed, the rpm or manifold pressure will rise to a setting greater than that before application of the heat. The engine should also run more smoothly.

Whenever the throttle is closed during flight, the engine cools rapidly and vaporization of the fuel is less complete than if the engine were warm. Also, the engine is more susceptible to carburetor icing. Therefore, if the pilot suspects carburetor-icing conditions and anticipates closed-throttle operation, he should turn carburetor heat full-on before closing the throttle. The heat should be left on during the closed-throttle operation. The heat will help in better fuel vaporization and carburetor ice prevention. Periodically, however, the throttle should be opened smoothly for a few seconds to keep the engine warm, since otherwise the carburetor heater may not provide enough heat to prevent icing.

Use of carburetor heat tends to reduce the output of the engine and also to increase the operating temperature. Therefore, the heat should not be used when full power is required (as during takeoff) or during normal engine operation except to check for the presence of, or to remove, carburetor ice.

In extreme cases of carburetor icing, after the ice has been removed it may be necessary to apply just enough carburetor heat to prevent further ice formation. *However, this must be done with caution. Check the manufacturer's recommendations on the use of carburetor heat for the airplane you fly.*

The carburetor heat should be checked for proper operation during the preflight check. Follow the manufacturer's recommendations in making this check.

Fuel Injection   Fuel injectors have replaced carburetors in some airplanes. In the fuel injection system, the fuel is normally injected into the system either directly into the cylinders or just ahead of the intake valve; whereas, in the carburetor, the fuel enters the airstream at the throttle valve. The fuel injection system is generally considered to be less susceptible to icing than the carburetor system.

Idling Procedure

Whenever the throttle is closed during flight, the engine cools rapidly and vaporization of fuel is less complete. Furthermore, the airflow through the carburetor system under such conditions is not sufficiently rapid to assure a uniform mixture of fuel and air. Consequently, the engine may stop because it is receiving too lean a mixture ("starving") or too rich a mixture ("loading up"). A sudden opening or closing of the throttle may aggravate this condition, and the engine may cough once or twice, sputter, and stop.

Three precautions should be taken to prevent the engine from stopping while idling. First, make sure that the ground-idling speed is properly adjusted (about 550 to 660 rpm minimum for most light engines.) Second, do not open or close the throttle abruptly. Third, keep the engine warm during glides by frequently opening the throttle for a few seconds.

Starting the Engine

Before starting the engine, move the airplane to a position clear of other aircraft, where the propeller will not stir up gravel or dust to damage the propeller, injure property, or cause annoyance. The wheels should be held firmly, either by adequate parking brakes or blocks in front of the wheels.

Engines Equipped With a Starter   The exact starting procedure differs among engines, and the pilot should be familiar with the operating manual starting procedure for his particular engine. If the engine has a starter, the pilot should make sure no one is in front of the propeller. He should always check to be sure the area is clear, call "clear," and wait for a response before engaging the starter.

As soon as the engine starts, advance the throttle to obtain recommended warmup rpm and *check the oil pressure gauge immediately*. Unless the gauge indicates oil pressure within a few seconds, stop the engine and discover what is causing lack of oil pressure. If oil is not circulating properly, the engine can be seriously damaged in a short time.

The engine must reach normal operating temperature before it will run smoothly and dependably. Temperature is indicated by the cylinder-head temperature gauge. If the airplane is not equipped with this gauge you must depend on the oil-temperature gauge. Remember, in this case, that oil warms very slowly in cold weather.

Just before takeoff check engine operation thoroughly—including each magneto separately. Check for proper operation of carburetor heat at magneto-checking rpm. *Follow the manufacturer's recommendations when performing all checks.* Use a check list—do not rely on memory.

To enable the pilot to check operation quickly and easily, engine instruments are marked in much the same way as the airspeed indicator. A red line indicates maximum or minimum limits and a green arc indicates normal operating range.

Engines Not Equipped With a Starter   If the airplane has no self-starter, the person who is to turn the propeller calls "Gas on, switch off, throttle closed, brakes on." The pilot will check these items and repeat the phrase. The switch and throttle must not be touched again until the person swinging the prop calls "contact." The pilot will repeat "contact" and *then* turn on the switch—never turn on the switch and then call "contact."

If you are swinging the prop yourself, a few simple precautions will help you avoid accidents.

When touching a propeller, always assume that the switch is on, even though the pilot may confirm your statement "Switch off." The switches on many engine installations operate on the principle of short-circuiting the current. If the switch is faulty, as sometimes happens, it can be in off position and still permit the current to flow to the spark plugs just as if it were on.

Be sure the ground is firm. Slippery grass, mud, grease, or loose gravel might cause you to slip and fall into or under the propeller.

Never allow any portion of your body to get in the way of the propeller. This applies even though the engine is not being cranked; occasionally, a warm engine will backfire after it has been stopped for a minute or two.

Stand close enough to the propeller to be able to step away as it is pulled down. If you stand too far away from the propeller, you must lean forward to reach it. This throws you off balance and you may fall into the blades as the engine starts. Stepping away after cranking is a safeguard in case the brakes give way.

In swinging the prop, always move the blade downward by pushing with the palms of the hands. If you push the blade upward, or grip it tightly with your fingers, backfiring may break your fingers or draw your body into the path of the blades.

If you are to remove blocks from in front of the wheels, remember that the propeller, when revolving, is almost invisible. Cases are on record in which people, intending to remove the blocks, attempted to walk directly through the propeller.

Relationship Between Manifold Pressure and Propeller RPM An airplane equipped with a fixed-pitch propeller has only a throttle power control. In this case, the setting of the throttle controls the propeller rpm and engine rpm.

An airplane equipped with a controllable-pitch, constant-speed propeller has two power controls—a throttle and a propeller control. The throttle controls the power output of the engine which is registered on the manifold pressure gauge. The propeller controls the rpm of the propeller (and also the rpm of the engine), which is registered on the tachometer. As throttle setting (manifold pressure) is increased, the pitch angle of the propeller blades is automatically increased through the action of the propeller governor system. The increase in propeller pitch increases the load on the propeller so that the rpm remains constant. As throttle setting (manifold pressure) is decreased, the pitch angle of the propeller blades is automatically decreased. The de-

crease in propeller pitch decreases the load on the propeller so that the rpm remains constant.

For any given propeller rpm, there is a manifold pressure that should not be exceeded. If an excessive amount of manifold pressure is carried for a given rpm, the maximum allowable pressure within the engine cylinders could be exceeded, placing undue stress on them. If repeated too frequently, this undue stress could weaken the cylinder components and eventually cause engine structural failure.

What can the pilot do to avoid conditions that would possibly overstress the cylinders? First, be constantly aware of the tachometer indication (propeller rpm), especially when increasing the throttle setting (manifold pressure). Know and conform to the manufacturer's recommendations for power settings of a particular engine to maintain the proper relationship between manifold pressure and propeller rpm. Remember, *the combination to avoid is a high throttle setting (manifold pressure indication) and a low propeller rpm (tachometer indication).*

When both manifold pressure and propeller rpm need to be changed, the pilot can further help avoid overstress by making power adjustments in the proper order. When power settings are being decreased, reduce manifold pressure before rpm. When power settings are being increased, reverse the order —increase propeller rpm first, then manifold pressure. *If propeller rpm is reduced before manifold pressure, manifold pressure will automatically increase and possibly exceed manufacturer's tolerances.*

Summarizing: In an airplane equipped with a controllable-pitch (constant-speed) propeller, the throttle controls the manifold pressure and the propeller control controls the propeller rpm. Avoid high manifold pressure settings with low propeller rpm. When decreasing power, first decrease manifold pressure, then propeller rpm; when increasing power, first increase rpm, then manifold pressure.

SECTION V—FLIGHT INSTRUMENTS

19. The Pitot-Static System Flight Instruments

The pitot-static system (fig. 89) is a source of pressure for operations of the

(1) Altimeter;
(2) vertical-speed indicator; and
(3) airspeed indicator.

The pitot tube is mounted so there is minimum disturbance of the air due to the motion of the airplane. For this reason its location will vary on different types of aircraft. Static vents are generally located flush with the fuselage—one on either side.

Both the pitot-tube opening and the static-vent openings should be checked during the preflight inspection to see that they are not clogged. If clogged, call for a mechanic to clean them out. Clogged or partially clogged openings may cause inaccurate instrument readings. Do not blow into these openings. This can damage any of the three instruments.

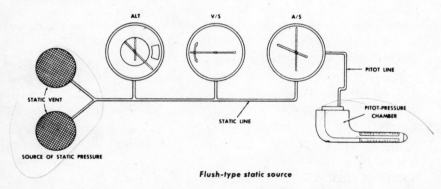

Flush-type static source

Figure 89. *Pitot-static system with instruments operated from it.*

The Altimeter

The altimeter (fig. 90) measures the height of the aircraft above a given level. Since it is the only instrument that gives altitude information, the altimeter is one of the most important instruments in the aircraft. To use his altimeter effectively, the pilot must thoroughly understand its principle of operation and the effect of barometric pressure and temperature on the altimeter.

Principle of Operation. Air is more dense at the surface of the earth than aloft. As altitude increases, the atmospheric pressure decreases. This difference in pressure at various levels causes the altimeter to indicate changes in altitude. The pressure altimeter is simply a barometer that measures the pressure of the atmosphere, and presents an altitude indication to the pilot in feet.

Effect of Nonstandard Pressure and Temperature Atmospheric pressure and temperature vary continuously. Rarely is the pressure at sea level 29.92 inches of mercury or the temperature exactly 59° Fahrenheit (standard sea level conditions). If no means were provided for adjusting altimeters to nonstandard pressure, flight could be very hazardous.

On a warm day the expanded air is lighter in weight per unit volume than on a cold day, and the pressure levels are raised. For example, the pressure level where the altimeter indicates 10,000 feet will be HIGHER on a warm day than under standard conditions. On a cold day the reverse is true, and the 10,000-foot level would be LOWER. The adjustment made by the pilot to compensate for nonstandard pressures does not compensate for nonstandard temperatures. Therefore, if terrain or obstacle clearance is a factor in the selection of a cruising altitude, particularly at higher altitudes, remember to anticipate that COLDER-THAN-STANDARD TEMPERATURE will place the aircraft LOWER than the altimeter indicates.

Setting the Altimeter Most altimeters are equipped with an altimeter setting window (sometimes referred to as the Kollsman window) which gives the pilot a way to adjust his altimeter for the atmospheric pressure variations discussed previously. FAA regulations provide the following concerning altimeter settings:

The cruising altitude of an aircraft below 18,000 feet MSL shall be maintained by reference to an altimeter *that is set to the currently reported altimeter setting of a station along the route of flight within 100 nautical miles.* If there is no such station, the current reported altimeter setting of an appropriate available station shall be used—and provided further that, in an aircraft having no radio, the *altimeter shall be set to the elevation of departure or an appropriate altimeter setting available before departure.*

Many pilots confidently expect that the current altimeter setting will compensate for irregularities in atmospheric pressure at all altitudes. Unfortunately, this is not always true. Remember that the altimeter setting broadcast by ground stations is the *station pressure corrected to mean sea level.* The altimeter setting does not account for distortion at higher levels, particularly the effect of nonstandard temperature.

However, it should be pointed out that if each pilot in a given area were to use the same altimeter setting, each altimeter would be equally affected by temperature pressure variation errors, making it possible to maintain desired altitude separation between aircraft.

When flying over high mountainous terrain, remember that certain atmospheric conditions could cause your altimeter to indicate an altitude of 1,000 feet or more HIGHER than you actually are. Allow yourself a generous margin of altitude—not only for possible altimeter error, but also for possible downdrafts which are particularly prevalent if high winds are encountered.

As an illustration of the use of the altimeter setting system, we will follow a flight from Love Field, Dallas, Texas, to Abilene Municipal Airport, Abilene, Texas, via the Mineral Wells VOR. Before takeoff from Love Field, Dallas, Texas, the pilot receives a current altimeter setting of 29.85 from the control tower. He applies this setting to the altimeter setting window of his altimeter. He then compares the indication of his altimeter with the known field elevation of 485 feet. If his altimeter is perfectly calibrated, the altimeter should indicate the field elevation of 485 feet. (However, since most altimeters are not perfectly calibrated, an indication of plus or minus 75 feet is generally considered acceptable. If an altimeter indication is off more than 75 feet, the instrument should be recalibrated by an instrument technician.)

When the pilot is over the Mineral Wells VOR, he makes a position report to the Mineral Wells FAA Flight Service Station. He receives a current altimeter setting of 29.94, which he applies to the altimeter setting window of his altimeter. Before entering the traffic pattern at Abilene Municipal Airport, he receives a new altimeter setting of 29.69 along with other landing instructions from the Abilene tower. Since he desires to fly the traffic pattern at approximately 800 feet above terrain—the field elevation at Abilene is 1,778 feet—he maintains an indicated altitude of approximately 2,600 feet. Upon landing, his altimeter should indicate the field elevation at Abilene Municipal (1,778 feet.)

Let's assume that the pilot neglected to adjust his altimeter at Abilene to the current setting. His traffic pattern would have been approximately 250 feet below the proper traffic pattern altitude, and his altimeter would have indicated approximately 250 feet more than the field elevation upon landing.

Actual setting	29.94
Proper setting	29.69
	.25

.25 (1 inch equals) approximately 1,000 feet)

.25 x 1,000 feet = 250 feet

The importance of properly setting and reading the altimeter cannot be overrated.

Altimeters and Altimetry

Altitude   Knowing the aircraft's altitude is vitally important to the pilot for several reasons. He must be sure that he is flying high enough to clear the highest terrain or obstruction along his intended route; this is especially important when visibility is poor. To keep above mountain peaks, the pilot must note the altitude of the aircraft and elevation of the surrounding terrain at all times. To reduce the potential of a midair collision, the pilot must be sure he is flying the correct altitudes in accordance with air traffic rules (on flights conducted at more than 3,000 feet above the surface). Often he will fly a certain altitude to take advantage of favorable winds and weather conditions. Also, a knowledge of the altitude is necessary to calculate true airspeeds. (See Exam-O-Gram No. 9, appendix I.)

Types of Altitude   Altitude is vertical distance above some point or level used as a reference. There may be as many kinds of altitude as there are reference levels from which to measure. However, pilots are usually concerned with five types of altitudes:

ABSOLUTE ALTITUDE—The altitude of an aircraft above the surface of the terrain over which it is flying.

INDICATED ALTITUDE—That altitude read directly from the altimeter (uncorrected) after it is set to the current altimeter setting.

PRESSURE ALTITUDE—The altitude read from the altimeter when the altimeter setting window is adjusted to 29.92. (Used for computer solutions for density altitude, true altitude, true airspeed, etc.)

TRUE ALTITUDE—The true height of the aircraft above sea level—the actual altitude. (Often expressed in this manner: "10,900 ft. MSL"—

Figure 90. *Sensitive altimeter. The instrument is adjusted by the knob (lower left) so the current altimeter setting (30.34 here) appears in the window to the right.*

the MSL standing for MEAN SEA LEVEL.) Airport, terrain, and obstacle elevations found on charts and maps are true altitudes.

DENSITY ALTITUDE—This altitude is pressure altitude corrected for nonstandard temperature variations. (An important altitude, since it is directly related to the aircraft's takeoff and climb performance.)

Vertical Speed Indicator

The vertical speed indicator (fig. 91) shows whether the aircraft is climbing, descending, or in level flight. The rate of climb or descent is indicated in feet per minute. If properly calibrated, this indicator will register zero in level flight.

Principal of Operation Before he can use this instrument properly, the pilot must understand one important fact. When the aircraft enters a climb or descent, or levels off, there is a short interval before the instrument gives the correct rate indication. This lag is a result of the time necessary for pressure changes to take place inside the instrument. If pitch changes are small and are made slowly, the indication on the instrument will be a very close representation of the correct rate at any given instant. When a rapid pitch change, or a large pitch change or a combination of the two is made, the instrument may lag far behind the correct indication (*Note*: A vertical speed indicator is now being manufactured which does not have this lag and gives a correct, instantaneous indication of the rate of climb or descent.)

Using the Vertical Speed Indicator If a pilot understands the lag in this instrument and overcomes the tendency to "chase the needle," the vertical speed indicator can be an aid to smooth precision flying. For example, during straight-and-level flight, small changes in altitude are detected almost instantly by this instrument. Therefore, the vertical speed indicator can be an invaluable aid in maintaining level flight when used with the altimeter.

The Airspeed Indicator

The airspeed indicator (fig. 92) is a sensitive, differential pressure gauge which measures and shows promptly the difference between (1) pitot, or impact pressure, and (2) static pressure, the undisturbed atmospheric pres-

Figure 91. *Vertical speed indicator.*

Figure 92. *Airspeed indicator.*

Calibrated Airspeed Calibrated airspeed is indicated airspeed corrected for installation error and instrument error. Although aircraft and instrument manufacturers attempt to keep airspeed errors to a minimum, it is not possible to entirely eliminate these errors throughout the airspeed operating range. At certain airspeeds and with certain flap settings, the installation error and instrument error may amount to several miles per hour. This error is generally greatest in the low airspeed range. In the cruising and high airspeed range, indicated airspeed and calibrated airspeed are normally approximately the same.

Airspeed limitations such as those found on the color-coded face of the airspeed indicator, on placards in the cockpit, or in the Airplane Flight Manual or owner's handbook, are calibrated airspeeds (sometimes referred to as TIAS—True Indicated Airspeed). Therefore, it may be important for the pilot to refer to the airspeed calibration chart to allow for possible airspeed errors. The airspeed calibration chart may be posted near the airspeed indicator, or it may be included in the Airplane Flight Manual or owners handbook.

The airspeed indicator should be calibrated periodically to make sure it is working properly. Leaks may develop in the tubing, or moisture may collect. Vibrations may destroy the sensitivity of the diaphragm. The instrument may be ruined by blowing into the pitot tube. Dirt, dust, ice, and snow collecting at the mouth of the tube may obstruct air passage and prevent correct indications.

True Airspeed The airspeed indicator registers true airspeed under standard sea level conditions—that is, when the pressure is 29.92 and the temperature is 15° C. Because air density decreases with an increase in altitude, the airplane has to fly faster at higher altitudes to cause the same pressure difference between pitot impact pressure and static pressure. Thus, for a given true airspeed, indicated airspeed decreases as altitude increases.

To put it another way, for a given indicated airspeed, true airspeed increases with an increase in altitude. A pilot can find his true airspeed by two methods.

The first method, which is more accurate, involves using a computer (see chapter 25). In this method, the calibrated airspeed is corrected for temperature and pressure by the airspeed correction scale on the computer.

Approximate true airspeed can be computed by a second "rule of thumb" method. This is done by adding to the indicated airspeed 2% of the indicated airspeed for each 1,000 feet of altitude.

sure at flight level. These two pressures will be equal when the aircraft is parked on the ground in calm air. When the aircraft moves through the air, the pressure on the pitot line becomes greater than the pressure in the static lines. This difference in pressure is registered by the airspeed pointer on the face of the instrument, which is calibrated to give the pilot his airspeed in miles per hour, or knots, or both.

Kinds of Airspeed There are three kinds of airspeeds that the private pilot should understand: (1) indicated airspeed; (2) calibrated airspeed; and (3) true airspeed.

Indicated Airspeed The direct instrument reading the pilot obtains from the airspeed indicator, uncorrected for variations in atmospheric density, installation error, and instrument error.

Sample Problem:

Given:

IAS .... 140 mph

Altitude .... 6,000 feet

Find: True Airspeed (TAS)

Solution:

$2\% \times 6 = 12\%$ (.12)

$140 \times .12 = 16.8$

$140 + 16.8 = 156.8$ mph (TAS)

The Airspeed Indicator Markings   Airplanes of 12,500 lbs. or less manufactured after 1945 and certificated by FAA are required to have airspeed indicators that conform to a standard color-coded marking system. This system of color-coded markings, pictured in figure 93, enables the pilot to determine at a glance certain airspeed limitations which are of vital importance to the safe operation of his aircraft. For example, if during the execution of a maneuver, the pilot notes that his airspeed needle is in the yellow arc and is rapidly approaching the red line, he should react immediately and take necessary corrective action to reduce his airspeed. Of course, at high airspeeds it is essential for the pilot to use smooth control pressures to avoid severe stresses upon the aircraft structure.

The private pilot should understand the airspeed limitations indicated by the color-coded marking system of the airspeed indicator. (See also Exam-O-Gram No. 8, appendix I.)

FLAP OPERATING RANGE (the white arc)

POWER-OFF STALLING SPEED WITH THE WING FLAPS AND LANDING GEAR IN THE LANDING POSITION (the lower airspeed limit of the white arc)

MAXIMUM FLAPS EXTENDED SPEED (the upper airspeed limit of the white arc). This is the highest airspeed at which the pilot should extend full flaps. If flaps are operated at higher airspeeds, severe strain or structural failure may result.

NORMAL OPERATING RANGE (the green arc)

POWER-OFF STALLING SPEED WITH THE WING FLAPS AND LANDING GEAR RETRACTED (the lower airspeed limit of the green arc)

MAXIMUM STRUCTURAL CRUISING SPEED (the upper airspeed limit of the green arc). This is the maximum speed for normal operation.

CAUTION RANGE (the yellow arc). The pilot should avoid this area unless in smooth air.

NEVER-EXCEED SPEED (the red line). This is the maximum speed at which the airplane can be operated in smooth air. No pilot should ever exceed this speed intentionally.

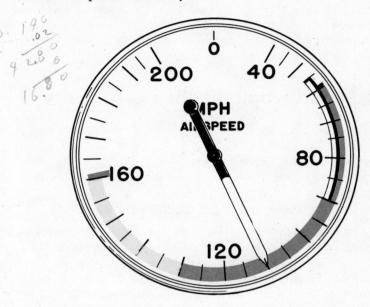

Figure 93. *Airspeed indicator showing color-coded marking system.*

Other Airspeed Limitations   There are other important airspeed limitations *not* marked on the face of the airspeed indicator. These speeds are generally found on placards in view of the pilot and in the Airplane Flight Manual or owner's handbook.

For example, one of the speeds, a very important one, is the MANEUVERING SPEED. This is the pilot's "rough air" speed and the maximum speed for abrupt maneuvers. If during flight rough air or severe turbulence is encountered, the airspeed should be reduced to maneuvering speed or less to reduce the stress upon the airplane structure.

Other important airspeeds include LANDING GEAR OPERATING SPEED, the maximum speed for the safe operation of the landing gear for aircraft equipped with retractable landing gear; the BEST ANGLE OF

CLIMB SPEED, important when a short field takeoff to clear an obstacle is required; and the BEST RATE OF CLIMB SPEED, the airspeed that will give the pilot the most altitude in a given period of time. The private pilot who flies the increasingly popular light twin engine aircraft must know his aircraft's MINIMUM CONTROL SPEED, the minimum flight speed at which the aircraft is satisfactorily controllable when an engine is suddenly made inoperative with the remaining engine at takeoff power.

Descriptions of these airspeed limitations are, through choice, limited to layman language.

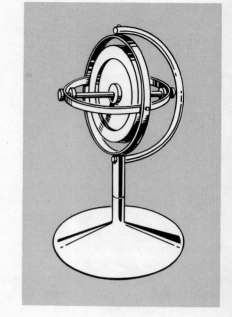

Figure 94. *Model gyroscope.*

20. Gyroscopic Flight Instruments

The following flight instruments contain gyroscopes (fig. 94):
(1) Turn and bank indicator
(2) Heading indicator (directional gyro)
(3) Attitude indicator (artificial horizon or gyro-horizon)

Turn and Bank Indicator

The turn and bank indicator was one of the first modern instruments used for controlling an aircraft without visual reference to the ground or horizon (fig. 95). It is a combination of two instruments, a ball and a turn needle. The ball part of the instrument is actuated by natural forces, while the turn indicator depends upon gyroscopic properties for its indications.

The Ball   The ball instrument checks the pilot's coordination. It is actually a balance indicator, because it indicates the relationship between the angle of bank and the rate of turn. *It tells the pilot the "quality" of the turn*—whether the aircraft has the correct angle of bank for its rate of turn.

In a coordinated turn, the ball assumes a position between the reference markers (fig. 96, left).

In a skid, the rate of turn is too great for the angle of bank, and the excessive centrifugal force causes the ball to move to the outside of the turn (fig. 96, center). To correct to coordinated flight calls for increasing the bank or decreasing the rate of turn, or a combination of both.

In a slip, the rate of turn is too slow for the angle of bank, and the lack of centrifugal force causes the ball to move to the inside of the turn (fig. 96, right). To correct to coordinated flight requires decreasing the bank or increasing the rate of turn, or a combination of both.

The Turn Needle   The turn needle indicates the rate (number of degrees per second) at which the aircraft is turning about its vertical axis. Unlike the attitude indicator (artificial horizon), it does not give a direct indication of the banking attitude of the aircraft. However, for any given airspeed, there is a definite angle of bank necessary to maintain a *coordinated* turn at a given rate. The faster the airspeed, the greater the angle of bank required to obtain a given rate of turn. Thus, the turn needle gives only an *indirect* indication of the aircraft's banking attitude or angle of bank.

Since the turn and bank indicator is one of the most reliable flight instruments used for recovery from unusual attitudes, the pilot should understand and learn to interpret its indications.

Types of Turn Needles   There are two types of turn needles—the "2 minute" turn needle and the "4 minute" turn needle. On a 2 minute turn needle, a 360° turn made at a rate indicated by a one needle width deflection would require 2 minutes to complete. In this case, the aircraft would be turning at a rate of 3° per second, which is considered a standard rate turn. With the 4 minute turn needle, a 360° turn made at a rate indicated by a one needle width deflection would require 4 minutes to complete. In this case, the aircraft

Figure 95. *Turn and bank indicator.*

is turning at a rate of 1½° per second. A standard rate turn of 3° per second would be indicated on this type of turn needle by a two needle width deflection. You may find a turn-and-bank indicator marked as a "2-minute" turn needle but calibrated so that a two-needle width deflection represents a standard rate of turn of 3° per second.

The Heading Indicator

The heading indicator (or directional gyro) is fundamentally a mechanical instrument designed to facilitate the use of the magnetic compass. Errors in the magnetic compass are numerous, making straight flight and precision turns to headings difficult to accomplish, particularly in turbulent air. The heading indicator (fig. 97), however, is not affected by the forces that make the magnetic compass difficult to interpret.

To use the heading indicator properly, the pilot must be able to adjust the card. To do this, the pilot turns a caging knob that rotates the card to the desired heading. It is important to check the indications frequently and reset the heading indicator with the magnetic compass when required.

Check the heading indicator at least every 15 minutes against the magnetic compass. Use great care when reading the magnetic compass. *Adjust the heading indicator to the magnetic compass indication only* when the aircraft is in wings-level, unaccelerated flight.

The pilot should be familiar with the limits of the heading indicator. The limits of operation vary with the particular design and make of instrument. However, on the type of instrument generally found in light airplanes, the limits for all practical purposes are 55° of pitch and 55° of bank. When either of these attitude limits is exceeded, the instrument "tumbles" or "spills" and no longer gives the correct indication until reset. After the instrument has been spilled, it may be reset with the caging knob.

The Attitude Indicator

The attitude indicator, or artificial horizon or gyro-horizon, with its miniature aircraft and horizon bar is the one instrument that gives a picture of the

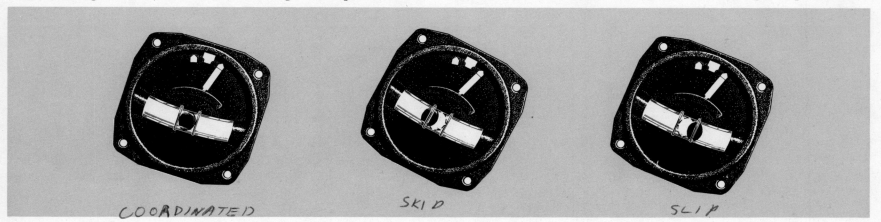

Figure 96. *Indications of the ball in various types of turns.*

93

Figure 97. *Heading indicator.*

Figure 98. *Attitude indicator.*

the wings overlap the horizon bar when the real airplane is in straight-and-level cruising flight.

Some models of attitude indicators are equipped with a caging mechanism. If the instrument is equipped with a caging mechanism, *it should be uncaged only in straight-and-level flight;* otherwise, it will not give proper indications. When uncaging this instrument, uncage it fully; otherwise, it may tumble at lower limits.

The pitch and bank limits depend upon the make and model of the instrument. Limits in the banking plane are usually from 100° to 110°, and the pitch limits are usually from 60° to 70°. If either of these limits is exceeded, the instrument will tumble or spill and will give incorrect indications until reset with the caging mechanism.

Every pilot should be able to interpret the banking scale (fig. 99). The banking scale indicator moves in the opposite direction from that in which the plane is actually banked. This will confuse the pilot if he uses this indicator to determine the direction of bank. This scale should be used only to obtain precision. The relationship of the miniature aircraft to the horizon bar should be used for an indication of the direction of bank of the real aircraft. (An attitude indicator is being manufactured with banking scale indicator that moves in the same direction as the bank.)

The attitude indicator is a reliable instrument. It is the most realistic flight instrument on the instrument panel. Its indications are very close approximations of the actual attitude of the aircraft itself.

attitude of the real aircraft (fig. 98). The relationship of the miniature aircraft to the horizon bar is the same as the relationship of the real aircraft to the actual horizon. This instrument gives an instantaneous indication of even the smallest changes in attitude. It has no lead or lag and is very reliable, if properly maintained.

To aid the pilot in interpreting this instrument's readings, an adjustment knob is provided with which he may move the miniature aircraft upward or downward inside the case. Normally, the miniature aircraft is adjusted so that

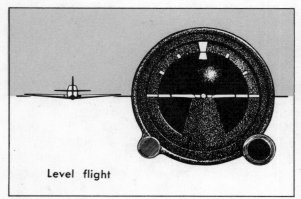

Level flight

Climbing turn to the left

Descending turn to the left

Figure 99. *Various indications on the attitude indicator.*

21. Magnetic Compass

The magnetic compass (fig. 100) is a simple instrument whose basic component consists of two magnetized steel needles mounted on the float, around which is mounted the compass card. The compass card has letters for cardinal headings, and each 30°-interval is represented by a number, the last zero of which is omitted. For example, 30° would appear as a 3 and 300° would appear as 30. Between these numbers, the card is graduated for each 5 degrees.

Compass Errors

Variation. Although the magnetic field of the earth lies roughly north and south, the earth's magnetic poles do not coincide with its geographic poles. Consequently, at most places on the earth's surface, the direction-sensitive steel needles which seek the earth's magnetic field, will not point to True North Pole but to Magnetic North Pole. Furthermore, local magnetic fields from mineral deposits and other conditions distort the earth's magnetic field and cause an additional error in position of the compass' north-seeking magnetized needles with reference to True North. The angular difference between True North and the direction indicated by the magnetic compass—excluding deviation error—is *variation*. Variation is different for different points on the earth's surface and is shown on the charts as broken lines connecting points of equal variation. These lines are *isogonic lines*. The line where the magnetic variation is zero is an *agonic line*. Variation was discussed in section III.

Deviation. Actually, a compass is very rarely influenced solely by the earth's magnetic lines of force. Magnetic disturbances from magnetic fields produced by metals and electrical accessories in an aircraft disturb the compass needles and produce an additional error. The difference between the direction indicated by an undisturbed magnetic compass, and that indicated by a magnetic compass in an aircraft, is *deviation*.

If an aircraft changes heading, the compass' direction-sensitive, magnetized needles will continue to point in about the same direction while the aircraft turns with relation to it. As the aircraft turns, metallic and electrical equipment in the aircraft change their position relative to the steel needles; hence, their influence on the compass needle changes and deviation changes. Thus, deviation depends, in part, on the heading of the aircraft. Although compensating magnets on the compass are adjusted to reduce this deviation on most headings, it is impossible to eliminate this error entirely on all headings. Therefore, a deviation card, installed in the cockpit in view of the pilot,

Figure 100. *Magnetic compass.*

enables him to maintain his desired magnetic headings. Deviation was discussed in section III.

Using the Magnetic Compass Since the magnetic compass is the only direction-seeking instrument in most aircraft, the pilot must be able to turn his aircraft to a magnetic compass heading and maintain it. Remember these characteristics of the magnetic compass:

1. If the aircraft is on a northerly heading and a turn is made toward east or west, the indication of the compass lags or indicates a turn in the opposite direction.

2. If the aircraft is on a southerly heading and a turn is made, the compass needle will indicate a greater amount of turn than is actually made.

95

3. If the aircraft is on an east or west heading, no error is apparent while entering a turn to north or south.

4. If the aircraft is on an east or west heading, an increase in airspeed causes the compass to indicate a turn toward north.

5. If the aircraft is on an east or west heading, a decrease in airspeed causes the compass to indicate a turn toward south.

6. If the aircraft is on a north or south heading, no error is apparent while climbing, diving, or changing airspeed.

As you can see, the compass should be read only when the aircraft is flying straight and level at a constant speed. *Reading the compass only under these conditions will reduce errors to the minimum.*

Precision turns to magnetic compass headings are made difficult by these characteristics. If only the magnetic compass is available for making turns to headings, use the following procedure: While in straight-and-level, unaccelerated flight, note the indication on the magnetic compass. Determine the number of degrees you need to turn to reach the desired heading. Then, using reference points on the ground, turn this approximate number of degrees. Recheck the magnetic compass indication when again in straight-and-level, unaccelerated flight. If you have not obtained correct heading, follow the procedure again.

If the pilot thoroughly understands the errors and characteristics of the magnetic compass, that instrument can become his most reliable means of determining heading.

SECTION VI—AIRCRAFT PERFORMANCE

22. Weight and Balance

All airplanes are designed for certain limit loads and balance conditions. Responsibility for making sure that the weight and balance limitations are met before takeoff *rests with the pilot.* Any pilot who takes off in an airplane that is not within the designated limit load and balance condition is not only violating the FAA regulations but inviting disaster.

Three kinds of weight must be considered in the loading of every aircraft. These are empty weight, useful load, and gross weight.

Empty Weight The weight of the basic airplane—the structure, the power-plant, and the fixed equipment, all fixed ballast, the unusable fuel supply, undrainable oil, and hydraulic fluid.

Useful Load (Payload) The weight of pilot, passengers, baggage, usable fuel, and drainable oil.

Gross Weight The empty weight plus the useful load is the gross weight of the airplane at takeoff. When an airplane is carrying the maximum load for which it is certificated, the takeoff weight is called the *maximum allowable gross weight.*

Understand that although your airplane is certificated for a specified maximum gross weight, it will not safely take off with this load under all conditions. For example, conditions that affect takeoff and climb performance—high elevations, high temperatures, and high humidity (high density altitudes), may require the "off loading" of fuel, passengers, or baggage. (Other factors to consider—runway surface, runway length, the presence of obstacles—will be discussed in chapter 23.)

In most modern airplanes, the pilot has a loading option. *He must decide the type mission to be flown and load his airplane accordingly.* For example, if all the seats are occupied and maximum baggage is carried, gross weight limitations may require less than full fuel. On the other hand, if the pilot is interested in range, he may elect to carry a full fuel load and carry fewer passengers and less baggage.

Balance Not only must the pilot consider the amount of load he carries, he must also determine that the load is arranged to fall within the allowable center of gravity range specified in the airplane weight and balance data. The center of gravity location, often indicated by the letters "CG," is the point where an airplane will balance. The allowable range where the CG may fall is called the *CG range.* The exact location of the range, usually near the forward part of the wing root, is specified for each type of airplane. Obtaining this balance is simply a matter of placing loads so that the average arm of the loaded airplane falls within the CG range. *In most modern aircraft, this can be accomplished by using common sense in distributing the load by following placards listed in the aircraft.* Do not exceed the maximum allowable weight that can be carried in the baggage compartment. In the absence of placards the pilot should refer to the weight and balance data in the Airplane Flight Manual to be sure the load is distributed so the airplane is in proper balance. An airplane loaded outside this range, even though gross weight limitations are met, may develop very undesirable flight characteristics.

The addition of equipment may have changed the CG and empty weight from that listed in the Owner's Manual. Be sure to use the latest weight and balance information in the FAA-Approved Airplane Flight Manual or other permanent aircraft records as appropriate.

Figure 101 (top) shows an airplane loaded forward of the CG range. Some of the undesirable characteristics for this airplane would be:

Excessive loads on the nose wheel (tendency to nose over on tail-wheel type airplanes)

Decreased performance

Higher stalling speeds

Higher stick forces

Figure 101 (center) shows an airplane loaded properly.

Figure 101 (bottom) shows an airplane loaded to the rear of the CG range. Some of the undesirable characteristics of this airplane would be:

Decreased static and dynamic longitudinal stability. Under some conditions the airplane may be impossible to control.

Violent stall characteristics

Very light stick forces (easy to overstress the airplane inadvertently)

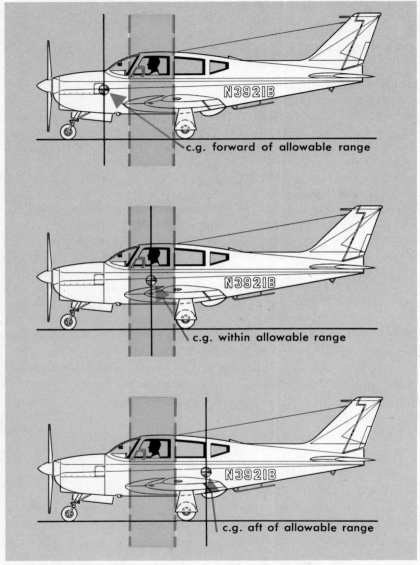

Figure 101. *Before takeoff, be sure the load is distributed correctly to assure proper balance. Flight can be very hazardous if the center of gravity is not within the allowable CG range.*

Sample Weight and Balance Problem In this sample weight and balance problem for an airplane with a maximum allowable gross weight of 2,650 pounds, the pilot is seeking the answers to two problems: (1) *Is the gross weight within the maximum allowable gross weight?* and (2) *Does the airplane meet balance requirements (is the CG within the allowable CG range)?*

The answer to the first question is relatively simple. Add the weight of items comprising the useful load (pilot, passengers, fuel, oil, and baggage) to the licensed empty weight of the airplane. Then check *total weight* to see that it does not exceed *maximum allowable gross weight*.

The solution to the second question can usually be found by common sense distribution of the load, following the placards in the aircraft or the loading instructions in the weight and balance data.

	Weight
EMPTY WEIGHT (licensed)	1,591.0
OIL (10 qts.) at 7.5 lbs. per gallon	19.0
PILOT AND FRONT SEAT PASSENGER	347.0
REAR PASSENGERS	303.0
FUEL (maximum) 55 gal. at 6 lbs. per gallon	330.0
BAGGAGE	20.0
Total	2,610.0

Since the maximum allowable gross weight for this airplane is 2,650 pounds and the gross weight falls within this figure, the weight requirements are met with this particular load. Assuming the loading placards are followed, balance requirements are also met with this load.

23. Aircraft Performance

Takeoff Performance Data

Far too many takeoff accidents have occurred simply because the pilots involved did not realize the effect of density altitude on airplane performance. This subject was covered in detail in sections I and II; here it will be discussed only briefly with other factors affecting takeoff distances.

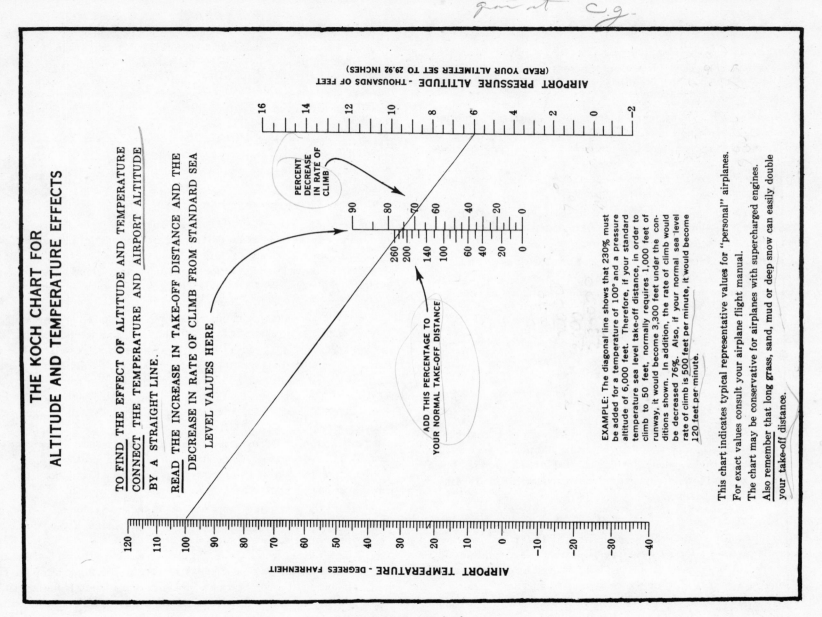

quiet c.g.

THE KOCH CHART FOR
ALTITUDE AND TEMPERATURE EFFECTS

TO FIND THE EFFECT OF ALTITUDE AND TEMPERATURE
CONNECT THE TEMPERATURE AND AIRPORT ALTITUDE
BY A STRAIGHT LINE.

READ THE INCREASE IN TAKE-OFF DISTANCE AND THE
DECREASE IN RATE OF CLIMB FROM STANDARD SEA
LEVEL VALUES HERE

AIRPORT PRESSURE ALTITUDE - THOUSANDS OF FEET
(READ YOUR ALTIMETER SET TO 29.92 INCHES)

PERCENT
DECREASE
IN RATE OF
CLIMB

ADD THIS PERCENTAGE TO
YOUR NORMAL TAKE-OFF DISTANCE

EXAMPLE: The diagonal line shows that 230% must
be added for a temperature of 100° and a pressure
altitude of 6,000 feet. Therefore, if your standard
temperature sea level take-off distance, in order to
climb to 50 feet, normally requires 1,000 feet of
runway, it would become 3,300 feet under the conditions shown. In addition, the rate of climb would
be decreased 76%. Also, if your normal sea level
rate of climb is 500 feet per minute, it would become
120 feet per minute.

This chart indicates typical representative values for "personal" airplanes.
For exact values consult your airplane flight manual.
The chart may be conservative for airplanes with supercharged engines.
Also remember that long grass, sand, mud or deep snow can easily double
your take-off distance.

AIRPORT TEMPERATURE - DEGREES FAHRENHEIT

Figure 102. *Koch chart.*

Factors Affecting takeoff Distances

1. *Pressure Altitude.*—The elevation read from the altimeter when the altimeter setting window (Kollsman window) is adjusted to 29.92. Generally, the higher the pressure altitude, the longer the takeoff distance required.

2. *Temperature.*—While most pilots understand the effects of pressure altitude on airplane performance, many do not realize the extent to which temperature variations can affect performance. Higher than standard temperatures may raise the density altitude of a field by several thousand feet. (Pressure altitude corrected for nonstandard temperature variations is *density altitude.*)

3. *Humidity.*—As previously pointed out, an airplane will require a longer takeoff ground-run when the air is saturated with moisture than under similar conditions in dry air.

4. *Gross Weight.*—Takeoff distances vary with gross weights. Under certain conditions—high density altitude, short runways, etc.—it might become necessary to "off load" part of the useful load to obtain a takeoff margin of safety.

5. *Runway Surface.*—The takeoff figures in your Airplane Flight Manual or owner's handbook are generally based on takeoffs from hard-surface runways. Remember that long grass, sand, mud, or deep snow can easily double your takeoff distances.

6. *Headwind Component.*—See takeoff data chart (figure 103) for headwind effect on takeoff distances.

Use of Flaps for Takeoff
Some airplanes require the use of partial flaps for best takeoff performance; others no flaps, since the additional drag caused by flaps more than offsets the lift advantage acquired from their use. The pilot should always use the takeoff flap setting recommended in his Airplane Flight Manual or owner's handbook.

The Koch Chart
This chart (fig. 102) gives the pilot information about altitude-temperature effects on airplane performance. The chart indicates typical representative values for personal-type airplanes. It is a valuable aid to the pilot whose airplane has no Airplane Flight Manual or owner's handbook containing takeoff data. Use of the chart is explained in the instructions within the chart. The sample problem involves a takeoff from a field with a pressure altitude of 6,000 feet and a temperature of 100° F.

Exercise No. 2
Using the Koch chart, find—

(1) the percentage of increase of takeoff distance length; and

(2) takeoff distance length under the following conditions:

Pressure altitude (feet)	Temperature (°F)	Takeoff distance standard sea-level conditions (feet)
1. 3,000	100	500
2. 4,500	100	730
3. 1,000	120	960
4. 9,500	30	1,100
5. 6,500	66	850

NOTE: See appendix II for correct answers.

Takeoff Data Chart
A takeoff data chart appears in many Airplane Flight Manuals and owner's handbooks. From this chart the pilot can determine (1) the length of the takeoff ground-run, and (2) the total distance required to clear a 50-foot obstacle under various airplane weights, headwinds, pressure altitudes, and temperatures. Of course, the chart for each airplane will be different. Figure 103 shows one such chart.

The first column of the chart illustrated gives three possible gross weights (2,100 pounds, 2,400 pounds, and 2,650 pounds). The second column lists three wind speeds (0, 15, and 30 mph) opposite each gross weight. The remainder of the chart consists of pairs of columns each pair having a main heading of a pressure altitude and temperature standard for that altitude (sea level, 59°F.; 2,500 feet, 50° F.; 5,000 feet, 41° F.; and 7,500 feet, 32° F.). The first column of each pair is headed "ground-run"; the second "to clear a 50-foot obstacle."

At the bottom of the chart is this note: "Increase distances 10 percent for each 25° F. above standard temperature for particular altitudes."

To determine the takeoff ground run for a given set of conditions, the following procedure should be used:

(1) Locate the computed gross weight in the first column.

(2) Locate the existing headwind in the second column and on the same row as the computed gross weight in (1).

(3) Follow the headwind row out to the first column (headed by "ground-run") of the pair of columns headed by the flight altitude. The number at the intersection of this row and column is the length of the ground-run in feet for the given set of conditions, provided the temperature is standard for the altitude.

(4) Increase the number found in (3) by 10 percent for each 25° F. of temperature above standard (for that altitude). The resulting figure is the length of the ground-run.

The same procedure is followed to find the distance to clear a 50-foot obstacle except that in (3) the headwind row would be followed out to the second column (headed by "to clear a 50-foot obstacle") of the pair of columns headed by the altitude. To find distances based on conditions in between those listed in the chart, you must interpolate.

Sample Problem.—What will be the *takeoff ground-run distance* with the following conditions?

Gross weight .... 2,100 lbs.
Pressure altitude .... 2,500 ft.
Temperature .... 75° F.
Headwind .... 15 mph

Solution.—Applying steps (1), (2), and (3) to the performance chart, we obtain a figure of 225 feet. Since the temperature is 25° above standard, step (4) must also be applied. Ten percent of 225 is 22.5, or approximately 23. Adding 23 to 225 gives a total of 248 feet for the takeoff ground-run. Putting this in tabular form, we have:

	Feet
Basic distance exclusive of correction for above standard temperature	225
Correction for above standard temperature (225 × 0.10)	23
Approximate takeoff distance required	248

Sample Problem.—What will be the *distance required to takeoff and clear a 50-foot obstacle* with the same airplane and with the following conditions?

Gross weight .... 2,650 lbs.
Pressure altitude .... 5,000 ft.

TAKE-OFF DATA

TAKE-OFF DISTANCE WITH 20° FLAPS FROM HARD SURFACE RUNWAY.

GROSS WEIGHT LBS.	HEAD WIND MPH	AT SEA LEVEL & 59°F.		AT 2500 FT. & 50°F.		AT 5000 FT. & 41°F.		AT 7500 FT. & 32°F	
		GROUND RUN	TO CLEAR 50' OBSTACLE	GROUND RUN	TO CLEAR 50' OBSTACLE	GROUND RUN	TO CLEAR 50' OBSTACLE	GROUND RUN	TO CLEAR 50' OBSTACLE
2100	0	335	715	390	810	465	935	560	1100
	15	185	465	225	540	270	625	330	745
	30	75	260	95	305	125	365	160	450
2400	0	440	895	525	1040	630	1210	770	1465
	15	255	600	310	700	380	835	475	1020
	30	115	350	150	420	190	510	245	640
2650	0	555	1080	665	1260	790	1500	965	1835
	15	330	735	405	865	490	1050	655	1345
	30	160	445	205	535	255	665	335	845

Note: Increase distances 10% for each 25°F above standard temperature for particular altitude.

Figure 103. *Takeoff performance data chart.*

Temperature .... 91° F.
Headwind .... Calm

Solution.—Following the four-step procedure, except using the "to clear a 50-foot obstacle" column, the solution of this problem gives these results.

	Feet
Basic distance exclusive of correction for above standard temperature	1,500
Correction for above standard temperature (1,500 × 0.20)	300
Approximate distance required to take off and clear a 50-foot obstacle	1,800

Exercise No. 3   Find the takeoff ground run distance and the distance necessary to clear a 50-foot obstacle under each of the following sets of conditions.

	Gross weight (lbs.)	*Headwind (mph)*	*Altitude (feet)*	*Temperature (°F.)*
1.	2,100	30	Sea level	59
2.	2,650	Calm	7,500	57
3.	2,400	15	2,500	50
4.	2,650	Calm	Sea level	109
5.	2,250	15	5,000	41

NOTE: See appendix II for correct answers.

Cruise Performance Data

Cruise performance charts (fig. 104), which are compiled from actual tests, are a valuable aid in planning cross-country flight. However since the number of variables involved rules out great accuracy, an ample fuel reserve should be provided. Fuel consumption depends largely on altitude, power setting (manifold pressure and propeller rpm), and mixture setting.

This sample problem will show how to use the cruise performance chart in figure 104.

Sample Problem.—How many flight hours of fuel remain under the following conditions?

Altitude	5,000
Propeller rpm	2,300
Manifold pressure (mp)	22 inches of mercury
Mixture	Lean
Fuel remaining	40 gal.

CRUISE PERFORMANCE CHART

Altitude	RPM	M P.	BHP	%BHP	TAS MPH	Gal/Hr.
2500	2450	23	175	76	158	14.2
		22	166	72	154	13.4
		21	157	68	151	12.7
		20	148	63	148	12.0
	2300	23	164	71	154	13.1
		22	153	67	149	12.2
		21	143	62	145	11.5
		20	135	59	142	11.0
	2200	23	153	67	149	12.1
		22	144	63	146	11.4
		21	135	59	142	10.8
		20	126	55	138	10.2
Maximum Range Settings	2000	20	107	47	126	8.7
		19	99	43	121	8.2
		18	89	39	113	7.5
		17	81	35	105	7.0
5000	2450	23	179	78	163	14.5
		22	169	73	159	13.6
		21	161	70	156	13.0
		20	150	65	151	12.2
	2300	23	167	73	158	13.4
		22	158	69	155	12.6
		21	148	64	151	11.9
		20	139	60	146	11.2
	2200	23	157	68	155	12.4
		22	148	64	151	11.7
		21	138	60	146	11.0
		20	131	57	143	10.5
Maximum Range Settings	2000	19	103	45	126	8.5
		18	94	41	118	7.9
		17	86	37	111	7.3
		16	79	34	103	6.8
7500	2450	21	163	71	161	13.1
		20	153	67	157	12.4
		19	143	62	152	11.7
		18	133	58	147	11.0
	2300	21	151	66	156	12.2
		20	142	62	151	11.6
		19	133	58	147	11.0
		18	125	54	142	10.5
	2200	21	143	62	152	11.4
		20	134	58	148	10.7
		19	126	54	143	10.2
		18	118	51	138	9.7
Maximum Range Settings	2000	19	107	47	131	8.7
		18	98	43	123	8.1
		17	90	39	116	7.6
		16	82	36	107	7.0

Data based on lean mixture, standard conditions, and maximum gross weight

Figure 104. *A cruise performance chart.*

Solution—

(1) Locate the altitude (5,000 feet) in the altitude column (first column).

(2) Locate the rpm (2,300) in the rpm column (second column) opposite the altitude (5,000 feet) just found in (1).

(3) Locate the manifold pressure (22 inches of mercury) in the mp column (third column) opposite the rpm (2,300) just located in (2).

(4) Follow this manifold-pressure row out to the column headed by "Gal/Hr," where the figure 12.6 is read. This is the rate of fuel consumption in gallons per hour.

(5) Divide fuel remaining (40 gallons) by rate of fuel consumption just found (12.6 gal/hr). The result is 3.17, the number of flight hours remaining. The 3.17 hours is equivalent to 3 hours and 10 minutes (multiply 0.17 by 60 minutes).

NOTE: The true airspeed (TAS) with this power setting would be 155 mph (next to last column).

Sample Problem.—If in the preceding sample problem, a power setting of 18 inches of manifold pressure and 2,000 rpm were used, how much more flight time would be available?

Solution—

(1) Following the same steps as in the preceding problem (except using the new rpm and mp), a fuel consumption rate of 7.9 gallons per hour is found.

(2) Dividing the fuel remaining (40 gallons) by 7.9 gives a total remaining flight time of 5.06 hours. When converted, this is equivalent to 5 hours 4 minutes.

(3) Subtracting 3 hours 10 minutes from 5 hours 4 minutes gives an increase in flight time (endurance time) of 1 hour 54 minutes.

Exercise No. 4   Find the true airspeed (TAS), rate of fuel consumption, and total flight time available under the following conditions:

	Altitude (feet)	RPM	Manifold pressure	Fuel available (gals.)
1.	2,500	2,450	23	55
2.	5,000	2,200	22	45
3.	7,500	2,000	16	25
4.	2,500	2,000	17	25
5.	5,000	2,300	23	50

NOTE: See appendix II for correct answers.

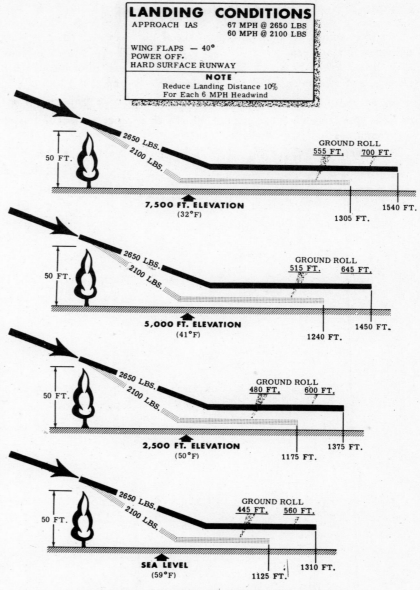

Figure 105. *A landing performance data chart.*

103

Landing Performance Data

Variables similar to those affecting takeoff distances also affect landing distances, although generally to a lesser extent. Consult your Airplane Flight Manual or owner's handbook for landing distance data, recommended flap settings, and recommended approach airspeeds. (See fig. 105.)

Sample Problem.—With a power-off approach speed of 60 mph and 40° of flaps, approximately what ground roll will be required under the following conditions?

Elevation	Sea level
Gross weight	2,100 lbs.
Temperature	59° F.
Headwind	Calm

Solution.—Approximately 445 feet.

Sample Problem.—With a power-off approach speed of 67 mph and 40° of flaps, approximately what total landing distance (including ground roll) would be required to clear a 50-foot obstacle and land under the following conditions?

Elevation	2,500 feet
Gross weight	2,650 lbs.
Temperature	50° F.
Headwind	12 mph

Solution—

Basic landing distance before headwind correction	1,375 feet
Correction for headwind (1,375 × .20)	−275 feet
Approximate landing distance	1,100 feet

SECTION VII—FLIGHT INFORMATION PUBLICATIONS

24. Airman's Information Manual

Introduction

The *Airman's Information Manual* (AIM)[1] presents, in a single document, all the information necessary for the planning and conduct of a flight within the conterminous United States. This excludes Alaska, Hawaii, and the United States possessions. Flight information for these areas is presented in separate publications.

The *Airman's Information Manual* is divided into six sections, each composed of a specific category or family of information, fashioned into a format consistent with the operational needs of aviation. It consolidates items of similar information and segregates Air Traffic Control procedural information with a sequencing arranged for operational use.

The *AIM* is intended for cockpit use either collectively or independently by sections. The manual is published as loose-leaf pages, and is three-hole punched to fit a standard three-ring binder.

Each section of the *AIM* will be published at varying intervals during the year, depending on the frequency of change of information. The various sections and the revision cycle of each are:

Section I—Basic Flight Manual—Semi-Annually

Section II—ATC Operations & Procedures—Quarterly

Section III—Flight Data & Special Operations—Every 28 days

Section IIIA—Notices to Airmen (NOTAMS)—Every 14 days

Section IV—Airport Directory—Semi-Annually

Section IVA—Airport/Facility Directory—Every 28 days

A Master Alphabetical Index follows Section IVA and is also revised every 28 days.

[1] **The Airman's Information Manual** is available on annual subscription for $15.00, plus $4.00 additional for foreign mailing. Requests should be directed to the Superintendent of Documents, U.S. Government Printing Office, Washington, D.C. 20402. Orders should be accompanied by check or money order made payable to the Superintendent of Documents.

The above schedule provides a completely new manual every six months. New or amended textual or tabulated material (except in the Airport/Facility Directory) is indicated by a solid dot prefixing the heading, paragraph, or line.

Selected excerpts from *AIM* are presented at the end of this section. Although only a small portion of the information in *AIM* is presented in these excerpts, the material illustrated is of vital interest to the private pilot. The format is unchanged to better familiarize you with the nature of the manual.

Explanation of Sections

Section I — Basic Flight Manual This section contains, in layman's language, educational, instructional, and training information. This information is assembled and presented in a systematic format, categorized by subject matter. It provides the novice pilot with the information to orient himself on the basic fundamentals of aeronautical knowledge required to fly in the National Airspace System. The Basic Flight Manual also serves as an official medium for documentation and interpretation of aeronautical knowledge for the *general aviation pilot*. Subject matter topics in Section I are: (1) Air Navigation Radio Aids, (2) Airport, Air Navigation Lighting and Marking Aids, (3) Altimetry, (4) Good Operating Practices, (5) Medical Facts for Pilots, (6) Radar, (7) Radio Telephone Phraseology and Techniques, (8) Safety of Flight, (9) Weather, and (10) Aeronautical Publications.

Selected excerpts from Section I are contained in Figures 106, 107, 108, and 109.

Section II — ATC Operations and Procedures This section serves as an *official* means of disseminating pertinent traffic control information of interest to all pilots. Again, the material is presented in layman's language to lessen the ambiguity which sometimes results from individual interpretation of rules, regulations, and procedures.

AIR NAVIGATION RADIO AIDS

VHF OMNIDIRECTIONAL RANGE (VOR)

1. Omniranges operate within the 108-118 mc frequency band and have a power output of approximately 200 watts. The equipment is VHF, thus, it is subject to line-of-sight restriction, and its range varies proportionally to the altitude of the receiving equipment. There is some "spill over," however, and reception at an altitude of 1000 feet is about 40 to 45 miles. This distance increases with altitude.

2. There is voice transmission on the omni-frequency, and all information broadcast over L/MF ranges is also available over the VOR's.

3. The effectiveness of the VOR depends upon proper use and adjustment of both ground and airborne equipment.

   a. **Accuracy:** The accuracy of course alignment of the omnirange is excellent, being generally plus or minus 1°.

   b. **Roughness:** On some VORs, minor course roughness may be observed, evidenced by course needle or brief flag alarm activity (some receivers are more subject to these irregularities than others). At a few stations, usually in mountainous terrain, the pilot may occasionally observe a brief course needle oscillation, similar to the indication of "approaching station." Pilots flying over unfamiliar routes are cautioned to be on the alert for these vagaries, and in particular, to use the "to-from" indicator to determine positive station passage.

   (1) Certain propeller RPM settings can cause the VOR Course Deviation Indicator to fluctuate as much as ±6°. Slight changes to the RPM setting will normally smooth out this roughness. Helicopter rotor speeds may also cause VOR course disturbances. Pilots are urged to check for this propeller modulation phenomenon prior to reporting a VOR station or aircraft equipment for unsatisfactory operation.

4. The only positive method of identifying an omnirange is by its Morse Code identification or by the recorded automatic voice identification which is always indicated by use of the word "VOR" following the range's name. Reliance on determining the identification of an omnirange should never be placed on listening to voice transmissions by the Flight Service Station (FSS) (or approach control facility) involved. Many FSS remotely operate several omniranges which have different names from each other and in some cases none have the name of the "parent" FSS.

SIMULTANEOUS VOICE TRANSMISSIONS FROM A SINGLE LOCATION

1. At several FAA facilities, simultaneous voice transmissions are made from a single location. For example, the New York FSS controls the transmitters at Kennedy, Hampton, Riverhead, Deer Park, Hempstead L/MF and VOR facilities.

2. To provide a uniformly brief announcement, generally for broadcast purposes, the name of the controlling facility, followed by the word AREA will be used, e.g., THIS IS NEW YORK AREA RADIO, etc.

3. Call from aircraft will be answered using the name of the station as stated by the pilot, e.g., a pilot calling "Riverhead Radio" will be answered by the New York FSS, "THIS IS RIVERHEAD RADIO, etc."

4. The word "AREA" signifies that the transmission from the named (controlling) location is emanating simultaneously from two or more remotely controlled facilities, having a different name or names.

FREQUENCY UTILIZATION PLAN

AIR NAVIGATION AIDS

108.1-111.9 mc: ILS localizer with simultaneous radio-telephone channel operating on odd-tenth decimal frequencies (108.1, 108.3 etc.).

108.2-111.8 mc: VOR's operating on even-tenth decimal frequencies (108.2, 108.4 etc.).

112.0-117.9 mc: Airway track guidance. (VORs)

COMMUNICATIONS

118.0-121.4 mc: AIR TRAFFIC CONTROL COMMUNICATIONS

121.5 mc: EMERGENCY (WORLD-WIDE)

121.6-121.95 mc: AIRPORT UTILITY

122.1, 122.2 mc: PRIVATE AIRCRAFT ENROUTE

122.5, 122.7, 122.6, 122.4 mc: PRIVATE AIRCRAFT TO TOWERS

122.8, 123.0 mc: AERONAUTICAL ADVISORY STATIONS (UNICOM)

122.9 mc: AERONAUTICAL MULTICOM STATIONS

123.1-123.55 mc: FLIGHT TEST AND FLYING SCHOOLS

123.6-128.8 mc: AIR TRAFFIC CONTROL COMMUNICATIONS

126.7 mc: FLIGHT SERVICE STATIONS

128.85-132.0 mc: AERONAUTICAL ENROUTE STATIONS (AIR CARRIER)

132.05-135.95 mc: AIR TRAFFIC CONTROL COMMUNICATIONS

Figure 106. *Air navigation radio aids.*

GOOD OPERATING PRACTICES

It should be remembered that adherence to air traffic rules does not eliminate the need for good judgment on the part of the pilot. Compliance with the following Good Operating Practices will greatly enhance the safety of every flight.

Judgment in VFR Flight

Use reasonable restraint in exercising the prerogative of VFR flight, especially in terminal areas. The weather minimums and distances from clouds are minimums. Giving yourself a greater margin in specific instances is just good judgment.

Conducting a VFR operation in a Control Zone when the official visibility is 3 or 4 miles is not prohibited, but good judgment would dictate that you keep out of the approach area.

Use of Victor Airways

Pilots not operating on an IFR flight plan, and when in level cruising flight, are cautioned to conform with VFR cruising altitudes appropriate to direction of flight. During climb or descent, pilots are encouraged to fly to the right side of the center line of the radial forming the airway in order to avoid IFR and VFR cruising traffic operating along the center line of the airway.

Report

On a VFR flight, when making initial radio contact with a control tower or a Flight Service Station providing Airport Advisory Service, report position and altitude. This will make it easier for ground facility personnel and other pilots to locate your aircraft.

Student Pilots Radio Identification

The FAA desires to help the student pilot in acquiring sufficient practical experience in the environment in which he will be required to operate. To receive additional assistance while operating in areas of concentrated air traffic, a student pilot need only identify himself as a student pilot during his initial call to an FAA radio facility. For instance, "Dayton Tower, this is Fleetwing 1234, Student Pilot, over." This special identification will alert FAA air traffic control personnel and enable them to provide the student pilot with such extra assistance or consideration as he may need. This procedure is not mandatory.

Conformance with the above Good Operating Practices is not as simple as it sounds. It requires constant attention to innumerable details and a deep-seated realization that additional hazards incident to flight operations exist whenever vigilance is relaxed.

Figure 107. *Good operating practices.*

Traffic Patterns

At most airports and military air bases, traffic pattern altitudes for propeller driven aircraft generally extend from 600 feet to as high as 1500 feet above the ground. Also traffic pattern altitudes for military turbojet aircraft sometimes extend up to 2000 feet above the ground. Therefore, pilots of en route aircraft should be constantly on the alert for other aircraft in traffic patterns and avoid these areas whenever possible.

MEDICAL FACTS FOR PILOTS

ALCOHOL

Do not fly while under the influence of alcohol. An excellent rule is to allow twenty-four hours between the last drink and takeoff time. Even small amounts of alcohol in the system can adversely affect judgment and decision-making abilities.

Remember that your body metabolizes alcohol at a fixed rate, and no amount of coffee or medication will alter this rate.

By all means, do not fly with a hangover, or a "masked hangover" (symptoms suppressed by aspirin or other medication).

DRUGS

Self-medication or taking medicine in any form when you are flying can be extremely hazardous. Even simple home or over-the-counter remedies and drugs such as aspirin, antihistamines, cold tablets, cough mixtures, laxatives, tranquilizers and appetite suppressors, may seriously impair the judgment and coordination needed while flying. The safest rule is to take no medicine while flying, except on the advice of your Aviation Medical Examiner. It should also be remembered that the condition for which the drug is required, may of itself be very hazardous to flying, even when the symptoms are suppressed by the drug.

Certain specific drugs which have been associated with aircraft accidents in the recent past are: *Antihistamines* (widely prescribed for hay fever and other allergies); *Tranquillizers* (prescribed for nervous conditions, hypertension, and other conditions); *Reducing Drugs* (amphetamines and other appetite suppressing drugs can produce sensations of well-being which have an adverse affect on judgment); *Barbiturates, Nerve tonics or pills* (prescribed for digestive and other disorders, barbiturates produce a marked suppression on mental alertness).

Figure 108. *Medical facts for pilots.*

RADAR

GENERAL

1. FAA radar units operate continuously at the locations shown in the Airport/Facility Directory and their services are available to all pilots, both civil and military. Contact the associated FAA control tower or ARTCC on any frequency guarded for initial instructions, or in an emergency, any FAA facility for information on the nearest radar service.

2. Radar Traffic Information Service Procedures, Expanded Radar Service for Arriving and Departing Flights in Terminal Areas Procedures, and Terminal Radar Service Procedures are published under "ARRIVAL."

RADAR TRAFFIC INFORMATION

1. Radar traffic information is issued by air traffic controllers as a clock position with relation to the track of an aircraft. The examples depicted below point out the possible error in the position of this traffic when it is necessary for a pilot to apply drift correction to maintain this track. This error could also occur in the event a change in course is made at the time radar traffic information is issued.

In above example traffic information would be issued to the pilot of aircraft "A" as 12 o'clock. The actual position of the traffic as seen by the pilot of aircraft "A" would be one o'clock. Traffic information issued to aircraft "B" would also be given as 12 o'clock, but in this case, the pilot of "B" would see his traffic at 11 o'clock.

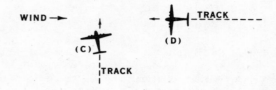

In above example traffic information would be issued to the pilot of aircraft "C" as two o'clock. The actual position of the traffic as seen by the pilot of aircraft "C" would be three o'clock. Traffic information issued to aircraft "D" would be at an 11 o'clock position. Since it is not necessary for the pilot of aircraft "D" to apply wind correction (crab) to make good his track, the actual position of the traffic issued would be correct. Since the radar controller can only observe aircraft track on his radar display, he must issue traffic advisories accordingly, and pilots should give due consideration to this fact when looking for reported traffic.

The information published, covering flight operations, air traffic services, and procedures within the conterminous United States is arranged and sequenced in accordance with that of a typical flight operation; i.e., preflight, departure, enroute, arrival, and landing.

In addition to the sequenced flight operations, are supporting general and emergency information and procedures. These include U. S. Entry and Departure Requirements, Air Defense Identification Zone (ADIZ), and SCATER procedures.

Section II concludes with emergency procedures. These procedures have been consolidated and placed last for ready reference.

Selected excerpts from Section II are contained in Figures 110, 111, 112, 113, and 114.

Figure 109. *Radar.*

SAFETY OF FLIGHT

WAKE TURBULENCE — Suggested Pilot Action

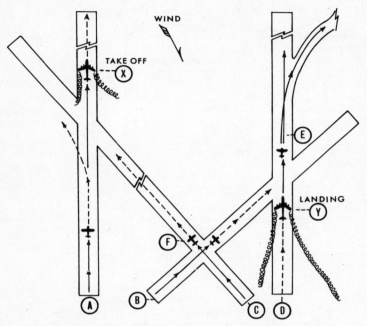

Example Take-off Landing Alternative courses of action.

| Large Aircraft | Small Aircraft | |
	Take-off*	Landing*
TAKE-OFF at X	B, D, C, A	D, C, B, A
LAND at Y	A, C, E, B	A, B, E, F

*Take-off and landing points listed in order of probable preference with regard to turbulence from take-off and landing of large aircraft.

Light aircraft especially are affected by the swirls of air in the wake of larger aircraft. These swirls of air are known as wing vortices but are generally referred to as wake turbulence. This invisible turbulence can be extremely dangerous during takeoff and landing. Numerous aircraft have encountered wake turbulence of such severity that complete loss of control of the aircraft resulted. The aircraft were, in some cases, at altitudes too low to recover. The most severe wake turbulence is produced by large commercial or military aircraft in landing or takeoff configuration. This hazardous phenomena is normally encountered within several minutes after passage of an aircraft, however, in calm surface winds, it may persist for periods exceeding five minutes. Complete information on wake turbulence and how best to avoid its hazards may be found in the current edition of the Airman's Information Manual and FAA Advisory Circular AC 90–23 dated February 24, 1965.

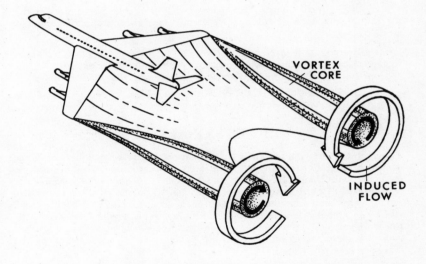

Example of wing tip vortices initial formation.

(Once formed, vortices extend and may be hazardous for an undetermined distance behind the generating aircraft.)

Figure 110. *Wake turbulence.*

COMMUNICATIONS

1. Pilots of departing aircraft should communicate with the control tower on the appropriate ground control frequency for taxi and clearance information and, unless otherwise advised, should remain on that frequency until they are ready to request take-off clearance. At that time, the pilot should communicate with the tower on the appropriate local control frequency.

2. The airport ground control frequencies 121.7 and 121.9 mc are normally provided to eliminate frequency congestion on the tower (local control) frequency. Provision of these frequencies for ground control and their use by aircraft and airport utility vehicles operated on the surface of the airport thus provides a clear VHF channel for arriving and departing aircraft. They are used for issuance of taxi information, clearances, and other necessary contacts between the tower and aircraft or other vehicles operated on the airport. Normally, only one of these ground control frequencies is assigned for use at an airport; however, at locations where the amount of traffic so warrants, both frequencies may be assigned with one or the other designated as a clearance delivery frequency.

3. Where the "ground control" frequency is not available (tower or aircraft), the tower normally will transmit to aircraft over an appropriate ground to air frequency.

4. Pilots of aircraft not equipped to transmit on a ground control frequency should transmit on the tower frequency and tune their receivers to the appropriate ground control frequency in accordance with the above.

NOTE.—See Airport Advisory Service (Non-Radar), under **ARRIVAL**, for communications procedures at airports not served by control towers.

LIGHT SIGNALS

1. The following procedures are used by airport traffic control towers in the control of aircraft not equipped with radio. These same procedures will be used to control aircraft equipped with radio if radio contact cannot be established. Airport traffic control personnel use a directive traffic control signal which emits an intense narrow beam of a selected color (either red, white, or green) when controlling traffic by light signals. Although the traffic signal light offers the advantage that some control may be exercised over non-radio equipped aircraft, all pilots should be cognizant of the disadvantages which are:

   a. The pilot may not be looking at the control tower at the time a signal is directed toward him.

   b. The directions transmitted by a light signal are very limited since only approval or disapproval of a pilot's anticipated actions may be trans-

mitted. No supplementary or explanatory information may be transmitted except by the use of the "General Warning Signal" which advises the pilot to be on the alert.

2. Portable traffic control light signals:

Color and Type of Signal	On the Ground	In flight
STEADY GREEN	Cleared for take-off	Cleared to land
FLASHING GREEN	Cleared to taxi	Return for landing (to be followed by steady green at proper time)
STEADY RED	Stop	Give way to other aircraft and continue circling
FLASHING RED	Taxi clear of landing area (runway) in use	Airport unsafe — do not land
FLASHING WHITE	Return to starting point on airport	
ALTERNATING RED & GREEN	General Warning Signal — Exercise Extreme Caution	

3. Between sunset and sunrise, a pilot wishing to attract the attention of the air traffic control tower operator should turn on a landing light and taxi the aircraft in position so that light is visible to the tower operator. The landing light should remain on until appropriate signals are received from the tower.

4. Pilots should acknowledge light signals by moving the ailerons or rudder during the hours of daylight or by blinking the landing or navigation lights during the hours of darkness.

5. During the hours of daylight the lighting of the rotating beacon will mean that ground visibility is less than three miles and/or that the ceiling is less than 1000 feet. During the hours of darkness, flashing lights outlining the traffic direction indicator (tetrahedron, wind tee or other device) will mean that ground visibility is less than three miles and/or the ceiling is below 1000 feet. The lighting of either of these signals indicates that a clearance from Air Traffic Control is necessary for landing, take-off, or flight in the traffic pattern if the airport is within a control zone.

Figure 111. *Departure procedures.*

ENROUTE

LAKE, ISLAND, AND MOUNTAIN REPORTING SERVICE

1. Selected Flight Service Stations provide flight monitoring where regularly traveled VFR routes cross large bodies of water, swamps, and mountains, for the purpose of expeditiously alerting Search and Rescue facilities when required.

2. Areas covered, associated Flight Service Stations, and the name of the service, "Stoneface," "Overlake," etc., are indicated on charts published in Section III. To obtain this service, contact the FSS by telephone or radio giving present position, type aircraft, altitude, indicated airspeed, proposed route of flight, and mainland estimate.

3. After these arrangements have been made, a radio contact with the FSS is required every ten minutes while en route. If contact is lost for more than fifteen minutes, Search and Rescue is alerted.

Figure 112. *Enroute procedures.*

ARRIVAL

VFR ADVISORY INFORMATION

1. VFR advisory information is provided by numerous radar and nonradar *Approach Control* facilities to those pilots intending to land at an airport served by an approach control tower. This information includes: wind, runway, traffic and NOTAM information.

2. Such information will be furnished upon initial contact with concerned approach control facility. The pilot will be requested to change to the *tower* frequency at a predetermined time or point, to receive further landing information.

3. Where available, use of this procedure will not hinder the operation of VFR flights by requiring excessive spacing between aircraft or devious routing. Radio contact points will be based on time or distance rather than on landmarks.

4. Compliance with this procedure is not mandatory but pilot participation is encouraged.

AIRPORT ADVISORY SERVICE (NONRADAR)

1. Flight Service Stations (FSS) located at airports where there are no control towers in operation provide advisory information to arriving and departing aircraft. This service is offered for safety purposes; traffic control is not exercised.

2. Airport advisories provide: wind direction and velocity, favored runway, altimeter setting, pertinent known traffic, Notices to Airmen, airport taxi routes, airport traffic patterns, and instrument approach procedures. These elements are varied so as to best serve the current traffic situation. Pilots using other than the favored runways should advise the FSS immediately.

3. Recommended phraseologies and communications procedures are as follows:

AIRCRAFT DEPARTING: When ready to taxi, the pilot should notify the station of his intentions. Except for scheduled air carriers or other frequent users of the airport, this information should include not only the aircraft identification, but also the aircraft type, location, type of flight planned (VFR or IFR), and destination.

Example:

Aircraft: GRAND FORKS RADIO, THIS IS COMANCHE SIX ONE THREE EIGHT, ON TERMINAL BUILDING RAMP, READY TO TAXI, VFR TO DULUTH, OVER.

Station: COMANCHE SIX ONE THREE EIGHT, THIS IS GRAND FORKS RADIO, WIND THREE TWO ZERO DEGREES AT TWO FIVE FAVORING RUNWAY THREE ONE, ALTIMETER THREE ZERO ZERO ONE, TIME ONE TWO TWO FIVE, CESSNA ONE-SEVENTY MAKING TOUCH AND GO LANDINGS ON RUNWAY THREE ONE.

NOTE.—The take-off time should be reported to the FSS as soon as practicable. If the aircraft has limited equipment and it is necessary to use the navigational feature of the radio range immediately after take-off, advise the FSS of this before shifting frequency from 122.2 to the range. In such cases, advisories will be transmitted over both 122.2 and the range frequency.

AIRCRAFT ARRIVING: When operating VFR, a pilot should transmit position and altitude information to the FSS when 15 miles from the airport.

Example:

Aircraft: GRAND FORKS RADIO, THIS IS TRI-PACER ONE SIX EIGHT NINER, OVER KEY WEST, TWO THOUSAND, LANDING GRAND FORKS, OVER.

Station: TRI-PACER ONE SIX EIGHT NINER, THIS IS GRAND FORKS RADIO, OVER KEY WEST AT TWO THOUSAND, WIND ONE FIVE ZERO DEGREES AT ONE TWO, FAVORING RUNWAY ONE THREE, ALTIMETER TWO NINER EIGHT NINER, DC-3 TAKING-OFF RUNWAY ONE THREE, CESSNA ONE FORTY ON DOWNWIND LEG RUNWAY ONE THREE MAKING TOUCH AND GO LANDINGS, COMANCHE DEPARTED RUNWAY ONE THREE AT ONE SIX PROCEEDING EASTBOUND, OVER.

NOTE.—Pilots should guard 122.2 mcs. until clear of the runway after landing and report leaving the runway to the FSS.

Figure 113. *Arrival procedures.*

TRAFFIC PATTERN DIRECTION

1. The segmented circle system consists of the following components: A wind indicator (sock) will be found at the center of the circle. Associated with the wind indicator and also located at the center of the circle, is the landing direction indicator, which may be a tetrahedron or tee, either free swinging or set for a particular runway. Although appearing as a single unit, the L-shaped indicator located at various positions around the segmented circle or at the end of a runway actually consists of two parts. That portion of the L in alignment with or parallel to a runway is known as the landing strip indicator. The other section of the L running at a right angle to the runway is known as the traffic pattern indicator.

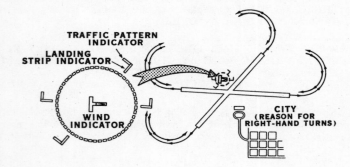

2. Preparatory to a landing, the pilot should concern himself with the indicator for the approach end of the runway to be used. If the pilot will mentally enlarge the indicator for the runway to be used, the base and final approach legs of the traffic pattern to be flown immediately become apparent. Similar treatment of the indicator at the departure end of the runway will clearly indicate the direction of turn to join the cross wind leg of the traffic pattern after takeoff.

3. A flashing amber light in the center of the segmented circle or on top the control tower or adjoining building indicates clockwise flow of traffic is in effect at that time and that right turns shall be made unless otherwise authorized by Air Traffic Control.

4. Right hand flow of traffic may be also be shown by indicators located at either the segmented circle or ends of the runway. A pilot may determine the direction of traffic flow by circling the airport at an altitude above the airport traffic area.

5. At airports where traffic control is exercised by a control tower, traffic and taxi patterns have been established to specify the desired flow of ground and air traffic operating on and in the vicinity of an airport. If the traffic pattern is not known, follow other traffic unless otherwise advised. Control tower operators issue clearances or other information to pilots as necessary for aircraft to generally follow the desired flight path (traffic patterns) when flying the airport traffic area/control zone and the proper taxi routes (taxi patterns) when operating on the ground.

6. The following terminology for the various components of a traffic pattern has been adopted as standard for use by control towers and pilots:

STANDARD TRAFFIC PATTERN COMPONENTS

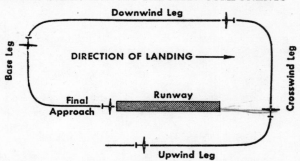

Upwind leg.	A flight path parallel to the landing runway in the direction of landing.
Crosswind leg.	A flight path at right angles to the landing runway off its upwind leg.
Downwind leg.	A flight path parallel to the landing runway in the direction opposite to landing.
Base leg.	A flight path at right angles to the landing runway off its approach end and extending from the downwind leg to the intersection of the extended runway center line.
Final approach.	A flight path in the direction of landing along the extended runway center line from the base leg to the runway.
Closed Runway or Taxiway.	

Figure 114. *Landing procedures.*

Section III — Flight Data and Special Operations This section contains operational Flight Data most subject to continuous change that is not appropriate for inclusion within other sections of the manual.

The information in Section III is presented in various tabulations or grouping arrangements appropriate to the specific items. Typical examples are: Changes/Additions to *AIM*, FSS Lake, Island, and Mountain Reporting Service, Oil Burner Routes, Special Notices, VFR Airport Traffic Patterns, and Sectional Chart Bulletin. A Glossary of Aeronautical Terms and a list of the Abbreviations in common use in *AIM* are included in this section and are reproduced in Figures 115 and 116 for your use in interpreting the various other excerpts from *AIM*.

Sectional Chart Bulletin This bulletin provides a tabulation of the major changes in aeronautical information that have occurred since the publication date of each Sectional Aeronautical Chart.

In general, these tabulations will contain only essential data such as changes in the airspace that present a hazardous condition or impose a restriction on the pilot, and major changes to airports and radio navigational aids. The bulletin should be used by the VFR pilot to update and maintain his Sectional Charts.

When the new edition of the chart is published, the corrective tabulation will be removed from this bulletin.

Figure 117 is a sample tabulation modified as appropriate for the 58th Edition of the Dallas Sectional Aeronautical Chart (The chart furnished with this handbook).

Lake, Island, and Mountain Reporting Service This service is supplied on request by the FSS in many areas of the United States. It is extremely valuable when flying over water or hazardous terrain. Figure 118 shows an example of this service.

Special Notices The excerpts from Special Notices (Figure 119) has been chosen to illustrate the type of information to be found in this part of Section III. Special Notices should be checked prior to a cross-country flight to see if they contain any information pertinent to your route of flight.

Oil Burner Routes Oil Burner Routes are areas wherein military high-speed aircraft conduct navigational flights at altitudes from 500 feet above the ground and up. There are at the present time 20 of these routes within the conterminous United States. Due to the high speed of the using aircraft and consequent rapid closure rate you should use extreme vigilance when traversing these routes. Figure 120 excerpt from Section III shows a typical Oil Burner Route.

Section III-A — Notices to Airmen (NOTAMS) This section is issued every 14 days and is primarily designed to supplement Section III of *AIM*. It contains much information that may well affect your flight. A newly constructed television tower that extends as much as 1,500 feet above the ground in the vicinity of your destination airport may not appear on your chart. Your intended destination airport may be temporarily closed because of construction, flooding, heavy accumulation of snow, or other conditions. Certain runways may be closed or certain areas of the airport may be unsafe for taxiing. There may be other hazards not normally expected. Perhaps the control tower has changed its transmitting frequency. Some of the air navigation radio aids you plan to use on your flight may be temporarily out of commission or may have had recent frequency changes.

The information in NOTAMS falls into two general categories, permanent and temporary. Data considered permanent is printed in bold face type and is usually cited only once; however, it will be transferred to the next revision of the Sectional Chart Bulletin (Figure 117) and carried there until a new Sectional Chart is published. You should note such changes on your charts and other records. Temporary data, printed in regular type, is continuously cited in the NOTAMS until the particular conditions no longer exist. These should not require a change to your Sectional Charts.

NOTAMS are presented alphabetically by states and by cities or localities within states. New or revised data are indicated by underlining the first line of the affected item. The new information is not necessarily limited to the underlined portion, which is used only to attract attention to the new insert.

Figure 121 shows the NOTAM section for Texas. The plain language interpretation of the Austin, Texas, tabulation (denoted with an arrow) is as follows:

> Mueller Municipal Airport: A 1,199 foot (2,049 feet above sea level) lighted TV tower has been constructed at a point 5.5 nautical miles west-northwest of the airport (true direction 287°), at latitude 30° 19′ 33″, longitude 97° 47′ 58″.

This information allows you to determine the exact position of the tower for noting it on the appropriate sectional chart.

You may wish to refer to the abbreviations (Figure 116) in interpreting the NOTAMS.

GLOSSARY OF AERONAUTICAL TERMS

AIR DEFENSE IDENTIFICATION ZONE (ADIZ) — The area of airspace over land or water within which the ready identification, the location, and the control of aircraft are required in the interest of national security. For operating details see ADIZ procedures.

AIRPORT ADVISORY AREA — The area within five statute miles of an uncontrolled airport on which is located a Flight Service Station so depicted on the appropriate Sectional Aeronautical Chart.

AIRPORT ADVISORY SERVICE — A service provided by a Flight Service Station to enhance the safety of terminal operations of airports where a station is operating but where there is no control tower.

AIRPORT TRAFFIC AREA — The airspace within a circular limit defined by a five statute mile horizontal radius from the geographical center of an airport at which an operative airport traffic control tower is located and extending upwards from the surface to, but not including, 2,000 feet above the surface.

APPROACH CONTROL SERVICE — Air traffic control service, provided by a terminal area traffic control facility for arriving and/or departing IFR flights and, on occasion, VFR flights.

CARDINAL ALTITUDES OR FLIGHT LEVELS — "Odd" or "even" thousand-foot altitudes or flight levels. Examples: 5000, 6000, 7000, FL 250, FL 260, FL 270.

CEILING — The height above the ground or water of the lowest layer of clouds or obscuration phenomena that is reported as "broken," "overcast," or "obscuration" and not classified as "thin" or "partial."

CONTERMINOUS U.S. — Forty-eight states and the District of Columbia.

CONTINENTAL CONTROL AREA — The area, which includes that airspace within the conterminous United States at and above 14,500 feet MSL, excluding airspace less than 1,500 feet above terrain, and prohibited and restricted areas (except certain specified restricted areas).

CONTINENTAL U.S. — Forty-nine states. The original 48 states and Alaska.

CONTROL AREA — Controlled airspace extending upwards from a specified height above the surface of the earth. Unless otherwise provided in appropriate cases, control areas extend upward from 700 feet above the surface until designated from 1,200 feet above the surface or from at least 500 feet below the MEA, whichever is higher, to the base of the continental control area.

CONTROL ZONE — Controlled airspace extending upwards from the surface of the earth. Control zones may include one or more airports and are normally circular areas 5 statute miles in radius with extension where necessary to include instrument approach and departure paths.

FINAL APPROACH—VFR — A flight path of a landing aircraft in the direction of landing along the extended runway center line from the base leg to the runway.

FIX — A geographical position determined visually, by reference to one or more radio navigational aids, by celestial plotting, or by another navigational device.

FLIGHT ADVISORY SERVICE — Advice and information provided by a facility to assist pilots in the safe conduct of flight.

FLIP — Flight Information Publication.

FLIGHT SERVICE STATION (FSS) — A facility operated by the FAA to provide flight assistance service.

IFR CONDITIONS — Weather conditions below the minimum prescribed for flights under VFR.

PROHIBITED AREA — Designated airspace within which the flight of aircraft is prohibited.

RADAR ADVISORY SERVICE — The provision of advice or information based on radar observation.

RADIAL — A radial is a magnetic bearing extending from a VOR, VORTAC, or TACAN.

TARGET — The indication displayed on a radar scope resulting from a primary radar return or a radar beacon reply.

TRANSITION AREA — An area extending upward from 1,200 feet or higher above the surface when designated to complement control zones; from 700 feet above the surface when designated in conjunction with an airport with no control zone but for which an instrument approach procedure has been prescribed; or from 1,200 feet or higher above the surface when designated in conjunction with airway route structures or segments. Unless otherwise limited, transition areas terminate at the base of the overlying control area or Continental Control Area.

VECTOR — A heading issued to the pilot for the purpose of providing navigational guidance by means of radar.

VISIBILITY, PREVAILING — The horizontal distance at which targets of known distance are visible over at least half of the horizon. It is normally determined by an observer on or close to the ground viewing buildings or other similar objects during the day and ordinary city lights at night. Under low visibility conditions the observations are usually made at the control tower. Visibility is REPORTED IN MILES AND FRACTIONS OF MILES in the Aviation Weather Report. If a single value does not adequately describe the visibility, additional information is reported in the "Remarks" section of the report.

Figure 115. *Glossary of aeronautical terms.*

Note: "s" may be added for plural, or as appropriate.

acft -------- aircraft	clrnc ------- clearnce	fld ---------- field	info--------- information
adjt -------- adjacent	cntr -------- center	flt ---------- flight	inop -------- inoperative
admin ------ administration	Co ---------- county	flwg -------- following	inst -------- instrument
AGL-------- above ground level	comm ------ communication	FM ---------- fan marker	int ---------- intersection
Airgi ------ Airguide	comsnd ---- commissioned	fone -------- telephone	intl --------- international
●AL -------- Approach and Landing Chart	comsng ----- commissioning	freq -------- frequency	intsv ------- intensive
alt ---------- altitude	config ------- configuration	FSS -------- Flight Service Station	J-bar ------- jet runway barrier
amdt-------- amendment	constr ----- construction		kc ---------- kilocycles
ANRA------ air navigation radio aids	constrd ---- constructed	GCA ------- ground control-led approach	
ant---------- antenna	cont -------- continuous/ continuously	gnd --------- ground	lat ---------- latitude
apch-------- approach	crs --------- course	GWT ------- gross weight	lcl ---------- local
apchg ------ approaching	CS/T ------ combined station/tower	●H ----------- Non-directional radio beacon (homing), power 50 watts to less than 2000 watts	lclzr --------- localizer
aprxly------ approximately	ctc --------- contact		lctd ---------- located
arpt -------- airport	ctl --------- control		lctn --------- location
arr --------- arrival/arrive	ctld -------- controlled		LFR ------- Low/Medium frequency radio range
ARTCC---- Air Route Traffic Control Center	dalgt ------ daylight	●HH --------- Non-directional radio beacon (homing), power 2000 watts or more	
ASDE------ airport surface detection equipment	demsnd ---- decomis-sioned		lgt --------- light
	demol ------ demolition		lgtd -------- lighted
ATC-------- air traffic control	DF --------- direction finder		lgtg -------- lighting
●ATIS ------ Automatic Ter-minal infor-mation Service	discntd ---- discontinued	hi ---------- high-	LMM ------- compass loca-tor at middle marker ILS
	DME ------- UHF standard (TACAN con-patible) dis-tance measur-ing equipment	hr ----------- hour	
		hvy -------- heavy	lnd --------- land
auto-------- automatic		hwy -------- highway	lndg-------- landing
aux -------- auxiliary	dptg-------- departing		LOM ------- compass loca-tor at outer marker ILS
avbl -------- available	dptr -------- departure	ident ------ identification	
awy -------- airway		●IFF ------- Identification Friend from Foe	long ------- longitude
	efctv ------ effective		
BC---------- back course	elev -------- elevation	IFR -------- Instrument Flight Rules	M ----------- magnetic (after a bearing)
bcn --------- beacon	emgcy------ emergency	IFSS ------- International Flight Service Station	MAA ------- maximum authorized altitude
bcst-------- broadcast	eng --------- engine		
bldg-------- building	eqpmt ------ equipment		
bndry ------ boundry	excp -------- except	ILS ------- instrument landing system	mag -------- magnetic
brg --------- bearing	extsn ------ extension		maj --------- major
btn --------- between	extsv ------ extensive	imdtly ----- immediately	max --------maximum
		inbnd ------ inbound	mc---------- megacycles
clsd -------- closed	facil ------- facility	indef ------ indefinitely	MCA ------- minimum cross-ing altitude
	flashg ----- flashing		

MEA ------ minimum en-route IFR altitude	quad ------- quadrant
meml ------- memorial	rad---------- radial
●MH --------- Non-directional radio beacon (homing), power less than 50 watts	RAE ------- Royal Aircraft Establishment visual glide slope indicator
mi ---------- mile	RAPCON - radar approach control
min --------- minimum or minute	RATCC --- radar air traffic control center
MM --------- middle marker ILS	rbn---------- radio beacon
MOCA ----- minimum ob-struction clearance altitude	rcv--------- receive
	rcvg-------- receiving
	rcvr-------- receiver
mod -------- modernization/ modification	rdo --------- radio
MRA ------ minimum recep-tion altitude	reconstr --- reconstruction
	REIL------- runway end identification lights
mrkd ------- marked	relctd ------ relocated
mrkg ------- marking	rgt ---------- right
MSL ------- mean sea level	rng --------- range
mun -------- municipal	rnwy ------- runway
natl -------- national	ruf ---------- rough
navaid----- navigational aid	RVR ------- runway visual range
ngt --------- night	RVV ------ runway visibil-ity values
nmi --------- nautical mile/s	
No --------- number	
	●SIF -------- Selective Iden-tification Feature (of the basic Mark X radar beacon system)
obstn ------ obstruction	
oct --------- octane	
OM -------- outer marker ILS	
operg ------ operating	sked-------- schedule
opern ------ operation	smi -------- statute mile/s
outbnd ----- outbound	SR ---------- sunrise
patn -------- pattern	SS ---------- sunset
permly ----- permanently	stn --------- station
p-line------ pole line	sys--------- system
pwr--------- power	

Figure 116. *Abbreviations.*

ABBREVIATIONS – Continued **Note:** "s" may be added for plural, or as appropriate.

T ---------- true (after a bearing)
TACAN --- UHF navigational facility – omnidirectional course and distance information
tet --------- tetrahedron
tfc --------- traffic
tkof -------- take-off
tmprly ----- temporarily
tmpry ------- temporary
trans ------- transcribed
trml -------- terminal
trng -------- training
tsmt -------- transmit
tsmtg ------ transmitting
tsmtr ------- transmitter
TV --------- television
twr --------- tower
txwy ------- taxiway
UFN ------- until further notice
unavbl ----- unavailable
uncltd ----- uncontrolled
unlgtd ----- unlighted
unmrkd ---- unmarked
VASI ------- visual approach slope indicator
vcnty ------ vicinity
VFR ------- visual flight rules
VOR ------- VHF navigational facility – omnidirectional, course only
VOR-DME- collocated VOR navigational facility and UHF standard navigational facility and UHF standard distance measuring equipment
VORTAC - collocated VOR and TACAN navigational facilities
VOT ------- a VOR receiver Testing Facility
vsby ------- visibility
wea -------- weather
WIP -------- work in progress
wt --------- weight

Figure 116. *Continued*

SECTIONAL CHART BULLETIN

DALLAS

58th Edition, February 6, 1964

Delete Block Ranch arpt 32°19′N, 97°14′W. Delete Diamond M Ranch arpt 32°41′N, 101°05′W. Add V62 airway from Lubbock to Abilene via the Lubbock 125°T & Abilene 306°T. Add obstn 1780′ MSL 33°36′35″N, 99°36′46″W. Add obstn 3570′ MSL 33°53′25″N, 101°51′08″W. Change Abilene VORTAC freq 112.6 ch 73 to 113.7 ch 84. Delete Rockwood FM 32°46′N, 97°22′W. Delete Dobbins arpt 33°41′N, 96°11′W. In Western border change Hobbs VOR freq 116.6 to 111.0. Add obstn 700′ MSL 32°04′27″N, 96°27′15″W. Add obstn 2714′ MSL 32°17′05″N, 99°38′38″W. Add obstn 937′ MSL 33°09′45″N, 97°06′18″W. Add obstn 878′ MSL 32°55′32″N, 96°24′16″W. Add obstn 932′ MSL 33°08′03″N, 96°07′35″W. Add obstn 2349′ MSL 33°34′43″N, 96°57′12″W.

Figure 117. *Sectional chart bulletin.*

LAKE, ISLAND AND MOUNTAIN REPORTING SERVICE
Flight Service Station (FSS)

This service provides flight monitoring where regularly traveled VFR routes cross large bodies of water, swamps, and mountains, for the purpose of expeditiously alerting Search and Rescue facilities when required.

Areas covered, associated Flight Service Stations, and the name of the Service, "Stoneface" "Overlake", etc., are indicated on the following charts. To obtain this service, contact the FSS by telephone or radio giving present position, type aircraft, altitude, indicated air speed, proposed route of flight, and mainland estimate.

After these arrangements have been made, a radio contact with the FSS is required every ten minutes while en route. If contact is lost for more than fifteen minutes, Search and Rescue is alerted.

Figure 118. *Lake, island, and mountain reporting service.*

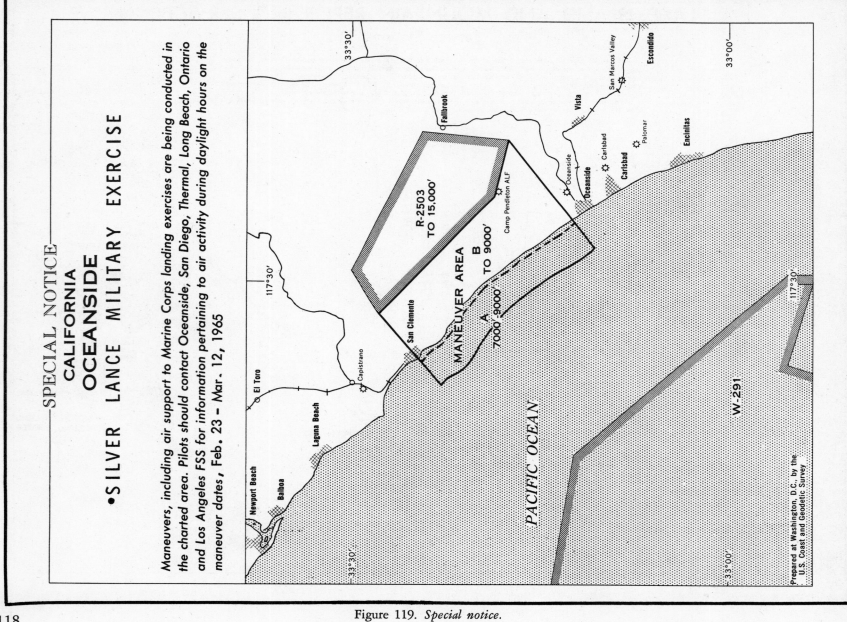

SPECIAL NOTICE

CALIFORNIA
OCEANSIDE

• SILVER LANCE MILITARY EXERCISE

Maneuvers, including air support to Marine Corps landing exercises are being conducted in the charted area. Pilots should contact Oceanside, San Diego, Thermal, Long Beach, Ontario and Los Angeles FSS for information pertaining to air activity during daylight hours on the maneuver dates, Feb. 23 – Mar. 12, 1965

Figure 119. *Special notice.*

OIL BURNER ROUTES

LEGEND

→ ► ► CLIMB OUT TRACKS
► ► ► ► ► ENTRY TRACKS
/////// MANEUVER AREA OF BOMB RUNS
BOMB RUN CORRIDOR
— — — — RE-ENTRY TRACKS
●—● POSITIONS SPECIFIED IN TEXT
500 VFR ALTITUDES (3000 CEIL - 5 MI VIS)
VFR & CONTOUR ALTITUDES (3000 CEIL-5 MI VIS)

COLORADO/KANSAS/NEW MEXICO/OKLAHOMA/TEXAS
ZERO HOUR — Effective November 1, 1964

Aircraft shall cross 34°22′N, 105°40′30″W (Corona, New Mexico VOR) (reporting point) at FL 250 or as assigned by ATC, then descend direct to cross 34°33′N, 105°33′W at or below 23,000′ MSL; then descend direct to cross 34°40′N, 105°28′W at 22,000′ MSL; then descend direct to cross 34°45′N, 105°12′W at or below 18,000′ MSL; then descend direct to cross 34°53′N, 104°48′W at 10,000′ MSL; then descend direct to cross the route entry point at 34°47′N, 104°29′W at 7000′ MSL, maintain 7000′ MSL direct to 35°24′N, 104°08′W, then 7000′ MSL direct to 36°37′N, 102°50′W; then descend direct to cross 36°49′N, 102°35′W at 6000′ MSL, maintain 6000′ MSL direct to 37°03′N, 102°17′W, then 6000′ MSL direct to 37°52′N, 103°10′W.

Short Look and Lay Down — After passing 37°52′N, 103°10′W aircraft shall maintain between 6000′ and 7000′ MSL thru the bomb run corridor (5 SM either side of centerline from 37°52′N, 103°10′W to 38°06′N, 103°25′W). After exiting

the route at 38°06′N, 103°25′W climb direct to cross 38°09′N, 103°26′W at 8000′ MSL, maintain 8000′ MSL direct to 38°22′N, 103°27′W, then 8000′ MSL direct to 38°21′N, 103°17′W; then 8000′ MSL direct to 38°02′N, 102°55′W; then direct to cross 37°53′N, 102°45′W at 9000′ MSL; then climb direct to cross 37°30′N, 103°09′W at FL 200; then maintain FL 200 direct to Tobe VORTAC.

Re-Entry — After completing the initial Short Look bomb run aircraft that are scheduled to execute an additional bomb run shall, after exiting the route at 38°06′N, 103°25′W, climb direct to cross 38°09′N, 103°26′W at 8000′ MSL, maintain 8000′ MSL direct to 28°22′N, 103°27′W, then 8000′ MSL direct to 38°21′N, 103°17′W, then 8000′ MSL direct to 38°04′N, 103°00′W, then 8000′ MSL direct to 37°38′N, 102°31′W; then turn right descending to cross 37°29′N, 102°45′W at 6000′ MSL, thence via the published route.

Alternate Entry — Aircraft shall cross 36°23′N, 103°13′W (Dalhart VORTAC 287/37) (reporting point) at 15,000′ MSL, maintain 15,000 MSL direct to 36°39′N, 102°49′30″W; then descend direct to cross 36°49′N, 102°35′W at 11,000′ MSL, maintain 11,000′ MSL direct to 37°03′N, 102°17′W; then descend direct to cross 37°14′N, 102°29′W at 6000′ MSL, thence via the published route.

Route Width — The route width from 34°47′N, 104°29′W to 35°24′N, 104°08′W is reduced to 5 SM on the east side of centerline.

Hours of Operation — 24 hours daily, 7 days per week.

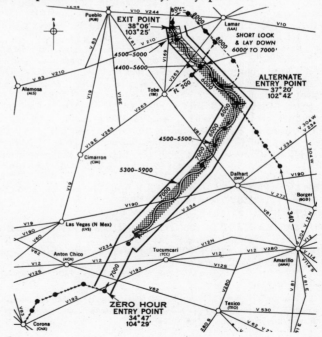

Figure 120. *Oil burner routes.*

TEXAS

AMARILLO: Controlled Firing Area lctd 10 mi NE of end of NE/SW rnwy of Amarillo AFB/Mun: Lat 35°-21'09'', long 101°37'04'' E to 35°21'12'', 101°32'26'', S to 35°17'56'', 101°32'26'' W to 35°17'56'', 101°37'04'', N to point of beginning. Time of Use: 24 hrs per day. Altitudes: up to 3552'.

AUSTIN, MUELLER MUN ARPT: 1199' (2049') lgtd TV twr constrd 5.5 nmi WNW (287° T) at lat 30°19'33'', long 97°47'58''.

BIG SPRING: Due intsv jet tfc at Webb operg Mon-Fri during dalgt hrs it is suggested all acft operg VFR remain at or above 9000' MSL when traversing area encompassed by 15 nmi arc of BGS VOR, excluding any overlap of V-66, including area W along V-16S to point 20 nmi SW of BGS VOR, and an extsn E to include area bounded N by S bndry of Trng Area Webb AFB/Reese Three, bounded S by N bndry of V-66, to N-S line drawn through town of Loraine, Tex. Concentrated jet trng within 10 nmi radius of Colorado City Aux Arpt lctd aprxly 38 nmi E Big Spring. VFR student jet tfc crossing airways within radius of 60 nmi BGS VOR utilizing appropriate VFR hemispherical crossing for tfc advisories.

BIG SPRING HAMILTON FLD: Caution, all alt 3,600' MSL and above intensive jet tfc. T-37 tfc pattern alt at Webb AFB 3,600' MSL.

BIG SPRING HOWARD COUNTY ARPT: Caution, all alt 4,100' MSL and above, intensive jet tfc. T-37 tfc pattern alt at Webb AFB 3,600' MSL.

BROWNSVILLE, RIO GRANDE VALLEY INTL ARPT: Rnwy 13R-31L clsd except that lgt acft may be cleared to land on rnwy 13R.

CLEAR SPRING ARPT: Civil acft requiring use of this fld when military acft are in the tfc patn, should fly a rectangular patn with turns in the opposite direction from the military patn and rock wings on downwind. Patn should be flown at 1200' MSL until military tfc is clear. Use rnwys only for lndgs. Rnwy 13-31 clsd ufn.

CONROE, MONTGOMERY CO ARPT: 304' (492' MSL) lgtd FM twr constrd 5 nmi E (098° T at) lat 30°20'07'', long 95°19'31''.

DALLAS, LOVE FLD: Two bldgs being erected 5 nmi SSE (144°T) at lat 32°47'00'', long 96°47'50''. Bldg A max tmpry hgt 661' (1115' MSL). Completed bldg will be 595.5'. (1039' MSL). Bldg B will reach max tmpry hgt 710' (1149' MSL) in Jan 1965. Completed bldg will be 609.5' (1049' MSL).

DENVER DITY ARPT: 350' (3830' MSL) lgtd rdo twr constrd 14 nmi S (175°T) at lat 32°43'50'', long 102°47'42''.

EDINBURGH MUN ARPT: Rnwys rough, Use Caution.

FT WORTH, SAGINAW ARPT: 208' (1008' MSL) lgtd rdo twr constrd 11nmi W (272° T) at lat 32°52'48'', long 97°36'06''.

HAMILTON MUN ARPT: 400' (1605' MSL) lgtd rdo twr constrd 3 nmi NNE (020° T) at lat 31°42'59'', long 98°07'54''.

JOHNSON CITY ARPT: Microwave twr under constr 1400' WSW 105' AGL will be obstn lgtd and painted.

JOHNSON CITY ARPT TWR: Mobile twr utilizing freqs 236.6, 243.0, 126.2, 121.5 caretake status except as notamed weather and altimeter setting avbl when twr is in opern.

KINGSVILLE, KLEBERG CO ARPT: 400' (474' MSL) lgtd TV twr constrd 7.5 nmi E (090° T) at lat 27°33'02'', long 97°52'35''.

LAREDO: Instv VFR jet trng conducted in Laredo ctl zone and in area 5 mi either side of 068° rad Laredo VOR extending 20 mi eastward of stn. It is urged that all VFR operns (civil and mil) be conducted at or above 9000' MSL in this area. If this is not feasible, ctc Laredo AFB apch ctl on 126.2 mc or 122.5 mc; rcv on 126.2 or 118.5 mc for tfc advisory service. Acft operg VFR and off awys within a 50-nmi radius of Laredo. Use extreme caution due extsv jet trng.

LIBERTY, HOUSE ARPT: 204' (237' MSL) lgtd rdo twr constrd 3.5 nmi W (277° T) at lat 30°03'32'', long 94°47'05''.

MIDLAND AIR TRML: Webb AFB T-38 acft will be making practice ILS apchs to transition from Webb 1 Intensive student jet trng area to the Midland ILS, acft will repart Webb 1 Intensive Student Jet Trng area northbound at 12,000' MSL descending to intercept W course of the Midland ILS lclzr. All transition and practice ILS apchs shall be during dalgt hrs in VFR conditions and only when Webb 1 Intensive Student Jet trng Area is in use.

OZONE MUN ARPT: 200' (2626' MSL) lgtd rdo twr constrd 2 nmi S (172° T) at lat 30°41'54'', long 101°11'42''.

PERRYTON MUN ARPT: 300' (3168' MSL) lgtd rdo twr constrd 2

SAN ANGELO, MATHIS FLD: 260' (2170' MSL) lgtd rdo twr constrd 3.5 nmi N (5° T) at lat 31°24'41'', long 100°28'29''.

SAN ANTONIO, CAMP BULLIS: Controlled Firing Area as follows: A circular area 1¼ smi in radius centered at lat 29°42'00'', long 98°33'50''. Altitude: surface to 3000' MSL (1500' AGL). Time and use: 0830 to 1200 hrs lcl time, Fri of each wk for destruction of ammunition by detonation.

SAN ANTONIO, RANDOLPH AFB: Due to jet and conventional acft making GCA apchs suggest all acft operg VFR that will traverse area N of Randolph remain at least 10 nmi from the base and above 3000' MSL. Hvy conventional and jet instrument acrobatic and transition trng in SE quadrant btn V198 and V163 and V163W 60 nmi radius of Randolph Mon-Fri. VFR jet tfc will be crossing V163 and V163W S of the City of San Antonio at the appropriate hemispherical crossing altitudes en route to Hondo Aux Arpt. Hvy IFR/VFR penetrations and apcrs will be made from the La Vernia VOR to Randolph AFB. Should necessity dicate flight in the close proximity of Randolph AFB, aircraft should contact Randolph Tower on 126.2 mcs for traffic advisories.

TEMPLE, DRAUGHON-MILLER ARPT: Runway 11-29 clsd until aprxly Mar 1, 1965.

TYLER, POUNDS FLD: ILS-13, Amdt. 5, ILS-31, Amdt. 5 and ADF 1, Amdt. 5 are revised as follows effective immediately: Delete straight-ih minimums.

VICTORIA CO-FOSTER ARPT: 420' (540 MSL) lgtd rdo twr constrd 5 nmi SSW (204°T) at lat 28°46'32'', long 96°57'12''.

WICHITA FALLS AIR TRML: 203' (1212' MSL) lgtd rdo twrs/4/constrd 3 nmi WSW (237° T) at lat 33°57'38'', long 98°33'42''.

Figure 121. *Notices to airmen.*

AIRPORT/FACILITY DIRECTORY LEGEND

LOCATION

The airport location is given in nautical miles (to the nearest mile) and direction from center of referenced city. This is followed by the bearing and distance from the principal NAVAID within 25 nautical miles of the airport. The distance is not specified if less than half mile from the field.

ELEVATION

Elevation is given in feet above mean sea level and is based on highest usable portion of the landing area. When elevation is sea level, elevation will be indicated as "00". When elevation is below sea level, a minus sign (−) will precede the figure.

RUNWAYS

The runway surface, length, reciprocal headings, and weight bearing capacity are listed for the longest instrument runway or sealane, or the longest active landing portion of the runway or strip, given to the nearest hundred feet, using 70 feet as the division point, i.e., 1468 feet would be shown as "14"; 1474 feet would be shown as "15". Runway lengths prefixed by the letter "H" indicates that runways are hard surfaced (concrete; asphalt; bitumen, or macadam with a seal coat). If the runway length is not prefixed, the surface is sod, clay, etc. The total number of runways available is shown in parenthesis.

RUNWAY WEIGHT BEARING CAPACITY

Add 000 to figure following S, T, TT and MAX for gross weight capacity, e.g., (S−000).

S—Runway weight bearing capacity for aircraft with single-wheel type landing gear. (DC−3), etc.

T—Runway weight bearing capacity for aircraft with twin-wheel type landing gear. (DC−6), etc.

TT—Runway weight bearing capacity for aircraft with twin-tandem type landing gear. (707), etc.

Quadricycle and twin-tandem are considered virtually equal for runway weight bearing considerations, as are single-tandem and twin-wheel.

A blank space following the letter designation is used to indicate the runway weight bearing capacity to sustain aircraft with the same type landing gear, although definate figures are not available, e.g., (T−).

MAX—Maximum runway gross weight bearing capacity for all aircraft.

Omission of weight bearing capacity indicates information unknown. Footnote remarks are used to indicate a runway with a weight bearing greater than the longest runway.

SEAPLANE BASE FACILITIES

A number preceding the parenthetical designation, indicates the number (quantity) available.

Beaching gear, consisting of the quantity and type of beaching gear available.

The number (quantity) if available, of Mooring Buoys (MB) and Crash Boats (CB) available. MB & CB indicates details of quantity are not available.

LIGHTING

B: Rotating Light (Rotating beacon). (Green and white, split-beam and other types.) Omission of **B** indicates rotating light is either not available or not operating standard hours (sunset-sunrise).

NOTE—Code lights are not codified, and are carried in Remarks.

L: Field Lighting (when code **L4-7** is indicated, lighting **4, 5, 6, 7** is available). An asterisk (*) preceding an element indicates that it operates on prior request only (by phone call, telegram or letter). Where the asterisk is not shown, the lights are in operation or available sunset to sunrise or by request (circling the field or radio call). **L** by itself indicates temporary lighting, such as flares, smudge pots, lanterns.

1—Strip lights or portable runway lights (electrical)
2—Boundry
3—Runway Floods
4—Low Intensity Runway
5—Medium Intensity Runway
6—High Intensity Runway
7—Instrument Approach (neon)
8A, B, or C—High Intensity Instrument Approach

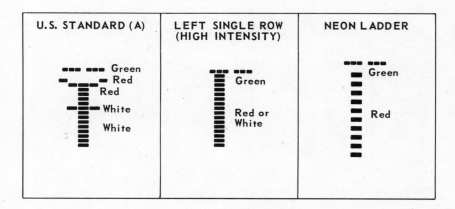

U.S. STANDARD (A)	LEFT SINGLE ROW (HIGH INTENSITY)	NEON LADDER
Green / Red / Red / White / White	Green / Red or White	Green / Red

9—Sequence Flashing Lights (3,000' out unless otherwise stated)
10—Visual Approach Slope Indicator (VASI)
11—Runway end identification lights (threshold strobe) (REIL)
12—Short approach light systems (SALS)

Figure 122a. Airport/facility directory legend.

Lighting (Con't)

13—Runway alignment lights (RAIL)
14—Runway centerline
15—Touchdown zone

Because the obstructions on virtually all lighted fields are lighted, obstruction lights have not been indicated in the codification.

SERVICING

S1: Storage
S2: Storage, minor airframe repairs.
S3: Storage, minor airframe and minor powerplant repairs.
S4: Storage, major airframe and minor powerplant repairs.
S5: Storage, major airframe and major powerplant repairs.

FUEL

F1   80 oct., at least.
F2   80/87 oct., or lower.
F3   91/96 oct., or lower.
F4   100/130 performance rating, or lower.
F5   115/145 performance rating, or lower.

TURBINE FUELS

TP-1   650 turbine fuels for civil jets.
JP-1   (Kerosene), JP-3, JP-4, JP-5.

OTHER

AOE—Airport of Entry.
VASI—Visual Approach Slope Indicator, applicable runway provided.
RVV—Runway visibility, applicable runway provided.
RVR—Runway Visual Range, applicable runway provided.
TPA—Traffic Pattern Altitude&This information is provided only at those airports without a 24-hour operating control tower or without an FSS providing Airport Advisory Service. Directions of turns are indicated only when turns of the pattern(s) are to the right (non-standard). TPA data is related to the runway listed under the tabulated airport information. Generally, only one altitude is listed; however, at some airports two altitudes have been established; one for conventional aircraft and one for high performance aircraft. They are shown in this manner, TPA 8/15-R (increments of 100 feet). The higher figure being the higher performance aircraft altitude.
FSS—The name of the controlling FSS is shown in all instances. When the FSS is located on the named airport, "on fld" is shown following the FSS name. When the FSS can be called through the local telephone exchange, (Foreign Exchange) at the cost of a local call, it is indicated by "(LC(" local call) with the phone number immediately following the name of the FSS, i.e., "FSS: WICHITA (LC481-5867)." When an Intephone line exists between the field and the FSS, it is indicated by "(DL)" (direct line) immediately following the name of the FSS, i.e., "FSS: OTTO (DL)."

AIRPORT REMARKS

"FEE" indicates landing charges for private or nonrevenue producing aircraft. In addition, fees may be charged for planes that remain over a couple of hours and buy no services, or at major airline terminals for all aircraft.

"Rgt tfc 13-31" indicates right turns should be made on landings and takeoffs on runways 13 and 31.

Limited—Intended for private use, but use by public is not prohibited.

Remarks data is confined to operational items affecting the status and usability of the airport, traffic patterns and departure procedures.

Obstructions.—Because of space limitations only the more dangerous obstructions are indicated. Natural obstructions, such as trees, clearly discernible for contact operations, are frequently omitted. On the other hand, all pole lines within at least 15:1 glide angle are indicated.

COMMUNICATIONS

Clearance is required prior to taxiing on a runway, taking off, or landing at a tower controlled airport.

When operating at an airport where the control tower is operated by the U.S. Government, two-way radio communication is required unless otherwise authorized by the tower. (When the tower is operated by someone other than the U.S. Government, two-way radio communication is required if the aircraft has the necessary equipment.)

Frequencies transmit and receive unless specified as: T—Transmit only, R—Receive only, X—On request. Primary frequencies are listed first in each frequency grouping, i.e., VHF, LF. Emergency frequency 121.5 is available at all TOWER, APPROACH CONTROL and RADAR facilities, unless indicated otherwise by a crossout: 121.5.

Radar available is listed under "RADAR SERVICES" Radar beacons are indicated by "(BCN)" after "RADAR SERVICES", when available.

VOICE CALL

The voice call for contact with the traffic control services listed at each airport is the airport name followed by the call of the particular service desired, i.e., "LAGUARDIA TOWER." In these instances, only the name of service is listed. When the voice call of the facility is not the same as the airport name, the complete voice call is listed.

Figure 122b. *Airport/facility directory legend.*

SERVICES AVAILABLE

(See ATC Operations and Procedures, Section II)

TOWER

Clearance Delivery (CLRNC DEL).
Approach Control (APP CON) Radar and Non-Radar.
Departure Control (DEP CON) Radar and Non- Radar.
VFR Advisory Service (VFR ADV) Non-Radar.
Traffic Information Service (TFC INFO) Radar.
Surveillance Radar Approach (ASR).
Precision Radar Approach (PAR).
Ground Control (GND CON).
VHF Direction Finding (VHF/DF).

FLIGHT SERVICE STATION (FSS)

Airport Advisory Service (AAS).
Flight Following Service.
Island, Mountain and Lake Reporting Service.

UNICOM

Private aeronautical station, operates same hours as the airport, transmits and receives on one of the following frequencies:

U – 1 –122.8 mc (at airports without a control tower).

U – 2 – 123.0 mc (at airports with a control tower).

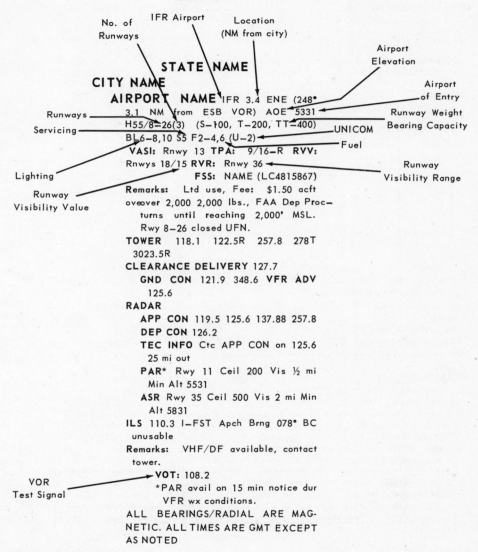

Figure 122c. *Airport/facility directory legend.*

TEXAS

ABERNATHY MUNI 4 E
3327 H50 (2) S5 F4   FSS: LUBBOCK

ABILENE
  ABILENE MUNI See Section IV-A

  BUTTERFIELD TRAIL 5 NW
  1670 H25 (1) L4 S5 F4 U-1
                                              FSS: ABILENE (LC OR4-6915)
  Remarks: P-line NW. Rnwy 7-25 ruf, emgcy only.

ARLINGTON
  ARLINGTON MUNI *IFR* 4 S
  630 H40 (1) L4 S5 F4
                              FSS: FORT WORTH (LC MA4-8444)
  VFR ADV For APP CON, DEP CON See FORT WORTH/
  GREATER SOUTHWEST INTL in Section IV-A
  -
  LUCAS 3 SW
  611 21 (3) S5   FSS: FORT WORTH (LC MA4-8444)
  Remarks: W, NW blkd. Wet.

ATHENS
  JONES MUNI 3 SE
  455 H37 (1) L4 F4   FSS: TYLER

AZLE
  ATWOOD 3 NW
  820 28 (3) S1 F2
  Remarks: N, NW blkd.
  -

  FLYING OAKS 4 S
  720 28 (1) S1
  Remarks: P-line S.

BRECKENRIDGE
  STEPHENS CO 2 S
  1282 H38 (3) BL4 S5 F4 U-1
                                        FSS: MINERAL WELLS

BRIDGEPORT MUNI *IFR* 2 S
971 21 (3) F2
Remarks: Make no low apchs, p-lines along all apchs.

CADDO MILLS MUNI 5 W
540 H40 (2)
Remarks: Fence N and NW. Drag races Sundays N/S strip.

CISCO MUNI 3 NW
1612 28 (4) F4   FSS: MINERAL WELLS
Remarks: P-line N.

CLEBURNE MUNI 3 W
856 H30 (1) BL4 S5 F4   FSS: FORT WORTH

COLORADO CITY
  COLORADO CITY 3 NE
  2168 30 (1) F2   FSS: MIDLAND
  Remarks: Unattended.
  -
  HARRELL FISHING CAMP 6 S
  2130 33 (1)   FSS: MIDLAND
  Remarks: P-line S.

CORSICANA
  ALLISON RANCH 3 NW
  410 H30 (2) F4 U-1   FSS: DALLAS
  Remarks: P-line SW.
  -
  CORSICANA MUNI 5 SE
  440 H34 (1) BL 4 S5 F4 U-1   FSS: DALLAS
  Remarks: P-line NE.

CROSBYTON
  PAULDER 1 E
  3017 H26 (1) F4   FSS: LUBBOCK
  Remarks: Low P-line N. Use rnwy. 3900' strip avbl.

DALLAS
  ADDISON See Section IV-A
  -
  DALLAS GARLAND *IFR* 9 NE
  614 H34 (2) L4 S5 F4 U-1

Figure 123a. *Airport directory*

AIRPORT DIRECTORY

FSS: DALLAS (LC RI 9-3502)

VFR ADV: For APP CON DEP CON See DALLAS/LOVE FLD
in Section IV-A

- -

HIGHLAND PARK 8 N
573 H24 (1) S5 F4 U-1   FSS: DALLAS (LC RI 9-3502)
Remarks: Use rnwys, txwys only.

- -

LOVE FLD See Section IV-A

- -

PARK CITIES 9 NW
483 H17 (1) L4 S5 F4 U-1
     FSS: DALLAS (LC RI 9-3502)
Remarks: P-line NW. Rgt tfc rnwys 13 and 17.

- -

RED BIRD See Section IV-A

- -

WHITE ROCK 6 NE
543 H21 (1) S5 F4 U-1   FSS: DALLAS (LC RI 9-3502)

_____

DECATUR MUNI 2 N
1059 28 (3) B S1 F4   FSS: FORT WORTH
Remarks: P-lines E, SW, W. Bcn operg on request.

_____

DENTON MUNI 3 W
652 H41 (1) L4 S3 F4   FSS: FORT WORTH
Remarks: P-lines E, SE.

_____

EASTLAND MUNI 1 N
1468 32 (4) L4 F4   FSS: MINERAL WELLS
Remarks: Unattended.

_____

FORT WORTH
    GREATER SOUTHWEST INTL, DALLAS-FT WORTH FLD See Section IV-A

- -

LUCK 10 S
700 H30 (1) L4 S2 F4   FSS: FORT WORTH (LC MA 4-8444)
Remarks: P-lines N and S. Attended days.

- -

MEACHAM FLD See Section IV-A

- -

OAK GROVE *IFR* 11 S
690 H20 (1) L4 S5 F4 U-1   FSS: FORT WORTH (LC MA 4-8444)
VFR ADV: For APP CON, DEP CON See FORT WORTH/ GREATER

SOUTHWEST INTL in Section IV-A
Remarks: Rgt tfc N.

_____

GAINESVILLE 3 W
833 H47 (4) *L4 S5 F5   FSS: ARDMORE

_____

GRAHAM MUNI 2 E
1120 H33 (1) BL4 S3 F4 U-1   FSS: MINERAL WELLS
Remarks: P-line W. Tower N. Soft when wet.

_____

GRAND PRAIRIE Adj S
550 H28 (3) *L4 F4 U-1   FSS: DALLAS (LC RI 9-3502)
Remarks: P-lines N, NE, SW; bldgs NW.

_____

GREATER SOUTHWEST INTL, DALLAS-FT WORTH FLD See FT WORTH,
GREATER SOUTHWEST INTL, DALLAS-FT WORTH FLD in Section IV-A

_____

GREENVILLE
    MAJORS See Section IV-A

_____

HAMILTON
    HAMILTON FLD See BIG SPRINGS

- -

    HAMILTON MUNI 2 S
1320 30 (2) B*L4 F2   FSS: WACO

_____

JACKSBORO
    PURSLEY FLD 4 NW
1100 33 (1) S1   FSS: MINERAL WELLS
Remarks: Unattended. P-line N.

_____

LEMESA MUNI 1 E
2994 H42 (2) L4 S5 F4 U-1   FSS: MIDLAND
Remarks: Threshold displaced 270' rnwy 15. P-lines apch rnwy 24.

_____

LUBBOCK
    LUBBOCK MUNI See Section IV-A

- -

    TOWN AND COUNTRY ARPK 6 S
3270 H21 (1) L4 S5 F4   FSS: LUBBOCK
Remarks: P-line W 3200 strip.

_____

McKINNEY
    FLYING M RANCH 5 W
760 25 (1) U-1   FSS: DALLAS
Remarks: P-line N.

Figure 123b. *Airport directory.*

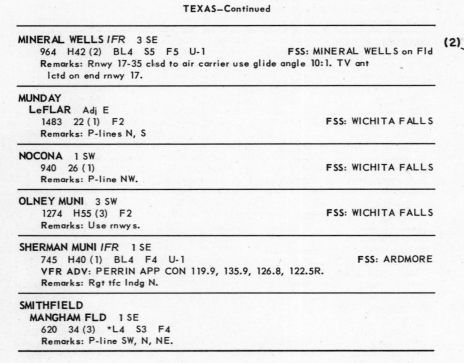

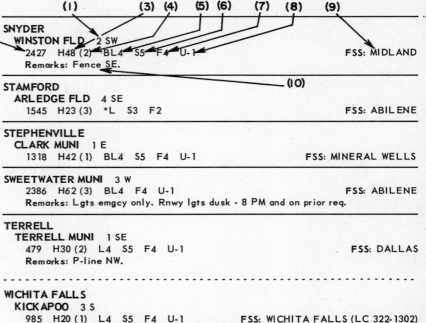

TEXAS—Continued

MINERAL WELLS *IFR* 3 SE
964 H42 (2) BL4 S5 F5 U-1   FSS: MINERAL WELLS on Fld
Remarks: Rnwy 17-35 clsd to air carrier use glide angle 10:1. TV ant
lctd on end rnwy 17.

MUNDAY
LeFLAR Adj E
1483 22 (1) F2   FSS: WICHITA FALLS
Remarks: P-lines N, S

NOCONA 1 SW
940 26 (1)   FSS: WICHITA FALLS
Remarks: P-line NW.

OLNEY MUNI 3 SW
1274 H55 (3) F2   FSS: WICHITA FALLS
Remarks: Use rnwys.

SHERMAN MUNI *IFR* 1 SE
745 H40 (1) BL4 F4 U-1   FSS: ARDMORE
VFR ADV: PERRIN APP CON 119.9, 135.9, 126.8, 122.5R.
Remarks: Rgt tfc lndg N.

SMITHFIELD
MANGHAM FLD 1 SE
620 34 (3) *L4 S3 F4
Remarks: P-line SW, N, NE.

SNYDER
WINSTON FLD 2 SW
2427 H48 (2) BL4 S5 F4 U-1   FSS: MIDLAND
Remarks: Fence SE.

STAMFORD
ARLEDGE FLD 4 SE
1545 H23 (3) *L S3 F2   FSS: ABILENE

STEPHENVILLE
CLARK MUNI 1 E
1318 H42 (1) BL4 S5 F4 U-1   FSS: MINERAL WELLS

SWEETWATER MUNI 3 W
2386 H62 (3) BL4 F4 U-1   FSS: ABILENE
Remarks: Lgts emgcy only. Rnwy lgts dusk - 8 PM and on prior req.

TERRELL
TERRELL MUNI 1 SE
479 H30 (2) L4 S5 F4 U-1   FSS: DALLAS
Remarks: P-line NW.

WICHITA FALLS
KICKAPOO 3 S
985 H20 (1) L4 S5 F4 U-1   FSS: WICHITA FALLS (LC 322-1302)
Remarks: P-line NW. 3600' strip avbl. Atndd daylight hours.

Figure 123c. *Airport directory.*

Section IV — Airport Directory This section contains a listing of all known airports, heliports, and seaplane bases available for civil use within the conterminous United States. It indicates the airport services and facilities available at each. Heliports and Seaplane Bases are tabulated separately following the Airport tabulation. Military Airports and privately owned and operated airports closed to civil aviation are not listed.

Airports are listed alphabetically by state and cities or towns within the state. Where the city and airport names are identical, the airport name is omitted. Airport names are sequenced alphabetically at locations having two or more airports. Airport names different from the city or town name are cross-referenced.

An Airport/Facility Directory Legend is contained in this section and serves both Section VI and Section VIA. Figures 122a, b, and c, show the complete legend.

The excerpted portions of the Texas Directory (Figures 123a, b, and c) show some of the airports contained on the Dallas Sectional Chart provided with this handbook. Using the entry for Snyder, Winston Field, (Figure 123c), as an example, the tabulated information would be interpreted as follows:

(1) 2SW — Winston Field is approximately 2 nautical miles Southwest of the center of the city of Snyder, Texas.

(2) 2427 — The field elevation is 2,427 feet above sea level.

(3) H48 — The longest runway is hardsurfaced with a length between 4770 feet and 4870 feet.

TEXAS

ABILENE MUNI *IFR* 3 SE (102° 9.5 NM from ABI VOR)
1778 H60/17-35 (2) (MAX-30) BL4, 6, 8 S5 F4 U2
RVV: Rnwy 35   **FSS:** ABILENE on Fld
REMARKS: NW-SE txwy used by lgt acft for lndg during high cross wind
  conditions. Rgt tfc rnwys 4 & 35.
TOWER 126.2 122.7R 120.1 278T   **GND CON** 121.9
RADAR SERVICES: (BCN)
  APP CON 126.5 134.1 126.2 113.7T 110.3T 109.2T
  DEP CON 125.0
ILS 110.3 I-ABI Apch Brg 350°

DALLAS

ADDISON *IFR* 9 N (ADS VOR on fld)
637 H45/15-33 (2) BL4 S5 F5, JP1 U2   **FSS:** DALLAS (LC R19-3502)
REMARKS: Rnwy 21 apch rest by poleline-glide angle 3 to 1.
TOWER 121.1 122.7R   **GND CON** 121.7
RADAR SERVICES:
  DALLAS APP CON 123.7[1] 125.2 119.8[2] 110.3T
  DALLAS DEP CON 119.5
REMARKS: [1] 127°-307° [2] 308°-126°

DALLAS

LOVE FIELD *IFR* 5 NW (178° 7.1 NM from ADS VOR)
485 H77/13-31 (2) (S-100, T-150, TT-330) BL4, 6, 8A, 10, 11
S5 F5, JP1, 4 U2   VASI: Rnwy 31
RVR: Rnwy 13   **FSS:** DALLAS on Fld
REMARKS: Rnwy 36 apch rest by pole line-glide andle 14 to 1.
  Ctc apch ctl for tfc info. Formation tkofs prohibited. 3500 ft N end
  rnwy 18 avbl for S lndgs & tkofs. US Customs lndg rts arpt
  1230 am - 230 pm Mon-Fri, 1230 am - 430 pm Sat. Req arr notice
  be forward customs when filing flt plan in Canada, Mexico or
  Cuba. Rnwy 36 clsd for lndgs & tkofs.
TOWER 126.2 122.5R 118.7 278T
  CLRNC DEL 121.6   **GND CON** 121.9
RADAR SERVICES:
  DALLAS APP CON 125.2 123.7[2] 122.5R 119.8[3] 111.4T 110.3T
  DALLAS DEP CON 119.5
  TFC INFO Ctc APP CON 25 mi out
  PAR Rnwys 13 Ceil 200 Vsby 1/2 mi Min Alt 685
  ASR Rnwys 13, 31[1] Ceil 400 Vsby 1 mi Min Alt 885
ILS 110.3 I-DAL Apch Brg 127°
VHF/DF available, contact tower
REMARKS: [1] Maint at least 1400 til 3.5 mi from apch end of rnwy 31

LOVE FIELD – (Continued)

and 1000 til 1.4 mi fm apch end of rnwy 31. [2] 127°-307° [3] 308°-126°.
Acft apch love field from W and S side of lclzr crs extended
should ctc Dallas APP CON on 123.7. Acft apch from N and E side
of lclzr crs should ctc Dallas APP CON on 119.8.
(1) VOT: 111.0

FORT WORTH

GREATER SOUTHWEST INTL *IFR* 16 NE (GSW VOR on fld)
(2) 568 H84/13-31 (2) (S-120, T-180, TT-400) BL4, 6, 8 S3 F5, JP5
  RVR: Rnwy 13   **FSS:** FORT WORTH (LC MA 4-8444)
  REMARKS: Ctn-const vic N end rnwy 17-35. Rnwy 17 threshold
(3)   displaced 500 ft S. 5800 ft avbl lndg & tkof both directions.
  SOUTHWEST TOWER 118.9 126.2 122.7R 317T
  SOUTHWEST GND CON 121.8
(4) RADAR SERVICES:
  FORT WORTH APP CON 118.1 126.2 122.7R 119.6 109.5T
  FORT WORTH DEP CON 123.9 122.7R
(5) TFC INFO Ctc APP CON 25 NM out on 118.1
  ASR Rnwys 13, 17, 31, 35 Ceil 400 Vsby 1 mi Min Alt 968
ILS 109.5 I-GSW Apch Brg 129°
VHF/DF available, contact tower
(6) REMARKS: VOT: 111.8

FORT WORTH

MEACHAM FIELD *IFR* 5 N (177° 2.1 NM from FTW RBn)
692 H52/17-35 (3) (S-60, T-80, TT-) BL4, 6, 7 S5 F5, JP5 U2
                        FSS: FORT WORTH on Fld
REMARKS: Rnwy 31 apch rgst by poleline-glide angle 6 to 1.
TOWER[1] 126.2 122.7R 118.3   **GND CON** 121.9
RADAR SERVICES:
  FORT WORTH APP CON 119.6 126.2 122.7R 118.1 109.5T
  FORT WORTH DEP CON 123.9 122.7R
ILS 109.9 I-FTW Apch Brg 174°
REMARKS: [1] Oper 1300-0500Z.
VOT: 108.2

GREENVILLE

MAJORS FIELD 4 SE (GVT VOR on fld)
544 H80/17-35 (3) (S-80, T-140, TT-220) BL4[1] S5 F4   **FSS:** DALLAS
REMARKS: Ngt lndg not advisible. Rnwy lgts on first 3500 ft rnwy 35
  only, remainder lgtd smudge dots prior reg. S 3300' rnwy 17 lgtd.
TOWER[1] 121.3 122.5R
REMARKS: [1] Oper 1330-2200Z excp Sat & Sun.

Figure 124. *Airport/facility directory.*

(4) (2) There are two runways available for use (both are not necessarily hardsurfaced).

(5) BL4 — There is a rotating beacon (alternating green and white) which operates continuously between sunset and sunrise, and low intensity runway lighting.

(6) S5 — There is hangar storage and major airframe and minor powerplant repair available.

(7) F4 — Fuel of 100/130 performance rating and possibly lower octane ratings is available.

(8) U-1 — An aeronautical advisory station ("Winston Unicom") is available on the frequency of 122.8 mc.

(9) FSS Midland — Midland is the controlling Flight Service Station. Ground communication would require a long distance phone call. Inflight communication in the vicinity of Snyder could be established through Big Spring VOR.

(10) Remarks: Fence SE — A fence is located immediately adjacent to the landing area on the Southeast portion of the airport.

Section IV-A — Airport/Facility Directory This section contains a tabulated listing of all major airports, heliports, and seaplane bases which have terminal navaids and communications facilities (control towers) available at the field, as well as all enroute navaids (VOR, radio beacons, etc.) in the conterminous United States. These airport tabulations combine airport, navaid, and communication facilities into a single listing.

Airports and navaids are listed alphabetically by state just as in Section IV. Section IV, the Airport Directory, also contains a listing of these major airports but directs the reader to Section IV-A, *The Airport/Facility Directory*, for the complete tabulation.

Some of the major Texas Airports and navaids appearing on the Dallas Sectional Chart have been excerpted from Section IV-A and appear in Figure 124.

Remember, the legend (Figures 122a, b, and c) contained in Section IV, serves both Section IV and Section IV-A.

Using the entry for Fort Worth, Greater Southwest International, as an example, the tabulated information would be interpreted as follows: (Note: Only the information of *interest to the VFR pilot*, and which has not been explained in the Section IV sample for Winston Field is covered here.)

(1) (LC MA-4844) — Local telephone number of the Fort Worth FSS.

(2) Remarks — the north 3,100 feet of runway 17-35 is closed due to construction leaving 5,900 feet available for use.

(3) Southwest Tower — This is the voice call "Southwest Tower" for radio communications. 118.9 mc is the primary frequency. The tower could also be contacted by transmitting on 122.7 mc and receiving on 118.9 mc.

(4) Southwest Gnd Con — The frequency for "Southwest Ground Control" is 121.8 mc. Since this is not one of the normal ground control frequencies (i.e. 121.7 mc or 121.9 mc) your aircraft may not be equipped to transmit on 121.8 mc. If this is the case, you should transmit to ground control on a tower frequency and listen on 121.8 mc.

(5) TFC Info — Radar Traffic Advisory Service is available on 118.1 mc. If you have the appropriate frequency, it is recommended that you contact "Fort Worth Approach Control" at a distance of 25 nautical miles from the airport for this service. (See Chapter 27).

(6) VHF/DF — Direction Finding Service ("Fort Worth Homer") is available. The standard emergency frequency of 121.5 mc will normally be used for this service (see Chapter 29).

A Checklist for Maintaining Currency of Sectional Charts

1. *Check the latest Sectional Chart Bulletin* (published every 28 days) for any additions, deletions or revisions for the appropriate sectional chart. Note particularly any airspace restrictions or hazards and airport or radio frequency changes as they apply to your intended flight.

2. *Check the latest NOTAMS* (published every 14 days) for more recent changes to information listed above. Remember, NOTAMS will normally be your only source of information for temporary changes.

3. *Check the Airport Directory* (published every 6 months) for information concerning the airports you intend to use. Although the revision cycle is approximately the same as that for Sectional Charts, the Directory may have a later publication date.

4. *Check the Airport/Facility Directory* (published every 28 days) for information concerning major airports and navaids you intend to use. Pay particular attention to communication and navaid frequencies for possible changes.

SECTION VIII—FLIGHT COMPUTER

25. Slide Rule Face

The computer illustrated and discussed in this handbook has two sides—the slide rule or calculator face (fig. 126) and the wind face (fig. 127). The slide rule face is used to solve problems involving time, distance, fuel consumption, speed, and nautical-to-statute-mile conversions. The wind face is used to compute certain values associated with the wind triangle, if enough of these values are known. In this handbook only one type of wind triangle problem will be considered. This will be the problem of computing the true heading and ground speed when the wind direction and speed, true course, and true airspeed are known. To plan his flight properly, the private pilot will have to solve this type problem during preflight planning.

Three Scales on the Slide Rule Face   The main portion of the slide rule face consists of the "miles," "minutes," and "hours" scales (fig. 125). The miles scale (arrow #1) is the outer scale and lies on the fixed portion of this face. The minutes scale (arrow #2) is the middle scale; and the hours scale (arrow #3) is the inner scale. Both the minutes and hours scales lie on a rotatable disk.

You will note in figure 128 that the graduations of the miles scale and minutes scale are the same. Those on the hours scale are different.

The outer, or miles, scale will also be used to represent gallons (of fuel) and true airspeeds. The middle, or minutes scale is also used to represent indicated airspeeds.[1] The hours scale is used only to represent hours and minutes.

Scale Graduations (Miles and Minutes Scales)   As noted above, the miles and minutes scales are graduated in exactly the same intervals. Two problems are associated with interpreting these scales properly.

The first problem is assigning the proper value to the intervals that are numbered. The numbered intervals begin with 10 and end with 90. Between

---

[1] Actually, the minutes scale is used to represent calibrated airspeed. However, since indicated and calibrated airspeeds are approximately the same in the cruising airspeed range, only indicated airspeeds will be used in the flight computer discussion.

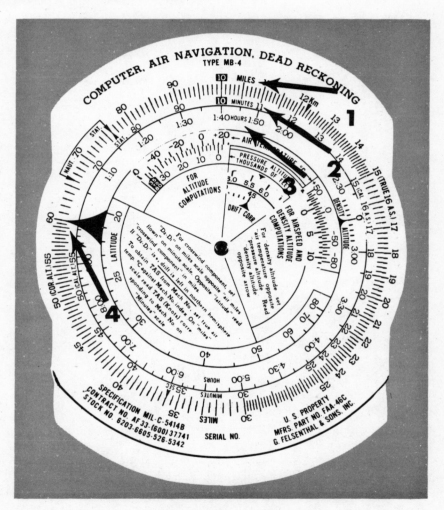

Figure 125. *Three scales and speed index. Arrow #1, miles scale; arrow #2, minutes scale; arrow #3, hours scale; arrow #4, speed index.*

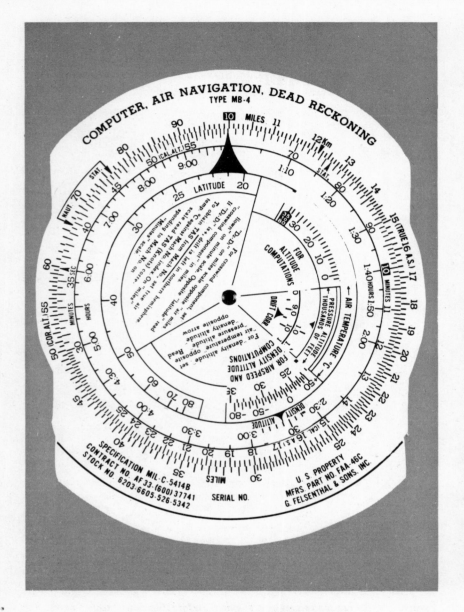

Figure 126. *Slide rule face of a flight computer.*

PRESS ALT FEET	F CORRECTION FACTORS FOR TAS							
	CALIBRATED AIRSPEED KNOTS							
	200	250	300	350	400	450	500	550
10.000	1.0	1.0	.99	.99	.98	.98	.97	.97
20.000	.99	.98	.97	.97	.96	.95	.94	.93
30.000	.97	.96	.95	.94	.92	.91	.90	.89
40.000	.96	.94	.92	.90	.88	.87	.87	.86
50.000	.93	.90	.87	.86	.84	.84	.84	.84

DIRECTIONS

USE CALIBRATED AIRSPEED AND PRESS ALT. TO OBTAIN F FACTOR. MULTIPLY F FACTOR BY TAB OBTAINED WITH COMPUTER TO OBTAIN TAB CORRECTED FOR COMPRESSIBILITY.

TRUE INDEX

TH = TC + Drift Left
− Drift Right

TH = MH + Var. East
− Var. West

MH = TH + Drift Right
− Drift Left

TC = TH − Drift Left
+ Drift Right

Figure 127. *Wind face of a flight computer.*

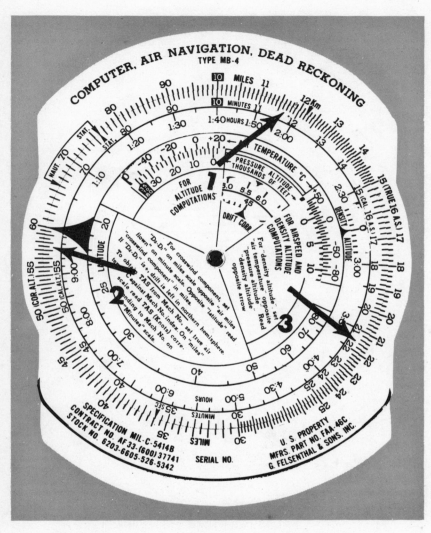

Figure 128. *Assigning values to the graduations of the scales.*

10 and 25, each unit interval is numbered (10, 11, 12, etc.). Between 25 and 60, each 5-unit interval is numbered (25, 30, 35, etc.). Between 60 and 90, each 10-unit interval is numbered (60, 70, etc.). We will choose 60 to illustrate the first problem. This particular mark on the scale could represent 0.6, 6, 60, 600, etc. In the case of calculations made by the private pilot, it will usually indicate 6, 60, 600.

The second problem is assigning the correct values to the subintervals. By subintervals we mean the graduations that lie between the numbered intervals. These will represent different values. Each subinterval between the numbered intervals from 10 to 15 represent one-tenth (.1) of the larger unit; between 15 and 30, each small subinterval represents two-tenths (.2) of a unit. The large intervals between 25 and 30 represent a unit (26, 27, 28, and 29). Between 30 and 60, each large subinterval represents a unit (31, 32, etc.) and each smaller subinterval five-tenths (.5) of a unit. Between 60 and 100 each subinterval represents one unit. Common sense must be used to determine what values to assign to the subintervals.

We will now take some examples and see how to assign values at various intervals on the scale. The *first step* should be to assign a value to the two numbered intervals on either side of the desired interval (unless the desired interval is numbered). The *second step* is to assign the proper value to the subintervals. To assign the proper value to the subintervals, we must first count the number of subintervals between the numbered intervals.

Now we are ready for examples. For the first example refer to arrow #1, figure 128. We will assign 11 and 12 to the two numbered intervals on either side of our desired interval (indicated by the arrow). There are 10 small subintervals between these two numbered intervals, so each one would have the value of one-tenth (.1). The arrow then points to a value of 11.7. If we assign 110 and 120 to the two numbered intervals, each subinterval has a value of one and the arrow would represent a value of 117.

A second example is indicated by arrow #2. First, we will assign the values 55 and 60 to the two numbered intervals. There are five large subintervals, each of which would have a value of one. Each of these intervals is further divided into two small subintervals having a value of five-tenths (0.5). The graduation indicated by arrow #2 then represents a value of 57.5. If 550 and 600 are assigned to the two numbered intervals, each subinterval has a value of 10 (large interval) and 5 (small interval), respectively, and the graduation represented by arrow #2 has a value of 575. If 5.5 and 6.0 are assigned to the numbered intervals, then by the same reasoning as above, the value of the graduation is 5.75.

A third example is illustrated by arrow #3. If 21 and 22 are assigned to the numbered intervals, each subinterval has a value of two-tenths and the arrow points to 21.6. If 210 and 220 are assigned, each subinterval is equal to two and the arrow points to 216.

Scale Graduations (Hours Scale) Between 1 hour and 2 hours on the hours scale, each 10-minute interval is numbered with subintervals for each 5 minutes. Between 2 hours and 5 hours, each half-hour interval is numbered with subintervals for each 10 minutes. Between 5 hours and 10 hours, each hourly interval is numbered with subintervals for each 10 minutes.

Speed Index The *Speed Index* is the large black arrow, or triangle-shaped symbol, located at the 60-minute or 1-hour position on the minutes scale (fig. 125, arrow #4). This index enables the operator to locate speeds much more rapidly and easily in time-and-distance problems.

Time, Speed, and Distance Problems

In chapter 15, we learned the relationship of time, ground speed, and distance and solved some problems by using simple arithmetic. We are now ready to solve these same types of problems on the slide rule face of the computer. If we know any two of the three quantities (time, ground speed, and distance), we can find the third quantity.

Determining the Amount of Time for a Flight In his preflight planning the pilot will compute his estimated ground speed for a flight based on the forecast winds aloft and his proposed true course as measured on the chart. After computing the ground speed, he will use it, along with the distance to be flown, to determine the total time for the flight.

Now the computer solution:

Sample Problem.—If a pilot maintains a ground speed of 140 mph, how long will it take him to fly 210 miles? (See fig. 129.)

Solution—

    Given: Ground speed .... 140 mph

               Distance to fly .... 210 miles

    Find: Time of flight.

(1) Rotate the minutes scale until the speed index falls under 14 on the "miles" scale (fig. 129, arrow #1). The 14 represents 140 mph.

(2) Under 21 (representing 210 miles) on the miles scale, read 90 on the minutes scale (fig. 129, arrow #2). This represents 90 minutes, or 1 hour and 30 minutes (1:30), which could have been read directly from the hours scale.

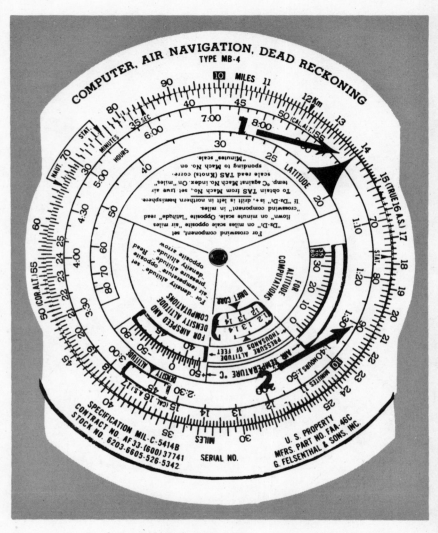

Figure 129. *Finding total flight time when ground speed and distance are known.*

132

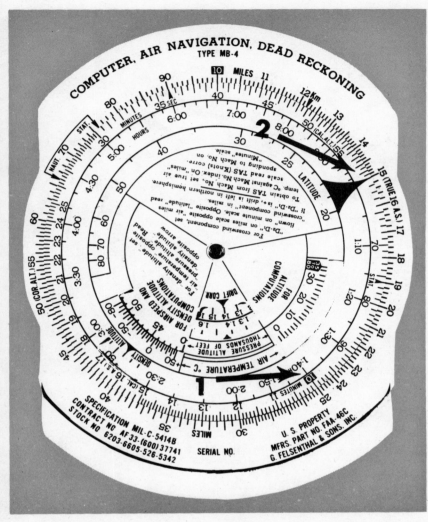

Figure 130. *Finding ground speed when flight time and distance flown are given.*

COMPUTER, AIR NAVIGATION, DEAD RECKONING
TYPE MB-4

Exercise No. 5 If a ground speed of (a) _____ is maintained, how much time will be required to fly a distance of (b) _____? Substitute the following quantities in blanks (a) and (b) and solve:

	(a) (mph)	(b) (miles)
1.	107	250
2.	123	320
3.	139	205
4.	152	365
5.	157	68
6.	135	43

NOTE: See appendix II for correct answers.

Determining Ground Speed During Flight During a flight, a pilot will wish to determine his actual ground speed. He will do this in the following way: Once he is on course at cruising altitude, airspeed, and power, he will check the time as he passes over a certain check point, which he locates on the chart. He then maintains a constant heading and checks the time when he passes over a second check point, which he also locates on the chart. He measures the distance between the check points on the chart and notes the length of time it took him to fly this distance. With these two figures, he can determine his ground speed. Now the computer solution:

Suppose the distance between the check points was 25 miles and the time to fly this distance was 10 minutes. Thus, our problem is:

Sample Problem.—If he flew 25 miles in 10 minutes, how many miles will he fly in 1 hour?

Solution—

Given: Distance flown .... 25 miles

Time flown .... 10 minutes

Find: Ground speed.

(1) Rotate the minutes scale until the 10 on this scale appears directly under the 25 on the miles scale (fig. 130, arrow #1).

(2) On the miles scale, opposite the speed index, read 15, which represents the ground speed of 150 mph (fig. 130, arrow #2).

Exercise No. 6 If an airplane flies (a)_____ miles in (b) _____ minutes, what is its ground speed? Substitute the following quantities in blanks (a) and (b) and solve:

133

	(a) (miles)	(b) (minutes)
1.	30	12
2.	10	5
3.	13	8
4.	27	15
5.	32	16
6.	27	10.5

NOTE: See appendix II for correct answers.

Fuel Consumption Problems

Fuel consumption problems may also be solved on the slide rule face of the computer in the same way as time, distance, and ground speed problems were solved. The miles, or outer, scale will be used to represent gallons and gallons per hour; the minutes scale will still be used to represent time.

One of the most important items a pilot should consider on any flight is: Do I have enough fuel to complete the flight with enough left in reserve to fly at least 45 minutes? A pilot should know the amount of usable fuel on board before taking off. He should also know the fuel consumption rate (gallons per hour) of the airplane he plans to fly for the altitude, power setting and mixture setting at which he plans to fly. This information is available in the Airplane Flight Manual.

Determining Total Flight Time Available One kind of fuel consumption problem a private pilot will have to solve is determining the total flight time available based on the fuel load.

Sample Problem.—If an airplane carries 60 gallons of usable fuel and the rate of fuel consumption is 12 gallons per hour, how much flight time is available?

Solution—

Given: Usable fuel .... 60 gallons

Rate of fuel consumption .... 12 gph

Find: Total flight time available.

(1) Rotate the minutes scale until the speed index falls under 12 on the miles scale (fig. 131, arrow #1). In this case 12 represents gallons and not miles.

(2) Under 60 on the miles scale, read 30 on the minutes scale. In this case, 30 represents 300 minutes, or 5 hours, which could have been read directly from the hours scale (fig. 131, arrow #2). Five hours is the total flight time available.

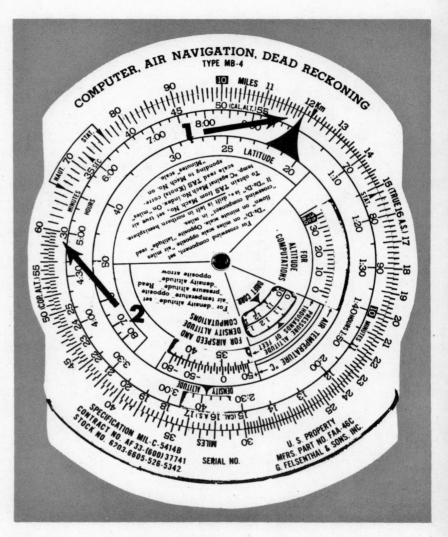

Figure 131. *Finding total available flight time when amount of fuel and rate of fuel consumption are known.*

134

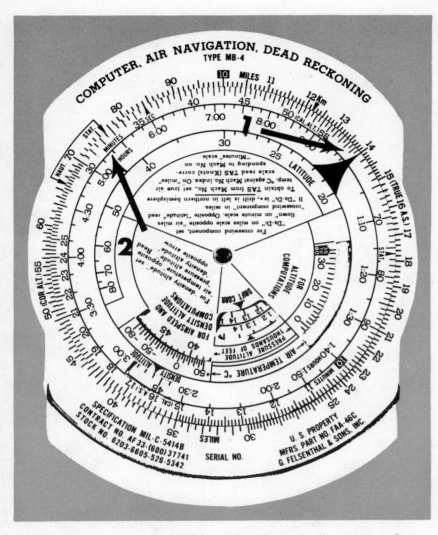

Figure 132. *Estimating amount of fuel to be used when estimated time enroute and fuel consumption rate are known.*

Exercise No. 7 If an airplane carries (a) _____ gallons of usable fuel and the rate of fuel consumption is (b) _____ gallons per hour, what is the total flight time available? Substitute the following quantities in blanks (a) and (b) and solve:

	(a) (gals.)	(b) (gph)
1.	36	9
2.	45	8.5
3.	37	7
4.	55	13
5.	18	6.3

NOTE: See appendix II for correct answers.

Determining Total Fuel to be Used on a Flight A second type of fuel consumption problem a private pilot should be able to solve is determining how much fuel will be used during a flight.

Sample Problem.—How much fuel will be used during a flight of 5 hours and 20 minutes if the rate of fuel consumption is 14 gallons per hour?

Solution—

Given: Time of flight.................................... 5:20 (320 minutes)
           Rate of fuel consumption .... 14 gph

Find: Total fuel used.

(1) Rotate the minutes scale until the speed index falls under 14 on the miles scale (fig. 132, arrow #1).

(2) Opposite 32 (representing 320 minutes) on the minutes scale, read 75 on the miles scale (fig. 132, arrow #2). Here 75 represents 75 gallons—the amount to be used on the flight.

The pilot must compare the above computed figure with the amount of usable fuel aboard so that he can determine his refueling points.

Exercise No. 8 How much fuel will be used during a flight of (a) _____ if the rate of fuel consumption is (b) _____ gallons per hour. Substitute the following quantities in blanks (a) and (b) and solve:

	(a) (time)	(b) (gph)
1.	3 hours	7
2.	3 hrs 30 min	11
3.	2 hrs 20 min	9.5
4.	4 hrs 15 min	10.3
5.	5 hrs 10 min	13.7

NOTE: See appendix II for correct answers.

True Airspeed Problems

To compute correctly his ground speed and heading, a pilot must know his true airspeed. To compute his true airspeed (TAS), he must know the pressure altitude at which he will be flying, the temperature in degrees Centigrade at this altitude, and his indicated airspeed (IAS).

The pilot will not know the pressure altitude during his preflight planning. In this case, he can use his proposed indicated cruising altitude. This introduces a slight error, but an insignificant one for the private pilot's use of airspeed readings. Once he reaches his cruising altitude, he can check the pressure altitude if he desires.

The pilot will not know the actual temperature at his proposed cruising altitude during his preflight planning. In this case, he can use the forecast temperature given in the winds-aloft forecast. After arriving at his cruising altitude, he can check his outside air temperature gauge for the actual temperature.

Determining True Airspeed Knowing the altitude, temperature, and indicated airspeed, the true airspeed may be determined on the computer in the sector labeled FOR AIRSPEED AND DENSITY ALTITUDE COMPUTATIONS (fig. 133, arrow #1). It is determined in the following way (fig. 133):

(1) Locate the proper free air temperature on the small scale labeled AIR TEMPERATURE °C (arrow #3).

(2) Rotate the disk, setting this temperature opposite the proper pressure altitude in the window marked PRESSURE ALTITUDE THOUSANDS OF FEET (arrow #2). (If the pressure altitude reading is not available, use indicated altitude.)

(3) On the minutes scale, locate the number corresponding to the indicated airspeed. For example, 13 if the airspeed is 130, etc.

(4) Opposite the indicated airspeed on the minutes scale, read the true airspeed on the miles scale.

Sample Problem.—What is the true airspeed of an airplane flying at an indicated airspeed of 120 mph at an altitude of 5,500 feet with an outside air temperature of +10° C.?

Solution—

Given: Altitude .... 5,500 feet
Air temperature .... +10° C.
Indicated airspeed (IAS) .... 120 mph

Find: True airspeed (TAS)

(1) Locate +10° on the small scale marked AIR TEMPERATURE °C. (fig. 134, arrow #1).

(2) Rotate the disk until 5,500 is located directly under +10 (fig. 134, arrow #1).

(3) Opposite 12 (representing 120 mph) on the minutes scale, read 132 on the miles scale, which represents a TAS of 132 mph (fig. 134, arrow #2).

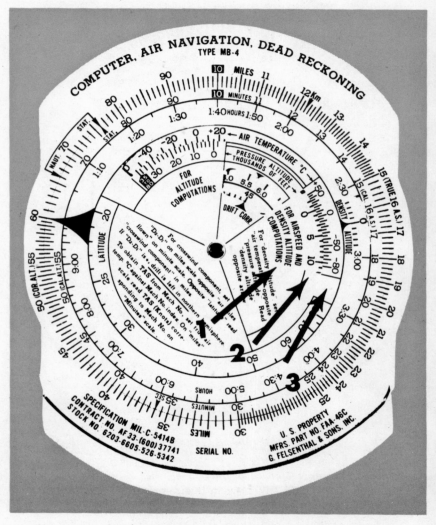

Figure 133. *Sector of computer used for true airspeed computations.*

136

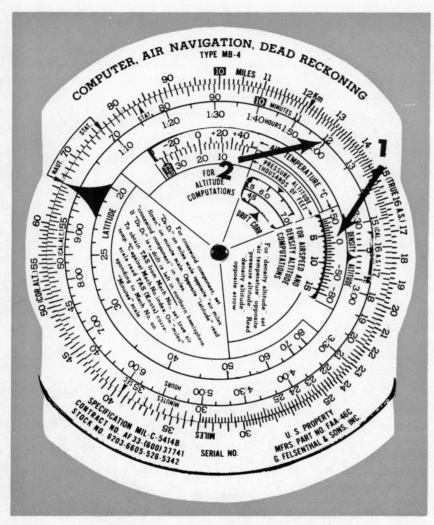

Figure 134. *Finding true airspeed when temperature, altitude, and indicated airspeed are known.*

Two mistakes are frequently made in this computation: One is using the wrong window. Be sure to use the window labeled FOR AIRSPEED AND DENSITY ALTITUDE COMPUTATIONS, and *not* the window labeled

FOR ALTITUDE COMPUTATIONS. The second mistake is forgetting that the temperature scale is reversed—the plus temperatures are on the left and the minus temperatures are on the right.

Exercise No. 9   Find the true airspeed (TAS) when the following pressure altitudes, temperatures, and IAS are given.

	Altitude (feet)	Temperature (°C.)	IAS (mph)
1.	5,000	0	120
2.	4,000	− 10	145
3.	4,000	+10	145
4.	7,500	+10	145
5.	6,500	− 15	150

NOTE: See appendix II for correct answers.

Converting Knots to Miles per Hour   Since the winds-aloft forecasts give the wind speed in knots, a private pilot must be able to convert knots to statute miles per hour to determine accurately his correct heading and ground speed. Since "knots" actually means "nautical miles per hour," our problem is converting nautical miles to statute miles. Computer solution of this conversion follows.

The conversion sector of the computer is shown in figure 135. The left arrow is labeled "naut." for nautical miles; the right arrow is labeled "stat." for statute miles.

Sample Problem.—Suppose we determine from the winds-aloft forecast that the wind speed at our proposed cruising altitude is 33 knots. What is the wind speed in miles per hour?

Solution—

(1) Rotate the minutes scale until 33 appears under the arrow labeled "naut." (fig. 135, arrow #1).

(2) On the minutes scale under the arrow labeled "stat." read 38 (arrow #2). This indicates that 33 nautical miles is equivalent to 38 statute miles, or 33K = 38 mph.

Exercise No. 10   If the following wind speeds are given in knots, find the speed in statute miles per hour.

1. 20 knots   4. 40 knots
2. 16 knots   5. 47 knots
3. 26 knots

NOTE: See appendix II for correct answers.

26. Wind Face

The wind face of the computer consists of a movable disk and a sliding grid. The outer rim of the movable disk (indicated by "compass rose" in figure 136) is graduated in degrees from 0° to 360°. The center portion of the movable disk is made from a piece of frosted plastic on which pencil marks may be made.

Sliding Grid   The sliding grid (fig. 136) consists of two sets of printed lines and slides up and down through the movable disk. The horizontal lines are arcs of concentric circles whose center is at the very bottom of the sliding grid. These circles, "speed circles," are equidistant, and each one represents 2 miles per hour. At each 10-mile interval, heavier "speed circle" lines appear and are numbered for easy reference. They are used for all measurements of speeds for the wind triangle—wind speed, ground speed, and true airspeed.

The second set of lines is a series of converging straight lines which meet at the center of the concentric circles (bottom of the grid). The center line of this series is the "true course" line,—it will always represent the *true course* in our discussion.[1] The other lines in this set are "true heading" lines, since they will show the number of degrees by which the *true heading* differs from the *true course*. In other words, the true heading lines represent degrees to either side of the center or true course line. Below the 150 speed circle, each line represents 2° and heavy lines appear and are numbered for each 10° interval. Above the 150 speed circle, each line represents 1° and heavy lines appear and are numbered for each 5° interval.

The sliding grid has two sides—a high-speed side and a low-speed side. The private pilot should use only the low-speed side, the only side used throughout this discussion. This side will give greater accuracy because the graduations of the scale are finer.

Compass Rose (or Azimuth Scale)   As noted above, the outer rim of the movable disk is graduated in degrees from 0° to 360°. It is indicated by the "compass rose" in figure 136. The four cardinal points of the compass, north, east, south, and west, are prominently indicated by N, E, S, and W. The compass rose, or azimuth scale, may be used to set any desired angular direction measured from true north.

The center portion of the compass rose is made from a piece of frosted plastic on which pencil marks may be made and erased. At the center of the compass rose is a small black circle, the grommet (fig. 136). The ground speed will be read under the grommet.

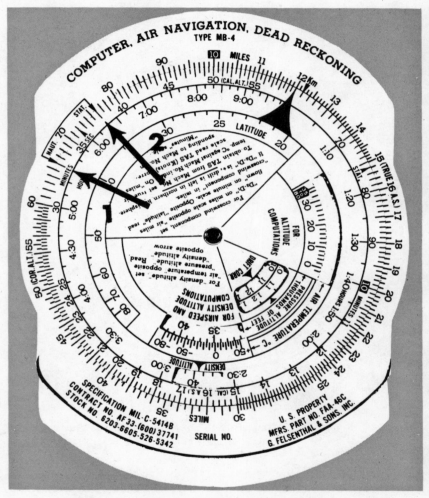

Figure 135. *Converting knots to miles per hour (33 knots equals 38 mph).*

---

[1] There are several correct methods of solving wind vector problems on the computer. The final answer is the same if the correct procedures are used, no matter which method is followed. The system used in this discussion was selected because:

(1) Only the most common type of wind vector problem will be solved in this handbook—that of finding the true heading and ground speed when the wind direction, wind speed, true course, and true airspeed are known.

(2) Using this method requires no juggling of the computer.

138

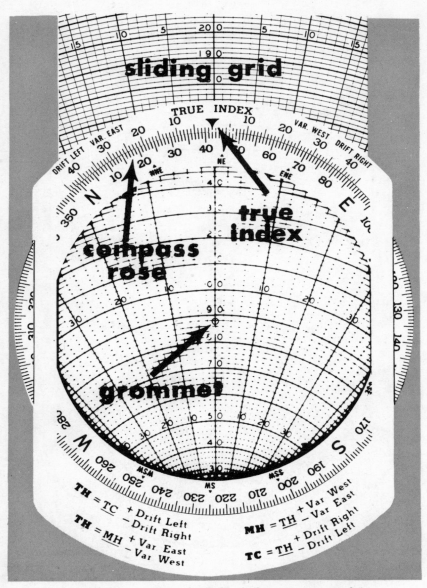

Figure 136. *Important parts of the flight computer wind face.*

True Index Just above and adjacent to the upper portion of the compass rose or azimuth scale is a fixed scale. Each line on this fixed scale represents 1°. At the middle of this fixed scale is a small black triangle with the apex pointing downward (fig. 136). This small black triangle is the true index. It lies directly above the center line of the sliding grid.

In wind triangle problems, the wind direction and true course will be positioned directly below the true index at various stages of solution.

Wind Triangle Representation

The various terms associated with a wind triangle were defined and discussed in the section on navigation. Before solving a wind triangle problem on the computer, we will review each term briefly and discuss its relationship or representation on the computer.

Wind Direction The wind direction is that direction *from* which the wind is blowing and is measured in degrees clockwise from true north.

In solving wind triangle problems on the computer, the wind direction will be placed directly below the true index by rotating the compass rose.

Wind Speed The wind speed is the rate of movement of the mass of air over the ground and is given in knots in weather reports and control tower instructions. Before the wind speed is represented on the computer, the speed in knots should be converted to miles per hour as previously shown.

The wind speed is represented on the computer by moving upward from the grommet along the center line of the grid a distance equivalent to the wind speed and making a pencil mark—either a small dot or small cross. In our discussion this pencil mark will be called the wind dot.

True Course True course is the direction of a proposed flight path as drawn on the chart measured in degrees clockwise from true north at the midmeridian.

The true course is always represented by the center line of the grid. In solving wind triangle problems, place the true course directly below the true index by rotating the compass rose.

True Airspeed The true airspeed of an airplane is its rate of progress through the air. In wind triangle solutions, always place the true airspeed speed circle under the dot.

Wind Correction Angle The wind correction angle is the correction that must be applied to the true course to establish the true heading that enables an airplane to make good a proposed true course. The angle is measured in degrees to the left or right.

The wind correction angle is represented on the computer as the number of degrees, left or right, from the true course line (center line of the grid) to the wind dot.

True Heading   True Heading is the actual heading of the airplane in flight, measured in degrees clockwise from true north. It is determined in wind triangle problem solutions by applying the wind correction angle to the true course.

Ground Speed   The ground speed of an airplane is its rate of progress over the ground. In wind triangle problem solutions, the ground speed is read under the grommet.

Wind Triangle Representation   Figure 137 shows the wind triangle as it should be visualized on the computer, although these lines will not actually be drawn. The following facts, closely related to our discussion, should be noted about this wind triangle:

(1) The *wind dot* is the point of intersection of the wind line (W) and the true heading-true airspeed line (TH-TAS). Notice that the wind arrow points toward the grommet. This is the way you should always picture the wind when using the computer (as described in this handbook) because it enables you to visualize the effect the wind is having on your airplane. This is important because you can immediately determine whether the ground speed will be less than or greater than the true airspeed by noting whether you have a headwind or a tailwind. You can also immediately determine whether the true heading will be to the left or right of the true course by noting whether there is a crosswind from the left or the right. In other words, by merely visualizing the relationship between the wind direction and the course line, you will not make the common mistake of applying the wind correction angle to the true course in the wrong direction. The length of the wind line represents the wind speed in miles per hour.

(2) The *true course* (TC) is represented by the center line of the grid. The *ground speed* (GS) is represented by the length of the TC-GS line and is read under the grommet. In this case, it is 160 mph.

(3) The *wind correction angle* is the angle between the true course (TC) line and the true heading line (TH). In the pictured triangle, it is 12° right. The little airplane, which lies on the true course line, has its longitudinal axis displaced to the right of the true course line (into the wind) an amount equal to the wind correction angle. In

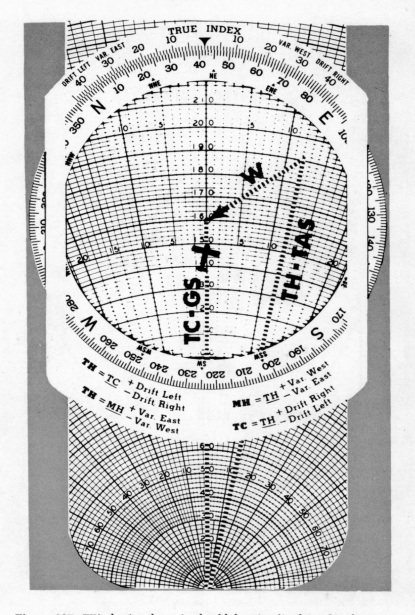

Figure 137. *Wind triangle as it should be visualized in this discussion.*

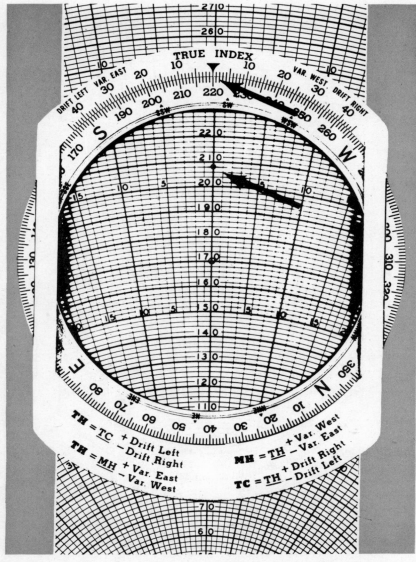

Figure 138. *First step in wind triangle solution — place wind direction under true index and measure up from the grommet (along center line) a length equivalent to the wind speed. Place dot at this point.*

other words, the longitudinal axis of the airplane is parallel to the true heading line.

(4) The *true airspeed* (TAS) is represented by the length of the TH-TAS line. The true airspeed circle is placed under the wind dot. In this case, it is 190 mph.

Solution of a Wind Triangle Problem

We are now ready to solve a wind triangle problem on the computer. The only type of problem we will illustrate in this handbook is the one the private pilot will encounter most often and should solve before taking off on a cross-country flight. This is the problem in which the true course, true airspeed, wind direction, and wind speed are known, and the pilot wants to find true heading and ground speed.

Sample Problem.—The pilot measures his true course on the chart and finds it to be 345°. He plans to cruise at a true airspeed of 140 mph. The winds-aloft forecast gives the wind direction and speed at his proposed cruising altitude as 220° and 33 knots. What is his ground speed and true heading for this flight.

Solution—

Given: Wind ....220°/33 knots

          True course (TC) ....345°

          True airspeed (TAS) ....140 mph

Find: Ground speed (GS)

      True heading (TH)

TAS	TC	WIND		WCA		TH	GS
		MPH	FROM	R+	L—		
140	345°	38	220°	?		?	?

(1) Convert the wind from knots to miles per hour, as shown in chapter 25. By this method, we find that 33 knots is equivalent to 38 mph. The known quantities are entered in a portion of a flight log.

(2) Slide the grid through the computer until one of the heavy horizontal lines lies under the center of the grommet. (The 170-mile grid line was chosen for this example.)

(3) Rotate the compass rose until the wind direction (220°) appears under the true index (fig. 138).

(4) Measure up from the grommet, along the center line, a length equivalent to 38 miles. (Note—Each horizontal line represents 2 miles.) At this point, place a pencil mark which we will refer to as the wind dot (fig. 138).

(5) Rotate the compass rose until the true course (345°) appears under the true index (fig. 139).

(6) Slide the grid through the computer until the *true airspeed* (140 mph) speed line lies directly under the wind dot (fig. 139).

| TAS | TC | WIND | | WCA | | TH | GS |
		MPH	FROM	R+ L—			
140	345°	38	220°	?		?	159

(7) Read the ground speed (159 mph) under the grommet.

(8) Find the wind correction angle by checking the number of degrees between the center line of the grid and the wind dot. In this case, it is 13°. (Note—Below the 150 mph line, each vertical line is equivalent to 2°; above the 150 mph line, each vertical line is equivalent to 1°.) Since the wind dot is to the left of the center line, the wind correction angle is 13° left.

(9) Since the wind correction angle is 13° L, the true heading is found by subtracting 13 from the true course. Thus, the true heading is 332° (345° — 13°).

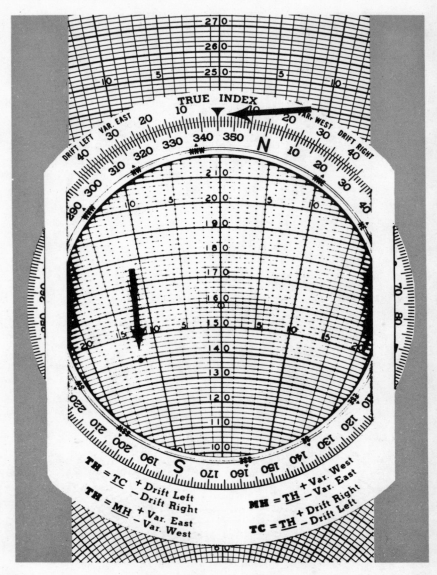

Figure 139. *The next step in wind triangle solution—place true course under true index and adjust sliding grid so the true airspeed circle lies under the wind dot. Then read ground speed and wind correction angle.*

TAS	TC	WIND		WCA R+ L—	TH	GS
		MPH	FROM			
140	345°	38	220°	—13°	332°	159

NOTE: After the wind correction angle was found, the true heading could have been determined in another way. On the outer fixed scale (either side of the true index), each mark represents 1°. To find the true heading in the example above, count 13° to the left (since the wind correction angle was 13° L) and directly under this mark read the true heading (332°) on the compass rose scale.

Exercise No. 11   If the following TAS, TC, wind speed, and wind direction are given, find the wind correction angle, true heading, and ground speed.

TAS	TC	WIND		WCA R+ L—	TH	GS
		Speed	From			
125	010°	35 mph	150°			
122	267°	42 mph	087°			
144	045°	15 mph	315°			
137	140°	36 mph	230°			
135	120°	20 knots	060°			

NOTE: See appendix II for correct answers.

SECTION IX—RADIO COMMUNICATIONS

27. Radio Communications

We have already studied briefly some of the basic principles of navigation. Until recently many pilots relied entirely on pilotage and dead reckoning when making VFR cross-country flights. Even now, some inexperienced pilots are reluctant to use radio navigation aids and communication facilities because they are not familiar with phraseologies, air traffic control procedures, and the convenience of radio aid in navigation.

However, private pilots can no longer afford to overlook the advantages and safeties made available by the radio. At busy airports throughout the country, arriving and departing air traffic is directed by control towers. Although light-gun signals are sometimes used when small airplanes are not radio-equipped, most airport traffic control instructions are given by radio. For operations of aircraft to, from, or on airports with FAA control towers, aircraft are now required to have both a radio receiver and a transmitter.

On cross-country flights many situations arise which make desirable use of two-way radio enroute. For example, a pilot may wish to obtain information about current weather along his course or the amount of ice or snow on the runways at his destination. Such information may be readily obtained by using the radio to call the nearest FAA Flight Service Station. However, if he files a VFR flight plan and requests *flight following service,* all this information and much more will be supplied by Flight Service Stations along the route designated in his flight plan. All he has to do is contact them.

Scheduled Weather Broadcasts on Range Frequencies   All airway communications stations having voice facilities on continuously operated navigation aids broadcast weather reports and other airway information at 15 and 45 minutes past each hour. The 45-minute-past-the-hour broadcast is an "airway" broadcast, consisting of weather reports from important terminals located on airways within approximately 400 miles of the broadcasting station. The 15-minute-past-the-hour broadcast is an "area" broadcast of weather reports from the stations within about 150 miles of the broadcasting station.

At each station, the material is scheduled for broadcast in this order:

(1) SIGMETS, AIRMETS, PIREPS, and RADAR reports when available.

(2) Local surface weather report including NOTAMS.

(3) Surface weather reports from other locations, including NOTAMS data.

(4) Repeat local surface weather report.

In addition, special weather reports and some Notice to Airmen data are broadcast off-schedule, immediately upon receipt. If you need special forecast service enroute, you may obtain it from any Flight Service Station.

The time of observation of weather reports included in a scheduled broadcast is 58 minutes past the hour preceding the broadcast. When the time of observation is otherwise, the observation time is given.

In-Flight Service   If your aircraft has two-way radio, you may call any FAA station along your route for any in-flight information or assistance, such as weather reports, special U.S. Weather Bureau advice (outlined below) to aid in establishing your position or locating an airport. You do not need to be thoroughly familiar with the standard phraseologies and procedures for air-ground communications.

A brief call to any FAA station, stating your message in your own words, will get immediate attention.

Personnel at FAA Flight Service Stations are trained to help pilots establish position by: (a) visual reference to terrain features; (b) VHF omnirange indications (triangulation); and (c) low frequency radio range orientation.

Pilot Weather Reports (PIREPS)   Whenever 5,000-foot or lower ceilings, 5-mile or lower visibilities, or thunderstorms and related phenomena are reported or forecast, FAA stations are required to solicit and collect PIREPS which describe conditions aloft. Pilots are urged to cooperate and volunteer reports of cloud tops, upper cloud layers, thunderstorms, ice, turbulence, strong winds, and other significant flight condition information. PIREPS should be given directly to FAA stations on normal enroute station frequencies.

PIREPS, SIGMETS, and advisories for light aircraft are included at the beginning of scheduled weather broadcasts by FAA stations within 200 miles of the area affected by the potentially hazardous weather. Also, pilots are advised of these reports during preflight briefings by FAA and Weather Bureau Stations and in air/ground contacts with FAA stations.

Weather Broadcast Format Scheduled weather broadcasts (15 and 45 minutes past each hour) will begin with the announcement of the station name, the time the broadcast is started, spoken in two digits or two digits and a fraction, and the title "Aviation Weather." Example:

THIS IS BIG SPRING RADIO. TIME ONE FIVE, AVIATION WEATHER. (If there are SIGMETS, AIRMETS, PIREPS, or RADAR REPORTS for the area, they will be broadcast at this time). BIG SPRING, BIG SPRING ZERO EIGHT ZERO ZERO OBSERVATION, ONE THOUSAND SCATTERED, MEASURED CEILING FIVE THOUSAND OVERCAST, VISIBILITY EIGHT, TEMPERATURE SEVEN TWO, DEW POINT SIX NINER, WIND ONE THREE ZERO DEGREES AT ONE FIVE, ALTIMETER TWO NINER EIGHT SEVEN. (Reports for approximately 10 additional stations follow, and the local weather report is repeated.) THIS IS BIG SPRING RADIO.

Special weather reports and advisories are broadcast when warranted by significant changes in the weather at a particular station or in a given area.

Radio Frequencies To take advantage of the communication and navigation features of the Federal Airways System, pilots should know something of the radio frequencies assigned for aviation use by the Federal Communications Commission. Aviation frequencies may be checked in the *Airman's Information Manual,* on aeronautical charts, or with the nearest FAA Flight Service Station, tower, or center. Use the most recent revision of the appropriate sections of AIM, rather than aeronautical charts, as the final check on these frequencies (see Chapter 24). Radio frequencies normally of interest to private pilots are:

AIRCRAFT RECEIVING FREQUENCIES

Low and medium frequencies ....200 to 415 kc
(Ranges, towers, beacons, etc.)

Omnirange (VOR) stations ....108.20 through 117.90 mc
(Airway track guidance and
enroute communications)

Air traffic control communications ....118.00 through 121.40 mc
122.20 mc, 126.70 mc

Emergency ....121.50 mc

Airport utility (ground control) ....121.90 mc, 121.70 mc

Aeronautical advisory station (UNICOM) ......122.80 mc, 123.00 mc
(If the airport has an operating tower, the UNICOM frequency is 123.00 mc. Aeronautical advisory stations that use these frequencies are operated by private agencies such as airport operators.)

Note: Private aircraft may receive and transmit on these frequencies.

AIRCRAFT TRANSMITTING FREQUENCIES

Private aircraft to towers ....122.40 mc, 122.50 mc,
122.60 mc, and 122.70 mc

(Check the *Airman's Information Manual* to determine frequencies that each tower guards.)

Private or commercial aircraft to FAA ....122.10 mc, 123.60 mc,
Flight Service Stations   and 126.70 mc

Low and medium frequencies are subject to considerable interference from static, whereas the very high frequencies (VHF) give relatively static-free radio communications. VHF reception distances vary with distance from the station and altitude of the aircraft.

Examples of normal VHF reception distances are shown in the following table for aircraft at several altitudes:

ALTITUDE OF AIRCRAFT (Above ground station)	RECEPTION DISTANCE (Statute miles)
1,000 feet	45 miles
3,000 feet	80 miles
5,000 feet	100 miles
10,000 feet	140 miles

NOTE: This table is based on zero elevation of the radio facility. Altitudes and distances shown are theoretical for flat terrain where no physical obstructions intervene.

Tuning a Radio Receiver   An aircraft radio is tuned to the station just as an ordinary home set is tuned. For best reception though, you must recognize certain peculiarities of the airplane radio.

Just as when reading other instruments, the pilot should view the frequency indicator from directly in front, preventing an error that might result in no signal or in reception of the wrong station. Another source of error is inaccuracy in frequency calibration, often caused by continued vibration or hard landings. Thus, a station which should be received on 116.40 mc may appear (on the radio dial) on 116.10 mc, 116.60 mc, or at some other frequency. If no signal is received when the set is tuned to a given frequency, turn selector in both directions until the station is tuned in. Then reduce the volume and adjust the frequency control slightly for best reception.

When a station is broadcasting intermittently (a control tower, for example), you may have to ask station personnel for a short or long count (counting from 1 to 5 or from 1 to 10) so that tuning may be completed. At busy locations though, requesting a count is both unnecessary and undesirable because it disrupts normal communications.

Range stations are identified either by code, or by voice recording alternated with code. *It is very important to check this identification to make sure the desired station is being received.*

Using an Aircraft Radio Transmitter   As already indicated, FAA recommends, and good operating practice demands, that pilots use their two-way radios for air-ground communications. To use a transmitter, however, you must obtain two licenses through the Federal Communications Commission (FCC). A radio station license is required for the aircraft transmitter itself, and the pilot must have a restricted radiotelephone operator permit.

When an aircraft has a VHF transmitter, the pilot should be sure he is transmitting on the proper frequency (normally 122.10 mc for Flight Service Stations, and 122.50 mc for towers).

When he is ready to transmit, the pilot should hold the microphone close to his mouth. After giving thought to what he is going to say, he should speak in a normal tone of voice. Although the message may be phrased in his own words, certain radiotelephone phraseologies are commonly used to reduce the length of transmissions and provide uniformity. The following are a few of these phraseologies:

Word or phrase	Meaning
ACKNOWLEDGE	Let me know that you have received and understand this message.
ROGER	I have received all of your last transmission. (Used to acknowledge receipt; should be used for no other purpose.)
AFFIRMATIVE	Yes.
NEGATIVE	That is not correct.
I SAY AGAIN	*Self-explanatory.*
SAY AGAIN	*Self-explanatory.*
STAND BY	*Self-explanatory.*
VERIFY	Check with originator.
OVER	My transmission is ended and I expect a response from you.
OUT	This conversation is ended; I do not expect a response from you.
CORRECTION	An error has been made in the transmission (or message indicated).

Remember, however, that it is not necessary for you to be thoroughly familiar with the standard phraseologies and procedures for air-ground communications. A brief call to any FAA station, stating your message in your own words, will receive immediate attention.

Airport and Enroute Communications Procedures   To illustrate two-way radio communication procedures, we will make an imaginary direct flight from Abilene Municipal Airport, Abilene, Texas, to Love Field, Dallas, Texas.

Follow the flight route on the Dallas Sectional Chart which accompanies this handbook.

The pilot goes in person to the Weather Bureau Airport Station where he checks the weather. Next, he files a VFR flight plan via interphone (if available), or telephone, with Abilene Flight Service Station, requesting flight following service (chapter 30). The FSS designates Mineral Wells as his flight watch station. He then completes all preparations and loads his airplane for the flight.

When ready to taxi, he calls the control tower on the ground control frequency (121.9 mc, in this case, as shown in *Airman's Information Manual* excerpt, chapter 24) giving the following information: aircraft identification, position, type of operation planned (VFR or instrument), and point of first intended landing.

Example

Pilot: ABILENE GROUND CONTROL THIS IS ASTROLARK THREE NINER TWO ONE BRAVO AT HANGAR TWO, READY TO TAXI, VFR FLIGHT TO DALLAS, OVER.

Tower: ASTROLARK THREE NINER TWO ONE BRAVO, CLEAR TO RUNWAY ONE FOUR. WIND ONE THREE ZERO DEGREES AT ONE SIX. ALTIMETER TWO NINER NINER EIGHT. TIME ZERO EIGHT THREE ONE.

Pilot: ASTROLARK THREE NINER TWO ONE BRAVO, ROGER.

After taxiing to run-up position and completing his pretakeoff check list, the pilot changes his radio transmitter and receiver to the appropriate tower frequency and calls the tower.

Pilot: ABILENE TOWER ASTROLARK THREE NINER TWO ONE BRAVO, READY FOR TAKEOFF.

The tower controller determines that there is no conflicting traffic and replies:

Tower: ASTROLARK THREE NINER TWO ONE BRAVO, CLEARED FOR TAKEOFF.

Pilot: ASTROLARK THREE NINER TWO ONE BRAVO, ROGER.

The pilot continues to guard the control tower frequency until leaving the airport traffic area. Then he retunes his VHF radio to the appropriate frequency—transmitter to 122.1 mc, receiver to the Abilene VOR frequency—and calls Abilene radio giving his time of takeoff so they can activate his flight plan.

Example

Pilot: ABILENE RADIO THIS IS ASTROLARK THREE NINER TWO ONE BRAVO, OFF AT ONE ZERO, VFR FLIGHT TO DALLAS. OVER.

Station: Acknowledges the transmission.

While proceeding on his flight, he continues to monitor Abilene radio until within receiving range of Mineral Wells radio, at which time he tunes in Mineral Wells. In the vicinity of Mineral Wells, he contacts Mineral Wells radio to give a position report. He first establishes contact with them, indicating the frequency on which a reply is expected.

Example:

Pilot: MINERAL WELLS RADIO THIS IS ASTROLARK THREE NINER TWO ONE BRAVO. REPLY ON VOR FREQUENCY. OVER.

Station: ASTROLARK THREE NINER TWO ONE BRAVO. THIS IS MINERAL WELLS RADIO. OVER.

The pilot then proceeds with his message, which usually includes position, time, flight altitude, and VFR flight plan from point of departure to destination.

Pilot: ASTROLARK THREE NINER TWO ONE BRAVO SIX MILES WEST OF MINERAL WELLS ZERO FIVE AT FIVE THOUSAND FIVE HUNDRED ON VFR FLIGHT PLAN ABILENE TO DALLAS. OVER.

Station: Mineral Wells radio acknowledges his position report and, being the flight watch station designated on his flight plan, will give him the latest weather information (including Dallas weather), NOTAMS, and other information pertinent to his flight.

Pilot: ASTROLARK THREE NINER TWO ONE BRAVO, ROGER, OUT.

While in the vicinity of Fort Worth, the pilot may wish to contact Greater Southwest or Britton radio for further information.

When approximately 25 miles west of Dallas, he calls Dallas approach control on 123.7 mc (as suggested in the remarks section for Love Field, figure 124).

Pilot: DALLAS APPROACH CONTROL THIS IS ASTROLARK THREE NINER TWO ONE BRAVO TWO FIVE MILES WEST AT THREE THOUSAND. LANDING AT LOVE FIELD. OVER.

At the specified point or distance from the airport, the pilot calls the tower in this area and will advise him at what point to contact the control tower. Approach control will give him wind and runway information, other traffic at Love Field.

Example:

Pilot: LOVE TOWER THIS IS ASTROLARK THREE NINER TWO ONE BRAVO, FIVES MILES WEST. REQUEST LANDING INSTRUCTIONS. OVER.

Tower: ASTROLARK THREE NINER TWO ONE BRAVO. FIVE MILES WEST. CLEARED TO ENTER TRAFFIC PATTERN, RUNWAY THREE SIX, WIND THREE FOUR ZERO DEGREES AT ONE FIVE. OVER.

Pilot: ASTROLARK THREE NINER TWO ONE BRAVO. ROGER.

The pilot then enters the traffic pattern on the downwind leg, and reports to the tower while turning on base leg. After receiving a clearance to land, he acknowledges and proceeds with his landing. While he is turning off the active runway, the tower instructs him to tune to ground control frequency for further taxi instructions. After clearing the active runway, he changes his radio transmitter and receiver to the ground control frequency, makes a radio check, and acknowledges all taxi instructions. He proceeds to the parking area, continuing to monitor this frequency until the airplane is parked. If he has not previously closed his flight plan by radio with the Dallas FSS (or tower), he should go to the nearest telephone, call the FSS station (or tower), and request that they close his flight plan from Abilene.

28. Radio Guidance in VFR Flying

In addition to the communications services discussed in the preceding chapter, the Federal Airways System of the Federal Aviation Agency provides several radio aids to air navigation. For example, the VHF omnirange (VOR) and the four-course low-frequency range are particularly useful to VFR pilots, both for navigation guidance and enroute communication. For assistance mainly to instrument pilots, there are such aids as radar and instrument landing systems (ILS).

New and improved types of electronic equipment are constantly being developed to make flying safer and easier. One such system is VORTAC (fig. 140). In addition to the bearing information obtained from the omnirange, this system supplies properly equipped airplanes with the distance of the plane from the station. With bearing and distance known, the pilot can determine his position, eliminating the need for bearings on two or more stations. Completion of all ground installations and widespread availability of low-cost equipment for use in personal planes will bring into fullest use this simplified means of determining position. However, an airplane equipped with a VOR receiver can still use a VORTAC station for bearing information just as it uses a normal VOR station. (NOTE: Throughout this handbook, VOR will be used to include both VOR and VORTAC stations.)

In recent years, the VHF omnirange (VOR) has replaced the low-frequency range as the basic radio aid to navigation. Frequencies of omnirange stations are in the VHF band, between 108 and 118 megacycles. The word

Figure 140. *A typical VORTAC station.*

"omni" means *all*, and an omnirange is a VHF radio range that projects courses in all directions from the station, like spokes from the hub of a wheel. Each of these spokes, or *radials*, is denoted by the outbound magnetic direction of the spoke. A *radial* is defined as "a line of magnetic bearing extending from an omnidirectional range (VOR)." In contrast to the situation with low-frequency ranges, which have only four range legs, it is possible to fly to and from omniranges in any direction.

A few of the advantages of flying omniranges are:

1. A flight may be made *to* a VOR from any direction, by flying the course to the station.
2. A flight may be made to any destination *from* the station by selecting the proper radial. Remember that VOR radials, as shown on charts, are always from the station, never toward.
3. When within range of two or more VOR's, a fix may be determined quickly and easily by taking bearings on the stations and determining position on a chart.

4. Static-free reception and the elimination of the complex orientation procedures often used by instrument pilots flying low-frequency ranges.

An important fact is that VOR signals, like other VHF transmissions, follow an approximate line-of-sight course. Therefore, reception distance increases with an increase in the flight altitude of an aircraft (fig. 141). A means is usually provided with omnireceivers to indicate when the signal is too weak for satisfactory reception.

In addition to their use in navigation guidance, VOR frequencies are used by FSS personnel for weather broadcasts and other communications. VOR stations are assigned three-letter identifications. At some stations these identification letters are broadcast continuously in code. Other stations are identified by a voice recording (example: Dallas VORTAC), alternating with the usual Morse Code identification (DALLAS VORTAC, ▬·· ·▬ ·▬··, DALLAS VORTAC, ▬·· ·▬ ·▬··, etc.).

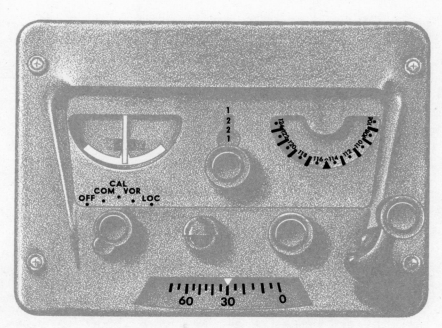

Figure 142. *Cockpit installation for a typical VOR receiver set. The vertical needle and "TO-FROM" indicator are combined into a single instrument (upper left). The course selector is the adjustable dial (bottom center).*

VOR Receivers VOR receivers are very simple to operate. The desired frequency is selected in the same manner as with other radio receivers. Three basic components are normally used by the pilot in VOR flying (fig. 142). One component is the omnibearing (course) selector, which enables the pilot to select the course he wants to fly. A second component is the "TO-FROM" indicator (also known as the ambiguity meter or sense indicator), which shows him whether the course is TO or FROM the station. The third is a deviation indicator (often called the "LEFT-RIGHT" indicator or vertical needle), which tells him when he is on course, or left, or right of course. Using these three components, the pilot obtains visual indications which give him a variety of information and guidance. The "TO-FROM" indicator and deviation indicator are often combined into a single display as they are in our illustration.

Because accuracy is an important factor in any navigation equipment, pilots should check their VOR receivers periodically to be sure they are functioning

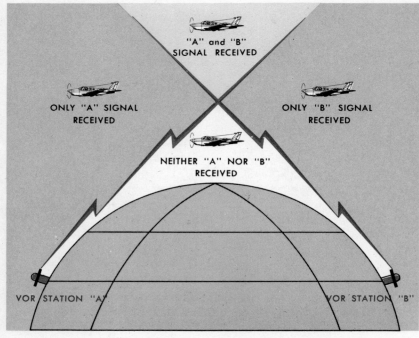

"A" and "B"
SIGNAL RECEIVED

ONLY "A" SIGNAL
RECEIVED

ONLY "B" SIGNAL
RECEIVED

NEITHER "A" NOR "B"
RECEIVED

VOR STATION "A"

VOR STATION "B"

Figure 141. *VHF transmissions follow a line-of-sight course.*

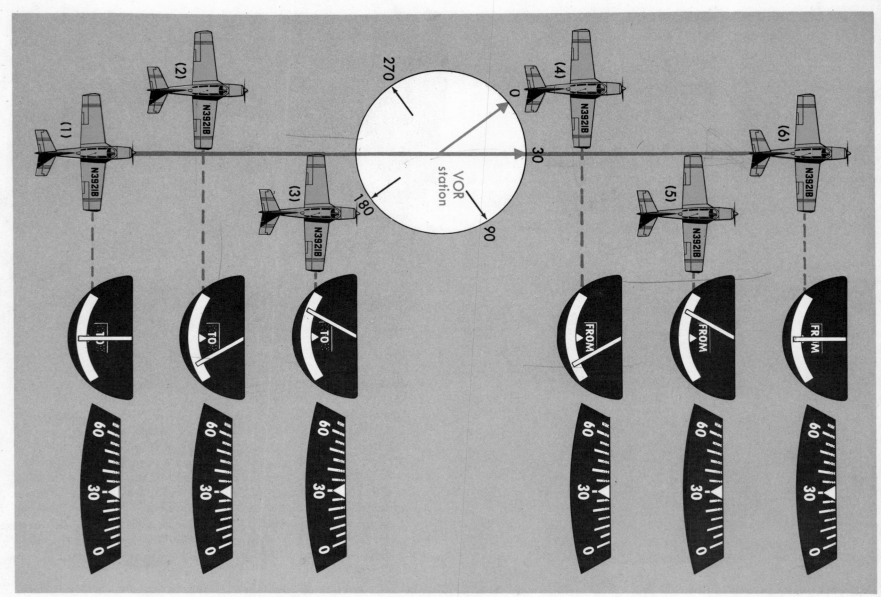

Figure 143. *VOR receiver instrument indications for various positions of an airplane relative to its desired course and the VOR station.*

properly. Procedures and locations for checking VOR receivers are published by FAA in the *Airman's Information Manual*.

When a pilot wishes to fly directly to a VOR facility, he should:

(1) Tune the receiver to the frequency of the VOR and *positively identify the station either by code* or voice recording. (The receiver is properly tuned when there is a positive indication on the TO-FROM indicator. If this indicates neither TO nor FROM or just partially indicates TO or FROM, or there is an oscillation, the signal is unusable.)

(2) Manually rotate the omnibearing (course) selector until the LEFT-RIGHT needle is centered at the bottom of the dial.

(3) Check to see that the TO-FROM indicator reads "TO." If it should read "FROM," merely turn the course selector 180° to obtain a "TO" reading, and the LEFT-RIGHT needle is again centered.

(4) Turn to the approximate heading that will maintain the magnetic course, i.e., the heading on the course selector that will take the airplane directly to the VOR station.

When a pilot wants to fly directly away from a VOR, he should:

(1) Follow the same procedure in (1) and (2) above.

(2) Check to see that the TO-FROM indicator reads "FROM." If it should read "TO," turn the course selector 180° to obtain a "FROM" reading, and the LEFT-RIGHT needle is again centered.

(3) Turn to the approximate heading that will maintain the magnetic course, i.e., the reading on the course selector that will take the airplane directly away from the VOR station.

Figure 143 shows various positions of an airplane relative to a VOR station and a desired course line, along with the indications of the VOR receiver components at each position. In referring to figure 143, turn the handbook so you are looking in the direction the airplane is flying.

In position No. 1, the pilot has found (by rotating his omnibearing selector) that his magnetic course TO the station is 030° and has already turned to a magnetic heading of approximately 030°. Note that the omnibearing selector is set on 30 (030°), the TO-FROM indicator reads TO, and the LEFT-RIGHT needle is centered. This indicates that the magnetic course to the station is 030°. If the pilot maintains these indications on his VOR receiver instruments, he will fly directly to the station. When the LEFT-RIGHT needle deviates from the centered position, the pilot should make small cor-

rections in heading to center it again, and in this way he will fly to the station. To get back on course he should make corrections in heading toward the needle.

Position No. 2 in figure 143 shows the component readings when the airplane is to the left of course. The LEFT-RIGHT needle is deflected to the right. It indicates the position of the desired course line relative to the pilot. It is deflected to the right, so the desired course is to the right and the pilot should turn to the right to get back on his course.

In position No. 3, the LEFT-RIGHT needle is deflected to the left, indicating that the desired course is to the left, and a turn to the left should be made.

As the airplane passes over the station, the TO-FROM indicator will change from TO to FROM.

In position No. 4, notice that the TO-FROM indicator now shows FROM, since the airplane has passed the VOR station. The course selector is still set on 30 (030°). The LEFT-RIGHT needle reacts in the same way as during flight TO the station. If the airplane strays to the left of course (as it has in position No. 4), the LEFT-RIGHT needle is to the right. This indicates that the course is to the right and a change in heading should be made to the right.

In position No. 5, the needle is deflected to the left, indicating that the airplane has strayed off course to the right. So, a turn should be made to the left to correct back to course.

In position No. 6, the airplane is back on course as is indicated by the centered LEFT-RIGHT needle.

Quite often when a pilot takes off on a cross-country flight, he already knows the approximate direction of the VOR station on which he wishes to "home in." So he may head in that direction and turn the course selector until the needle is centered but forget to check his TO-FROM indicator. Assume that he does fail to check this indication and further assume that it indicates "FROM." If he gets off course now and corrects by turning toward the needle, he will continue to get farther off course, because now the needle is deflected in the direction opposite his desired course.

The same situation exists when a pilot takes off and flies away from a VOR station, if he centers the needle with the course selector but the TO-FROM indicator reads "TO." A correction by turning toward the needle will get him farther off course.

Summarizing: If you wish to fly to a VOR station, center the needle with the course selector in such a way that the TO-FROM indicator reads "To," and fly the approximate heading shown on the course selector. If you wish to fly away from a VOR station, center the needle with the course selector so that the TO-FROM indicator reads "FROM" and again fly the approximate heading shown on the course selector. If you do it this way, you will always correct back to course by turning toward the needle. It may also help you to remember that, whether flying toward or away from the VOR station, your heading and the indication on the course selector should be approximately the same—never 180° out of phase.

The Low-Frequency Range Until the advent of the omnirange, the low-frequency radio range was the principal air navigation aid in the United States. The ranges were placed in use at a time when comparatively few airplanes were in operation, and four courses were ample for navigation and air traffic control. Beside the limited number of courses, low-frequency ranges have other limitations, such as poor reception because of static, and complex orientation procedures (mainly of concern to instrument pilots).

Despite these limitations, low-frequency ranges have certain advantages. They operate in the 200 to 400 kc band, and a low-frequency receiver is the only equipment needed to receive them. Under normal conditions, the low-frequency range is usable for distances of 50 to 100 miles, and can be received at low altitudes and on the ground.

Like omniranges, each low-frequency range station is assigned a letter-group identification. Unlike omniranges, however, this identifier may consist of a three-letter or two-letter group. This will depend upon whether there is an omnirange station using the same name as the low-frequency station. If an omnirange station and a low-frequency range station located in the same area have the same name, the omnirange will be identified by a three-letter group and the low-frequency range will be identified by a two-letter group. For example, the Lubbock, Tex., omnirange is identified by LBB (.—.. —... ....), and the low-frequency range by LX (.—.. —..—).

Range signals are interrupted every 30 seconds while the station identification signals are transmitted in code.

Figure 144 represents a typical four-course range. The signals in International Morse code for A (.—) and N(—.) are broadcast directionally from special antennas into opposite quadrants. Unless a pilot is flying on or near one of the four courses of the range, he will receive either "dit dah"(.—) or "dah dit"(—.) signals, depending on the quadrant in which the plane is

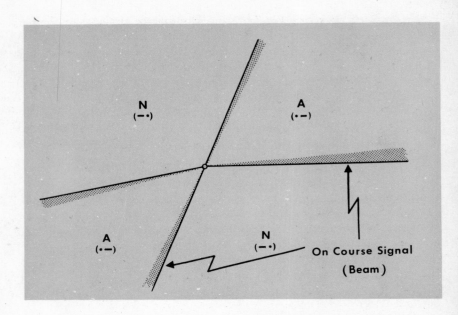

Figure 144. *Quadrants and courses of an LF/MF radio range. (Note: On sectional aeronautical charts, the "N" quadrants are outlined by lines along the range courses.)*

located. When the pilot is flying on a range leg, the A and N signals interlock, giving a monotone or steady on-course hum, popularly known as the beam. Beams (equisignal zones) are wedge-shaped zones approximately 3° wide. On aeronautical charts, the magnetic course to the station is printed on each range leg.

Areas in each quadrant adjacent to range courses are known as bisignal zones. Here the pilot receives the on-course hum with an A or N in the background, depending on the quadrant in which he is located. In those portions of each of the quadrants remote from the range legs, either an A or N will be received.

Pilots making VFR cross-country flights need not be proficient in complex orientation procedures on low-frequency ranges. They will, however, find these ranges most helpful when used in connection with pilotage, dead reckoning, and VOR flying, for directional guidance to determine position.

The Automatic Direction Finder Many personal-type airplanes are equipped with Automatic Direction Finder (ADF) radio sets which operate in the low- and medium-frequency bands. By tuning to low-frequency radio stations such as four-course ranges, radio beacons, and commercial broadcast stations, a pilot may use ADF for navigation in cross-country flying. Frequencies of radio aids to navigation are readily obtained from aeronautical charts. Changes since the published date of the latest sectional charts appear in the *Airman's Information Manual*. The sectional chart shows standard broadcasting stations most likely to be used by pilots. Positive identification of the station to which the set is tuned is extremely important.

Probably the most common use of ADF is that of homing by flying the needle to a station. Another useful practice is to first obtain bearings from two or more radio stations, and then plot radio lines of position on an aeronautical chart to establish position. This is known as plotting a radio fix. Since ADF does not account for wind drift and is susceptible to difficulties from thunderstorms and static, it lacks several of the advantages of VOR. When standard broadcast stations for homing are used, one of the principal disadvantages is the difficulty of positive identification. Nevertheless, pilots who do extensive cross-country flying will do well to make a thorough study of ADF and its uses.

VFR Flight Using Radio Aids To illustrate the use of radio aids in cross-country flying, assume that a pilot is making a flight, using the Dallas Sectional Chart (refer to the chart which accompanies this handbook). He decides to fly from Graham Airport (33° 06' N.; 98° 33' W.), Graham, Tex., direct to the Bridgeport VOR, and then fly direct to Majors Field (33° 04' N.; 96° 04' W.), Greenville, Tex. Draw these courses on the Dallas chart.

With his VOR receiver tuned to the frequency of the Bridgeport VOR (116.5 mc), he listens carefully for code or voice identification of Bridgeport radio. Next, he turns his course selector (omnibearing selector) until the LEFT-RIGHT (vertical) needle centers at the bottom of the dial and the TO-FROM indicator indicates "TO" the VOR. The course selector should then read 070°, which means his magnetic course to the station is 070°. Keeping the needle centered by making corrections toward the needle to return to course, he flies directly to the station. While he is passing over the station, the LEFT-RIGHT needle may swing sharply back and forth (directly over the station), and the TO-FROM indicator then settles on "FROM," indicating that he is now heading away from the station.

Correction for wind drift and magnetic variation have not been mentioned. Each is automatically compensated for when the pilot makes heading corrections to keep the LEFT-RIGHT needle centered. Since all radials from a VOR are magnetic rather than true bearings, magnetic variation is corrected in the VOR itself. Wind drift correction is made automatically by the pilot when he "crabs" the proper amount to keep the needle centered, which enables him to fly a straight-line course to the station.

After he has passed over the Bridgeport VOR, the pilot turns his course selector to 087°, the outbound bearing from the Bridgeport VOR to Majors Field. After making sure the TO-FROM indicator shows "FROM," he simply keeps the LEFT-RIGHT needle centered by turning toward the needle to stay on course.

Before getting out of range of the Bridgeport VOR, he obtains a fix using bearings from the Bridgeport and Greater Southwest VOR's. While tuned to Bridgeport, his LEFT-RIGHT needle is centered indicating that he is on course. Next, he tunes the VOR receiver to the Greater Southwest VOR (110.6 mc), identifies the station, and turns the course selector until the vertical needle centers and the TO-FROM indicator reads "FROM." From the course selector, he determines that his bearing from the Greater Southwest VOR is 005°. Upon plotting this bearing, he finds that it intersects the bearing from the Bridgeport VOR (the course which he is flying) at a point between a small arm and large arm of Garza-Little Elm Reservoir. This type of fix is most accurate when the cross bearings are approximately 90° apart, as are these two. In situations where more than two VOR's are within reception distance, additional radio bearings may be taken to confirm a fix.

During the latter portion of the flight (assuming he is at a relatively low altitude), he will be out of range of the Bridgeport VOR. However, he will be able to obtain bearings from the Dallas VOR to check progress along his course. For example, suppose he plans to start his letdown over the small lake adjacent to Lake Lavon, 27 miles west of Majors Field. The bearing from Dallas VOR to this point on his course is 032°. To confirm his position, he sets his course selector at 032° with the TO-FROM indicator showing "FROM" the station. Before reaching the point for reducing power for letdown, his vertical needle is to the RIGHT. While approaching this bearing (032° radial), the needle gradually moves toward the LEFT. When the needle becomes centered, he knows that the 032° radial (spoke of the wheel with an outbound magnetic direction of 032°) has been reached, and he double-checks his position by chart reading before beginning the letdown.

He notices from the chart that Majors Field lies on the 076° radial of the Dallas VOR. As an aid in letting him know when he is in the vicinity of the airport, he adjusts the course selector to 076° with the TO-FROM indicator showing "FROM" the station. The vertical needle will be to the RIGHT. When he approaches this radial, the needle gradually moves to the LEFT. When the needle becomes centered, he knows that the 076° radial has been reached and that he should be near the airport.

29. Emergency Radio Procedures

We would like to think that getting lost is something that always happens to "other pilots," never to us. Most of this handbook is devoted to information that should be used often and should enable a pilot to complete a flight successfully, confidently, and safely. This chapter is devoted to information to help a pilot complete a flight, but it is information which should seldom have to be used. However, it is information which no pilot should be without in case an emergency does arise and he becomes lost. The chapter explains what *you* must do if you get lost, what can be done *for you*, *who* can help you, and *how* they will help.

Because of inattention, poor visibility, or unusual wind conditions, a pilot may miss his check point and, as a result, become confused and reach that state of mind in which he thinks he is lost. He can follow a logical procedure to determine his position, locate satisfactory landmarks, and change his course, if necessary. *In no case should the pilot alter his course radically without first determining his position.* Circling aimlessly, doubling back on course, flying on hunches, etc., will only create confusion and make it impossible for him to follow any definite plan.

A recommended procedure is to continue on the established heading, watching prominent landmarks which can be identified on the chart. The pilot sometimes discovers that he has prematurely identified a check point, or has failed to observe one.

He should carefully check the visible landmarks available with his calculated position on the chart. The downwind side of the course should be checked first. If he fails to identify his position within 10 to 15 minutes, he should alter course slightly toward a conspicuous bracket (if available) provided he definitely knows which side of it he is on. He should then follow this bracket in the direction most likely to give him a definite fix. (A bracket

is a distinct feature of the terrain which bounds the course on one side and serves as a guide line. Ideal brackets are large rivers, prominent highways, railroads, and mountain ranges. Brackets are desirable on either side of the course. One at right angles to the course at or beyond the destination also is desirable as an end bracket.)

When a land mark is finally recognized, the pilot should accept it with caution and confirm his position by identifying other landmarks before proceeding with assurance. He should then determine the reason for error, and correct his heading to prevent flying off course again.

Because a majority of small airplanes are now equipped with radio, these procedures for determining position are normally combined with the use of radio aids.

Air markers of the type shown in figure 145 often prove a boon to pilots. In many instances, pilots who were lost, and low on gas, with radios inoperative, have located their positions from air markers, and have made emergency landings at nearby airports. Each air marker consists of the name of the town painted in large chrome yellow letters on a dark background; an arrow shows

Figure 145. *A typical air marker.*

the direction and distance to the nearest airport. These markers usually are painted on rooftops of large buildings conspicuous from the air. However, the number of markers is far too small to be relied upon for navigation.

Methods of Declaring an Emergency   If the above procedures fail, the lost pilot must call for help and he should not wait too long. In general, private pilots have two ways of declaring an emergency: (1) by transmitting an emergency message, and (2) by flying a triangular pattern.

Ground stations (Flight Service Stations, radar stations, control towers, etc.) have three electronic means of assisting: (1) by receipt of the emergency message transmitted by the pilot; (2) by radar detection of the triangular pattern; and (3) by DF (direction finding) bearings.

Transmitting Emergency Messages   When a pilot is in doubt about his position, or feels apprehensive for his safety, he should not hesitate to ask for help. That is his first means of declaring an emergency—*to use his radio transmitter and ask for help*. If he is in distress and needs help immediately, he may transmit the word MAYDAY several times before transmitting his message. This should get him immediate attention from all who hear. If he is only uncertain as to his position and wishes to alert ground stations, he may transmit the word PAN several times before transmitting his message. PAN indicates a lesser urgency than MAYDAY, but should get immediate attention.

An emergency message may be transmitted on any frequency; however, there are frequencies especially designated for such messages. The emergency frequency most likely available on the airplane radio used by the average private pilot would be the VHF frequency of 121.5 mc. He should be able to both transmit and receive on this frequency. This would be the best frequency to transmit and receive on during an emergency because almost all control towers, VHF direction finding (DF) stations, radar facilities, and Flight Service Stations guard this frequency. Regardless of which type of facility he contacts, that facility can help him, even if only by alerting other facilities to his difficulty.

Aid from Flight Service Stations   FAA Flight Service Station personnel are trained to assist pilots in establishing positions by: (a) visual reference to terrain features; (b) VHF omnirange indications (triangulation); and (c) low-frequency radio range orientation. One of these methods should help the pilot locate his position.

Aid From Radar Stations   Any radar station in the general area of a lost airplane will attempt to locate it on the radar screen. The pilot would be requested to make a series of turns or changes of heading that would enable the radar personnel to distinguish his plane from other airplanes on their screen. Listen carefully and follow their instructions. After positive identification by the radar station, the pilot will be notified of his position. He can then be given a heading to an airport or any point in the radius of coverage of the radar station.

Aid from DF (Direction Finding) Stations   A direction-finding station is a ground-based radio receiver capable of indicating the bearing from its antenna to a transmitting airplane. There are HF, VHF, and UHF direction-finding stations. However, only VHF stations will be discussed here since this is the type of radio transmitter most likely to be in the airplane of the average private pilot.

If a lost pilot is unable to establish communication with a VHF/DF facility, or if there is doubt about whether this service is available, he may ask for the service through any Flight Service Station or tower. His request will be relayed immediately to the appropriate DF facility. The pilot must remember that VHF transmissions follow line of sight; therefore, the higher his altitude, the better his chance of obtaining this service.

This example illustrates the procedure to be followed when using a direction-finding station:

1. Pilot calls VHF/DF station: "DALLAS HOMER, THIS IS ASTROLARK THREE NINER TWO ONE BRAVO REQUESTING *EMERGENCY* HOMING. OVER."

2. VHF/DF station acknowledges call up: "ASTROLARK THREE NINER TWO ONE BRAVO, THIS IS DALLAS HOMER, TRANSMIT FOR HOMING. OVER."

3. Pilot replies: "DALLAS HOMER, THIS IS ASTROLARK THREE NINER TWO ONE BRAVO" (pilot then transmits a 10-to-20-second voice signal, "AH-H-H," volume remaining as nearly constant as possible). This is followed by "ASTROLARK THREE NINER TWO ONE BRAVO. OVER."

4. VHF/DF station replies: "ASTROLARK THREE NINER TWO ONE BRAVO, THIS IS DALLAS HOMER, COURSE WITH ZERO WIND, ZERO THREE ZERO DEGREES. OVER."

5. Pilot acknowledges: "DALLAS HOMER, THIS IS ASTROLARK THREE NINER TWO ONE BRAVO. MY COURSE IS ZERO THREE ZERO DEGREES. OUT."

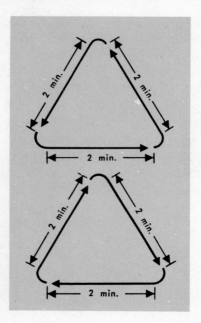

Figure 146. *If you are lost and the airplane radio is not operating properly, fly a triangular pattern. If only the transmitter is inoperative, fly the pattern to the right (bottom). If receiver and transmitter are inoperative, fly the pattern to the left (top).*

station could transmit instructions to him, even though he could not acknowledge them. We will divide the problem into two parts: (1) when only the transmitter is inoperative, and (2) when transmitter and receiver are inoperative.

With an inoperative transmitter and an operative receiver, the pilot can fly a triangular pattern to the RIGHT (fig. 146, bottom). He should hold each heading for 2 minutes and make the turns at a rate of approximately 1½° per second. A minimum of two such patterns should be completed before the original course is resumed. This pattern should be repeated at 20-minute intervals. While flying this pattern, the pilot should have the emergency frequency of 121.5 mc tuned in on his radio receiver. If his pattern is observed by radar controllers, instructions will be transmitted to him by the radar personnel.

If transmitter and receiver are both inoperative, the lost pilot should fly the same triangular pattern to the LEFT (fig. 146, top). If the pattern is observed by radar personnel, an escort airplane will be dispatched, if possible. If a pilot is lost in limited visibility conditions or at night, he may turn on his landing lights and navigation lights to aid the interceptor airplane. When a rescue airplane arrives, the pilot of the lost airplane should follow him.

The Four C's in an Emergency Situation   In any emergency situation, you should remember the FOUR C's:

1. *CONFESS* your predicament to any ground station. You should not wait too long. Give search and rescue a chance!

2. *COMMUNICATE* with his ground link station and pass as much of the distress message on the first transmission as possible. They need information for best search and rescue action.

3. *CLIMB* to a higher altitude, if possible, to get better radar and DF (direction finding) detection.

4. *COMPLY*—especially with advice and instructions received.

To the above Four C's might be added a fifth—*CONSERVE* fuel by using an economical or maximum endurance power setting. Such a setting can be determined from the Airplane Flight Manual, but the pilot should be familiar enough with his airplane to approximate the setting.

So a close check may be kept on the lost pilot, this procedure will be repeated as many times as are necessary to bring him safely to the station.

When the pilot transmits for homing, his transmission must be long enough for the station personnel to rotate their antenna to obtain a bearing on him. The transmission must be steady for them to get a good fix.

The course given the pilot by the DF station is the magnetic course to the station. However, unless the pilot has a good knowledge of wind conditions (which is unlikely, if he is lost), he will probably use the course given to him as a heading. If there is a strong crosswind, the course the station gives him will change each time he transmits for homing.

Emergency Lost Procedure With Radio Inoperative   What can a pilot do if he becomes lost and his radio is inoperative? His problem is how to let someone know he is lost. Perhaps only his transmitter is out and the receiver still operates. If he could only alert a radar station, personnel at this

SECTION X—FLIGHT PLANNING

30. Preflight Planning

What should the private pilot do to prepare himself for a cross-country flight?

FAA regulations state, in part, that before beginning a flight, the pilot in command of an aircraft shall familiarize himself with all available information appropriate to his intended flight. Preflight action for flights away from the vicinity of an airport shall include a careful study of available current weather reports and forecasts; consideration of fuel requirements; and provision for an alternate course of action if the flight cannot be completed as planned.

Careful preflight planning is extremely important. With adequate planning the pilot can complete his flight with greater confidence, ease and safety. Without it he may become a statistic—figures show *inadequate preflight planning* is a significant cause of fatal accidents.

Assembling Necessary Materials The pilot should collect the necessary material well before the flight to be sure nothing is missing. Appropriate, current sectional charts and charts of areas adjoining the flight route should be among this material. By having this information he will be prepared to circumnavigate weather or locate his position should he become lost. To determine the charts that cover surrounding areas, check the lower right-hand corner of the flight route chart. For example, the charts surrounding the Dallas chart are: Little Rock, Shreveport, Beaumont, Austin, El Paso, Roswell, Albuquerque, and Oklahoma City. This information can also be found around the margins of the chart just inside the black border.

The latest *Airman's Information Manual* should be among the material. It is available through the Superintendent of Documents, U. S. Government Printing Office, Washington, D. C. 20402. The *Airman's Information Manual* is available on an annual subscription basis (at present $15.00).

Additional equipment should include a computer, plotter, and any other item appropriate to the particular flight—for example, if a night flight, carry a flashlight; if a flight over desert country, carry a supply of water.

Weather Check You may wish to check the weather before you continue with other aspects of flight planning to see, first of all, if the flight is feasible and, if it is, which route is best. You should visit the local Weather Bureau airport station or the nearest FAA Flight Service Station (FSS), if available. A personal visit is best because you will have access to the latest weather maps and charts, area forecasts, terminal forecasts, SIGMETS and AIRMETS, hourly sequence reports, PIREPS, and winds-aloft forecasts.

If a visit is impractical, telephone calls are welcomed. Some Weather Bureau stations have "restricted" (unlisted) telephone numbers on which *only* aviation weather information is given. These numbers, along with other Weather Bureau and FSS numbers, are listed in the *Airman's Information Manual.* When telephoning for aviation weather information, identify yourself as a pilot; state your intended route, destination, intended time of takeoff, approximate time enroute; and advise if you intend to fly only VFR.

After receiving the weather briefing, you must determine if the flight can be made safely on the basis of the forecast and present weather. Beware of marginal conditions!

Using the Aeronautical Chart Draw the course to be flown on the sectional chart or charts. The course line should begin at the center of the airport of departure and end at the center of the destination airport. If the route is direct, the course line will consist of a single straight line. If the route is not direct, it will consist of two or more straight line segments—for example, you may choose a route via a VOR station which is off the direct route but which will make navigating easier.

Appropriate check points should be selected along your route and noted in some way. These should be easy-to-locate points such as large towns, large lakes and rivers, or combinations of recognizable points such as towns with an airport, towns with a network or highways and railroads entering and departing, etc. Normally choose only towns indicated by splashes of yellow on the chart. *Do not choose towns represented by a small circle*—these may turn out to be only a half-dozen houses. (In isolated areas, however, towns represented by a small circle can be prominent checkpoints.)

157

You should check along and to either side of your route for caution, restricted, and prohibited areas, military climb corridors, and Air Defense Identification Zones (ADIZ). Each area will have its restrictions printed either within the area or somewhere near the border, depending on its size. A further explanation will appear on the back of the chart. For example, a flight passing through the area south, southeast of Big Spring, Texas (lower left-hand corner of the Dallas chart), would encounter a military climb corridor. Altitude restrictions are listed just to the right of the corridor and within certain sections of the corridor itself. In addition, on the back of the chart you will find the reason for the corridor and the restriction, as well as a cross-sectional view of the corridor which should give you a better understanding of the altitudes to avoid in a given section.

Study the terrain along your route. This is necessary for several reasons. It should be checked to determine the highest and lowest elevations to be encountered so you can choose an appropriate altitude which will conform to FAA regulations. (If you are flying at, or above, 3,000 feet above the terrain, you must conform to the cruising altitude appropriate to the direction of flight.) Check your route for particularly rugged terrain so you can avoid it. Areas where a takeoff or landing will be made should be carefully checked for tall obstructions. Television transmitting towers may extend to altitudes over 1,500 feet above the surrounding terrain. It is essential for you to be aware of their presence and location. You must know the location of any such obstruction all along your route if the flight will be made at a low altitude.

Make a list of the navigation aids you will use along your route and the frequency on which you can receive each one. Indicate the aids that have voice facilities so you will know on which stations weather broadcasts can be received.

Use of the Airman's Information Manual

Make a list of the Flight Service Stations along your route and the frequencies which you can use for transmitting and receiving (in addition to the navigation aid frequencies selected from the chart). Check the correctness of navigation aid frequencies selected from the aeronautical chart. This can be done by checking the Sectional Chart Bulletin, NOTAMS, and the appropriate navigational aid information in section IV-A.

Study available information about each airport at which you intend to land. This should include a study of the following sections: NOTAMS; Airport Directory if the airport has no control tower; and Airport/Facility Directory if the airport has a control tower. Most of the information will be found in the Airport and Airport/Facility Directories. This includes location, elevation, runway and lighting facilities, available services, availability of UNICOM, types of fuel available (use to decide on refueling stops), FSS located on the airport, control tower and ground control frequencies, traffic information, remarks and other pertinent information. The NOTAMS section, issued every 14 days, should be checked for additional information on hazardous conditions or changes that have been made since issuance of the Airport and Airport/Facility Directory sections. Remember that the information in the Airport Directory section may be up to 6 months old and that in the Airport/Facility Directory should be no more than 28 days old.

The Sectional Chart Bulletin subsection should be checked for major changes that have occurred since the last publication date of each sectional chart you plan to use. Remember, your chart may be up to 6 months old. The published date of the chart appears on the front in the lower right-hand corner.

You can find much of the above information on the back of the sectional charts. However, the *Airman's Information Manual* will generally have the latest information and should be used in preference to the information on the back of the chart.

Airplane Flight Manual Data Check your Airplane Flight Manual to determine the proper loading of your airplane (weight and balance data). You must know the weight of the usable fuel and drainable oil aboard, the weight of the passengers, the weight of all baggage to be carried, and the empty weight of the airplane to be sure your total weight does not exceed the maximum allowable. You will also have to know the distribution of the load to tell if the resulting center of gravity is within limits. Be sure to use the latest weight and balance information in the FAA-approved Airplane Flight Manual or other permanent aircraft records, as appropriate, to obtain empty weight and empty weight CG information.

Determine the takeoff and landing distances from the appropriate charts, based on the calculated load, elevation of the airport, and temperature; then compare these distances with the amount of runway available. Remember, the heavier the load and the higher the elevation, temperature, and humidity, the longer your takeoff roll and landing roll and the lower your rate of climb will be. (See Exam-O-Gram No. 11, appendix I.)

Check the fuel consumption charts to determine the rate of fuel consumption at your estimated flight altitude and power settings. Calculate your rate of fuel consumption, then compare it with the estimated time for your flight so you can decide upon refueling points along your route.

Using the Plotter, Computer, etc. When you draw your course line on the aeronautical chart, use a protractor (or plotter) to determine your true course. Then determine the magnetic variation from the mid-isogonic line, apply it to your measured true course and obtain your magnetic course. You must know the magnetic course to decide whether to fly at an even-thousand-plus-five-hundred-feet level or an odd-thousand-plus-five-hundred-feet level. Then measure the length of your course line, *using the distance scale at the bottom of the chart* and NOT the scale on the plotter.

If after a thorough weather check you decide that the flight can be made safely, you should obtain the winds-aloft forecast and choose an altitude, with as favorable winds as possible, that will conform to FAA regulations. Of course, you may wish to sacrifice favorable winds at times in order to fly at an altitude where there is no turbulence. After determining your altitude and the forecast winds at that altitude, use this information and your estimated true airspeed, and measured true course, to compute (on your computer) the true heading and ground speed. From the computed true heading, determine your compass heading by applying variation (already obtained from the mid-isogonic line on the chart) and deviation (obtained from the compass correction card). From your computed ground speed and measured course distance, determine the total flight time. Then use the computed total time and your estimated fuel consumption rate to determine the amount of fuel you will consume during the flight.

After making the necessary computations, you are ready to file your flight plan. However, before we cover flight plans, let us discuss VFR *flight following service.*

VFR Flight Following Service Under the VFR flight following service, you file a FVFR flight plan, request the service, and contact designated flight watch stations as you pass over them enroute. Upon contact with a designated flight watch station, you receive a concise report of flight conditions ahead of you. These stations are specifically designated to monitor your route continuously for significant weather conditions and NOTAMS.

If your airplane has a two-way radio and your cross-country flight will last more than 1 hour, it is to your advantage to file a FVFR flight plan which is your *request for flight following service.*

VFR Flight Plan An examination of enroute accidents shows a striking relationship between the number of accidents by aircraft not on flight plans and those on flight plans. Filing a flight plan is not required by FAA regulations; however, it is good operating practice, since the information contained in the flight plan will be used in search and rescue operations in event of emergency.

Before departing, file a flight plan with the nearest FSS in person or by phone. To avoid congestion of already busy communication channels, use radio for filing flight plans *only* when it is impossible to file any other way.

Remember, there is every advantage in filing a flight plan; furthermore there is every advantage in requesting flight following service along with it if your flight warrants. The one thing you must not forget is to *close your flight plan upon arrival.* Do this by telephone with the nearest FSS, if possible, to avoid radio congestion. If there is no FSS near your point of landing, you may close it by radio with the nearest FSS on arriving over your destination.

Figure 147 shows the flight plan form a pilot files with the Flight Service Station. When you file a flight plan by telephone or radio, give the information in the order of the numbered spaces. This enables the FSS specialist to copy the information more efficiently. Most of the spaces are either self-explanatory or nonapplicable (such as item 13). However, some spaces may need explanation.

FEDERAL AVIATION AGENCY
FLIGHT PLAN

FORM APPROVED
BUDGET BUREAU NO. 04–R072.1

1. TYPE OF FLIGHT PLAN ☐ FVFR ☐ VFR ☐ IFR ☐ DVFR	2. AIRCRAFT IDENTIFICATION	3. AIRCRAFT TYPE	4. ESTIMATED TRUE AIR SPEED *(Knots)*	5. DEPARTURE TIME PROPOSED (Z)	ACTUAL (Z)
6. INITIAL CRUISING ALTITUDE / 7. POINT OF DEPARTURE	8. ROUTE OF FLIGHT				
9. DESTINATION *(Airport & City)*	10. ALTITUDE CHANGES EN ROUTE	11. ESTIMATED TIME EN ROUTE HOURS	MINUTES	12. FUEL ON BOARD HOURS	MINUTES
13. ALTERNATE AIRPORT	14. REMARKS				
15. NAME OF PILOT	16 ADDRESS OF PILOT OR AIRCRAFT HOME BASE				17. NO. OF PERSONS ABOARD
18. COLOR OF AIRCRAFT	19. FLIGHT WATCH STATIONS *(FAA use)*				

FAA FORM 398 (6–62).
USE PREVIOUS EDITIONS.
SEE REVERSE

CLOSE FLIGHT PLAN UPON ARRIVAL

Figure 147. *Flight plan form.*

Item 4 asks for the estimated true airspeed in knots. If you are able to convert your airspeed from miles per hour to knots, there is no problem. If you are not able, then report your airspeed in miles per hour.

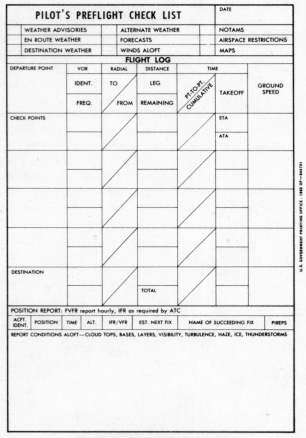

CLOSE FLIGHT PLAN UPON ARRIVAL

Figure 148. *Back of flight plan form.*

Item 5 asks for your proposed departure time in Greenwich Mean Time (indicated by the "Z"). If you are unable to convert local standard time to Greenwich Time, give the time as local standard and the FSS will convert it to Greenwich. To convert local standard time to Greenwich Mean Time, add 5 hours to Eastern Standard Time; add 6 hours to Central Standard Time; add 7 hours to Mountain Standard Time; and add 8 hours to Pacific Standard Time.

Item 6 asks for the proposed cruising altitude. Normally you can enter "VFR" in this block, since you will choose your own cruising altitude to conform to FAA regulations (on IFR flights, air traffic control designates the cruising altitude). However, if you request flight following service, the FSS specialist may ask for a specific altitude to go in this space.

Item 8 asks for the route of flight. If the flight is to be direct, enter the word "direct"; if not, enter the actual route to be followed such as via certain towns or navigation aids.

Item 12 asks for the fuel on board in hours and minutes. This is determined by dividing the total usable fuel aboard in gallons by your estimated rate of fuel consumption in gallons.

For item 19 the information will come from the FSS personnel. In this space will be entered the Flight Service Stations along your route designated to monitor your flight. As you pass over each designated station, contact it to make a position report. At this time, the station will give you all information pertinent to your flight. This will be done without your request—they will be expecting you.

Figure 148 shows the reverse side of the flight plan. This is used as check list for—and a place to enter—the information pertinent to your flight.

Even if you decide not to file a flight plan, make regular position reports to Flight Service Stations to receive altimeter setting, SIGMETS, and advisories to small aircraft. This will also enable search and rescue action to be focused in the proper area in case of an emergency. Remember, the Flight Service Stations are there for your use, so give them your business.

APPENDIX I—SELECTED EXAM-O-GRAMS

Exam-O-Gram No. 1

Situation

A pilot plans a VFR cross-country flight with his destination airport located in a control zone. The terminal forecast indicates that the ceiling and visibility will be decreasing but remain above VFR minimums until his estimated time of arrival. Upon arrival, he enters the control zone, contacts the tower, and indicates that he desires to land. He is cleared to land by the tower.

We shall assume that one or more of the following conditions actually existed at the time he entered the control zone:

(1) Flight or ground visibility was less than 3 miles but not less than 1 mile; and

(2) Ceiling was *less than* 1,000 feet

Analysis

1. WAS THE PILOT LEGAL? NO! The fact that the control tower operator cleared him to land *does not mean* that he is legal. The tower controller is concerned with the safe, orderly, and expeditious movement of air traffic. He will refuse landing only on the basis of other traffic.

2. WHY WAS THE PILOT NOT LEGAL? FAA regulations state in part that an aircraft shall not be flown VFR within a control zone when the ceiling is less than 1,000 feet, or the flight visibility is less than 3 miles. It further states that no person shall take off or land an aircraft or enter the traffic pattern of an airport within a control zone when the ground visibility is less than 3 miles.

3. WHAT ACTION SHOULD THE PILOT HAVE TAKEN TO BE LEGAL? He should have remained clear of the control zone, called the control tower, and requested an air traffic control clearance to land. He should remember that such a clearance does not constitute authority for

him to deviate from the *minimum safe altitudes* as given in FAA regulations.

4. WHAT ACTION IS DICTATED BY GOOD OPERATING PRACTICES? He should have used reasonable restraint in exercising the prerogative of VFR flight, especially in terminal areas. The weather minimums and distances from clouds are *minimums*. Giving oneself a greater margin in specific instances is just *good judgment*. Conducting a VFR operation in a control zone at weather minimums is not prohibited, but good judgment would dictate that pilots flying VFR keep out of the approach area.

Exam-O-Gram No. 3

An Invisible Hazard to Light Aircraft

The Civil Aeronautics Board listed the probable cause of a recent fatal light aircraft accident as structural failure of a light aircraft resulting from excessive airloads created by *wing-tip* vortices behind a large aircraft. The report also states: "The dangers of wake or vortex turbulence are still unknown to many pilots."

Discussion of Wing-Tip Vortices

1. WHAT ARE WING-TIP VORTICES? It is unfortunate that vortices are invisible. If you could see them, they would look like a pair of horizontal tornadoes stretching back from each wing-tip. These violent, compact, and fast-spinning air masses extend behind an aircraft for miles. Many pilots refer to this phenomenon as "prop wash" or "jet wash," but engineering studies have revealed this term a misnomer. The main source of this disturbance is not from the powerplant; it is from the wing-tips.

2. WHY ARE THEY DANGEROUS? They are dangerous because all tests to date indicate that *structural failure in the air* can occur in light aircraft upon penetration of the vortices behind larger transport aircraft. During take-off or landing, care should be taken to *avoid vortex disturbance.* Loss of control could be the result at a critical time when control is of prime importance to safety.

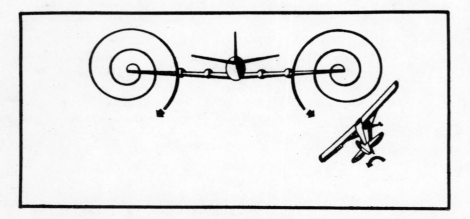

3. UNDER WHAT CONDITIONS ARE THEY MOST DANGEROUS? There are many factors affecting the intensity of wing-tip vortex, but it is a safe and practical generalization that *the bigger the ship the more violent and long-lived* will be the vortex disturbance. The source of this insidious danger can be out of sight by the time you encounter the wake. For example, when a large jet aircraft climbs at approximately 420 mph, the peak turbulence is *3½ miles* behind, and a relatively high degree of turbulence will exist for *7 miles.*

4. WHAT ACTION CAN THE PILOT TAKE TO AVOID OR REDUCE THIS HAZARD?

    a. Avoid passing behind any large aircraft.

    b. Avoid, when possible, places and altitudes frequented by large aircraft. Constantly monitor your radio for location of such aircraft.

    c. If you pass behind a crossing aircraft in flight, change altitude and slow down (at half the speed the shock will be only one-fourth as great).

    d. If you do get into a bad vortex in flight, your best procedure is to throttle back, "ride it out," and avoid "fighting the controls," since to do so may aggravate the condition.

    e. When taking off or landing behind large aircraft, be on the *alert* for the first sign of turbulence; allow adequate spacing, maintain higher than normal speeds, use the windward side of the runway, and maintain a flight path to the windward of the preceding aircraft.

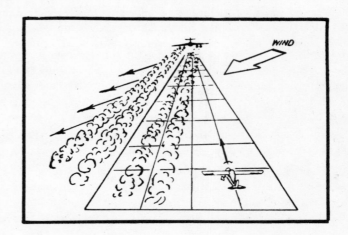

Exam-O-Gram No. 7

Getting Caught on Top of an Overcast

1. DO YOU HAVE ALL OF THE FOLLOWING REQUISITES FOR INSTRUMENT FLIGHT? (1) An Instrument Rating, (2) an aircraft fully equipped for instrument flight, and (3) recent instrument experience. If not, you should heed the following bit of advice concerning *flight over an extensive overcast cloud condition—DON'T!*

2. SHOULD YOU AVOID FLYING VFR OVER CLOUDS ENTIRELY? No. Many times it is both practical and desirable to select a cross-country cruising altitude above a *scattered* cloud condition to take advantage of smoother air, improved visibility, more favorable winds, or provide for more terrain and obstacle clearance, *provided* (1) you have *legal cloud separation* for climb, cruise, and destination descent, (2) weather conditions are stable or improving, and (3) you *stay alert* and take immediate action if the clouds beneath you increase and the "sucker holes" start to shrink. Don't wait too long to descend or make a 180° turn (one of aviation's oldest safety devices) if the situation warrants it.

3. WHAT OTHER PRECAUTIONS SHOULD YOU TAKE TO AVOID AN "ON-TOP-OF-AN-OVERCAST" TRAP? (1) Prior to your cross-country flight, visit the local Weather Bureau Airport Station or your nearest FAA Flight Service Station for a thorough weather briefing. Select an altitude that will be compatible with terrain and cloud separation requirements. (2) Use reasonable restraint in exercising the prerogative of VFR flight when conditions are close to minimums. Remember that with the right conditions, a low overcast can form under you in a matter of minutes. Consider the weather, the terrain you are flying over, and allow yourself a margin of safety commensurate with your experience level. (3) When you file your VFR flight plan with an FSS, request Flight Following Service in order to take advantage of special weather briefings from your enroute designated Flight Watch Station(s). Also, monitor appropriate frequencies for scheduled weather broadcasts at 15 and 45 minutes past each hour.

4. WHAT SHOULD YOU DO IF YOU GET CAUGHT ABOVE AN OVERCAST? You are admittedly "in a jam." Loss of orientation, a very probable sequel to loss of ground references, will further complicate your problem. However, you can improve your chances of avoiding disaster by following a few logical procedures. (See *Airman's Information Manual*—"Emergency Procedures.") For example, you should (1) establish communications with an FSS or other ground stations and *confess your predicament.* The personnel in these stations are well trained in assisting airmen in distress; give them a chance to help you before it's too late. If necessary, they can alert available VHF Direction Finding and Radar Stations (including military stations) to stand by for possible assistance. (2) If you have trouble establishing contact with a ground station, climbing will increase the range of your VHF radio equipment and improve the chances of ground radar detection. (3) Conserve your fuel by using an economical or maximum endurance power setting. (4) If you really need help, *comply* with instructions received from your ground station.

5. *Prevention* is a much better approach to this problem than the cure. If you are a VFR pilot, *AVOID GETTING CAUGHT ON TOP OF AN OVERCAST!*

Exam-O-Gram No. 8

Airspeed Indicator Markings

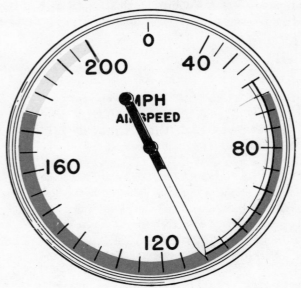

The above airspeed indicator depicts the airspeed limitation markings of a late model civilian airplane. *How many* of the airspeed questions below can you answer by studying the airspeed indicator pictured above?

1. *WHAT IS THE FLAP OPERATING RANGE?*
2. *WHAT IS THE POWER-OFF STALLING SPEED WITH THE WING FLAPS AND LANDING GEAR IN THE LANDING POSITION?*
3. *WHAT IS THE MAXIMUM FLAPS-EXTENDED SPEED?*
4. *WHAT IS THE NORMAL OPERATING RANGE?*
5. *WHAT IS THE POWER-OFF STALLING SPEED "CLEAN"— (GEAR AND FLAPS RETRACTED)?*
6. *WHAT IS THE MAXIMUM STRUCTURAL CRUISING SPEED?*
7. *WHAT IS THE CAUTION RANGE?*
8. *WHAT IS THE NEVER-EXCEED SPEED?*

Airplanes manufactured after 1945 and certificated under FAA regulations are required to have the standard system of airspeed indicator markings described in this Exam-O-Gram. In the interest of safety, it is important for you as a pilot to recognize and understand these airspeed limitation markings. And, too, this information will come in handy if you are planning to take a written examination for a pilot's certificate; current FAA written examinations contain questions on this subject. A short explanation of the airspeeds and airspeed ranges you need to know follows. The descriptions, through choice, are limited to layman language.

Air Speed
(See illustrations)

Starting with the *lower speeds and working up*, we have:

1. *FLAP OPERATING RANGE* (the white arc) ...... 60 to 110 mph
2. *POWER-OFF STALLING SPEED WITH THE WING FLAPS AND LANDING GEAR IN THE LANDING POSITION* (the lower limit of the white arc) .... 60 mph
3. *MAXIMUM FLAPS-EXTENDED SPEED* (the upper limit of the white arc). This is the highest airspeed at which you should put down full flaps. If flaps are operated at higher speeds, severe strain or structural failure may result .... 110 mph
4. *THE NORMAL OPERATING RANGE* (the green arc) .... 65 to 175 mph
5. *POWER-OFF STALLING SPEED "CLEAN"— WING FLAPS AND LANDING GEAR RETRACTED* (the lower limit of the green arc) .... 65 mph
6. *MAXIMUM STRUCTURAL CRUISING SPEED* (the upper limit of the green arc). This is the maximum speed for normal operation .... 175 mph
7. *CAUTION RANGE* (the yellow arc). You should avoid this area unless you are in smooth air .... 175 to 200 mph
8. *NEVER EXCEED SPEED* (the radial red line). This is the maximum speed at which the airplane can be operated in smooth air. No pilot should ever exceed this speed intentionally .... 200 mph

There are other airspeed limitations *not marked on the airspeed indicator* which you should know. They are generally found on placards in view of the pilot or in the Airplane Flight Manual. One of these speeds, a very important one, is the *MANEUVERING SPEED*. This is your "rough air" speed and the maximum speed for abrupt maneuvers. If during flight you should en-counter severe turbulence, you should reduce your airspeed to maneuvering speed or less in order to reduce the stress upon the airplane structure.

KNOW YOUR AIRSPEED LIMITATIONS
THIS KNOWLEDGE MAY SAVE YOUR LIFE

Exam-O-Gram No. 9

Altimetry

Your altimeter is a vitally important instrument. You will agree that flight without this instrument would, indeed, be a haphazard undertaking—yet, *HOW WELL DO YOU KNOW YOUR ALTIMETER?* Take this short quiz on altimetry; grade yourself by checking the answers and explanations that follow.

1. Check your ability to interpret altitude quickly by jotting down the readings of the six altimeters shown at the right. *Allow yourself 1 minute.*

2. FAA regulations require that you maintain your cruising altitudes (VFR as well as IFR) by reference to your altimeter. What do regulations require concerning the setting (or adjustment) of your altimeter?

3. If you are flying in very cold air (colder than standard temperatures), you should expect your altimeter to read—
   a. *higher* than your actual altitude above sea level.
   b. *lower* than your actual altitude above sea level.
   c. *the same* as your actual altitude above sea level.

4. Here are four altitudes with which you should be familiar. Briefly give the meaning of each. (1) *Indicated altitude.* (2) *Pressure altitude.* (3) *Density altitude.* (4) *True altitude.*

5. *Assume* that your proposed route crosses mountains with peaks extending to 10,900 feet above sea level. Before crossing this range, you adjust the altimeter setting window of your altimeter to the *current altimeter setting* reported by a Flight Service Station located in a valley near the base of this mountain range. If you maintain an indicated altitude of 11,500 feet by your altimeter, *can you be assured of at least 500 feet vertical clearance of these mountain peaks?*

Answers to Questions on Altimetry

1. (1) 7,500 ft. (2) 7,880 ft. (3) 1,380 ft. (4) 8,800 ft. (5) 12,420 ft. (6) 880 ft.

(1) 7,500

(2) 7780

(3) 1 380

(4) 8 800

(5) 12 420

(6) 8 90

If your altimeter is the three-pointer-type sensitive altimeter such as those pictured on the opposite side of this sheet, an orderly approach to reading your altitude is to first glance at the smallest hand (10,000 ft. hand); next read the middle hand (1,000 ft. hand); and last read the large hand (100 ft. hand). For the two-pointer altimeter, simply read the small hand first and the large hand next.

2. Your altimeter should be set to the *current reported altimeter setting* of a station along the route of flight. (Flight Service Stations, control towers, etc.). If your aircraft is not equipped with a radio, you should obtain an altimeter setting prior to departure if one is available, or *you should adjust your altimeter to the elevation of the airport of departure.*

3. If you are flying in cold air, you should expect your altimeter to indicate HIGHER than you actually are. There is an old saying—one well worth remembering—that goes something like this: "WHEN FLYING FROM A HIGH TO A LOW OR HOT TO COLD, *LOOK OUT BELOW!*" In other words, if you are flying from a high pressure area to a low pressure area or into colder air, you had better be careful because you probably aren't as high as you think—assuming, of course, that no compensations are made for these atmospheric conditions.

4. (1) *Indicated altitude*—That altitude read directly from the altimeter (uncorrected) after it has been adjusted to the current altimeter setting.

(2) *Pressure altitude*—The altitude read from the altimeter when the altimeter setting window is adjusted to 29.92. (This altitude is used for computer solutions for density altitude, true altitude, true airspeed, etc.)

(3) *Density altitude*—This altitude is pressure altitude corrected for nonstandard temperature variations. (It is an important altitude since *this altitude is directly related to the aircraft's takeoff and climb performance.*)

(4) *True altitude*—The true height of the aircraft above sea level—the actual altitude. (Often you will see a true altitude expressed in this manner: "10,900 ft. MSL"—The MSL standing for MEAN SEA LEVEL. Remember that airport terrain, and obstacle elevations found on charts and maps, are *true altitudes.*)

5. NO, you are not assured of 500 feet vertical clearance with these mountains. As a matter of fact, with certain atmospheric conditions, you might very well be 500 feet *BELOW* the peaks with this indicated altitude. (To begin with, 500 feet is hardly an adequate separation margin to allow on flights over mountainous terrain—1,500 to 2,000 feet is recommended in order to allow for possible altitude errors and downdrafts.)

A majority of pilots confidently expect that the current altimeter setting will compensate for irregularities in atmospheric pressure. Unfortunately, this is not always true. Remember that the altimeter setting broadcast by ground stations is the *station pressure corrected to mean sea level*. It does not reflect distortion at higher levels, *particularly the effect of nonstandard temperature*.

When flying over mountainous country, allow yourself a generous margin for terrain and obstacle clearances.

KNOW YOUR ALTIMETER

Exam-O-Gram No. 10

Fuel Contamination

EXCERPTS FROM A RECENT AIRCRAFT ACCIDENT REPORT: ". . . Subsequent examination of the engine and its components revealed large deposits of foreign material, sediment, and water in the fuel strainer, carburetor bowl, and fuel pump in sufficient quantities to cause stoppage. . . . Probable cause of accident: Inadequate preflight action by the pilot; subsequent *engine failure due to fuel contamination. . . .*"

DO YOU KNOW—AND PRACTICE—THE PRECAUTIONS YOU SHOULD TAKE TO AVOID FUEL CONTAMINATION? Perhaps you do, but there are many pilots who obviously do not—*as evidenced by the alarming increase in the number of fuel contamination-caused accidents*. The modern aircraft engine is a remarkably reliable and dependable mechanism, but it will not run on water, dirt particles, and other noncombustibles. Let's review this insidious problem by asking—and answering—a couple of rather pointed questions about this subject.

1. WHAT CAUSES FUEL CONTAMINATION?

a. *Storing aircraft with partially filled fuel tanks may cause condensation and water contamination.* You have, no doubt, often noticed moisture (or dew) on the outside of your aircraft early in the morning. When you noticed this, did it occur to you that this same moisture could form on the inside walls of your fuel tanks? Water is the worst offender in these contamination cases, and condensation inside the tank is one of the methods by which it finds its way into your fuel system.

b. *Servicing the aircraft from improperly filtered tanks, particularly small tanks or drums, is another principal source of fuel contamination.* This practice frequently introduces both dirt and water into the aircraft fuel system.

2. WHAT PRECAUTIONS SHOULD THE PILOT TAKE TO AVOID FUEL CONTAMINATION?

a. PREFLIGHT ACTION: Drain a generous sample of fuel (several ounces—not just a trickle or two) into a transparent container from each of the fuel sumps. (Notice that we specified each of the fuel sumps. This includes not only the main gascolator, but also the wing tank sumps.) Examine the sample of fuel from each sump for water and dirt contamination. Water *will not mix* with gasoline. If present, it will collect at the bottom of the transparent container and will be easily detected. If water or dirt appears, continue to drain fuel from that sump until you are sure the system is clear of all water and dirt. (NOTE: If your aircraft is not equipped with wing tank quick-drain petcocks, it is recommended they be installed. This can make the preflight check of the wing tank sumps much more convenient, as the frequent removal and replacement of wing tank sump drain plugs can be a time-consuming operation.)

b. POST-FLIGHT ACTION: (1) *Top off your tanks at the end of the day to avoid condensation and water contamination inside your fuel tanks.* Although this is a desirable procedure to follow at the end of each flying day (assuming your loading schedule for the next day will permit a full load of fuel), it is particularly important that this is done if the aircraft is to stand idle for several days—whether it is tied down out-of-doors or stored in a hangar. (2) Avoid, if possible, servicing your aircraft from small tanks or drums. *Should this become necessary, the fuel should always be strained through a chamois skin that is in good condition.*

c. PRECAUTIONARY MAINTENANCE ACTION: In addition to the previously discussed precautions, the following maintenance precautions should be performed on your aircraft at periodic intervals: (1) Inspect and clean the tank fuel outlet finger strainer. (2) Inspect and clean the inlet carburetor screen. (3) Flush the carburetor bowl.

BY FOLLOWING ALL OF THESE PRECAUTIONS, YOU CAN GREATLY REDUCE THE HAZARD OF ENGINE FAILURE DUE TO FUEL CONTAMINATION.

To better understand the reasons for the PREFLIGHT ACTION we have recommended, let's take a brief look at an actual water contamination test recently conducted by FAA—it's a real eye opener!

After all water was removed from the fuel system of a popular make high-wing monoplane, 3 gallons of water were added to the half-full fuel tank.

After a few minutes, the fuel strainer (gascolator) was checked for water. *It was necessary to drain 10 liquid ounces of fuel before any water appeared.* This is considerably more than most pilots drain when checking for water.

In a second test with the same aircraft in flying attitude (to simulate a later tricycle-geared model) the fuel system was again cleared of all water; then 1 gallon of water was added to the half-full tank. In a check of the fuel strainer (gascolator) quick drain, *more than a quart of fuel was drained before any water appeared.*

In both of the above-described tests, about 9 ounces of water remained in the fuel tank after the belly drain and the fuel strainer (gascolator) had ceased to show any trace of water. *This residual water could be removed only by draining the tank sumps.*

Two significant findings emerged from the above tests and from tests made on a plastic mockup of a similar fuel system:

1. When water was introduced into the fuel tank, it immediately settled to the bottom, but did not flow down the fuel lines to the fuel strainer until all fuel was drained from the lines.

2. Since it was found impossible to drain all water from the tank through the fuel lines, it was necessary to drain the fuel tank sumps in order to remove all water from the system.

HELP STAMP OUT FUEL CONTAMINATION!

Exam-O-Gram No. 11

Density Altitude and Its Effect on Aircraft Performance

A report of a recent accident was stated in the following words: "Takeoff was attempted on a 1,600-foot strip; the airplane cleared the fences but sank back and struck a ditch." The pilot states that he failed to consider the effect of the grassy, rough field, *the 90° temperature,* heavy load of fuel and passengers, and the calm wind.

This EXAM-O-GRAM discusses the effect that high temperature and other factors had on this takeoff.

1. WHAT IS DENSITY ALTITUDE? It is a measure of air density. Under nonstandard conditions, density altitude will differ from the elevation. As the air density decreases (i.e., air becomes thinner), density altitude increases, and vice versa. *Low atmospheric pressure, high temperature,* and *high humidity* all result in a decrease in air density and an *increase in density*

altitude. (Contrary to prevailing opinion, *moist air is less dense than dry air.* Water vapor actually weighs less than dry air—approximately five-eighths as much.)

2. WHAT EFFECT DOES AN INCREASE IN DENSITY ALTITUDE HAVE ON AIRCRAFT PERFORMANCE?

    a. Engine horsepower decreases (unless it is a supercharged engine).

    b. The propeller loses some of its efficiency, since it will not take as much of a bite out of the thinner air.

    c. Takeoff distance is increased and rate of climb is decreased because of the loss of engine power and propeller efficiency, and the higher true airspeed necessary to obtain the required lift in the thinner air. (In other words, if the density altitude is 8,000 feet at an elevation of 5,000 feet, the aircraft flies as though it were at 8,000 feet.)

3. UNDER WHAT CONDITIONS IS A HIGH "DENSITY ALTITUDE" MOST HAZARDOUS? When it is present with other factors that tend to increase the takeoff distance or require that this distance be limited, such as: heavy load; calm wind conditions; short runway; obstructions at or near the end of the runway; and unfavorable runway conditions (rough, tall grass, soft snow, up-grade, etc.).

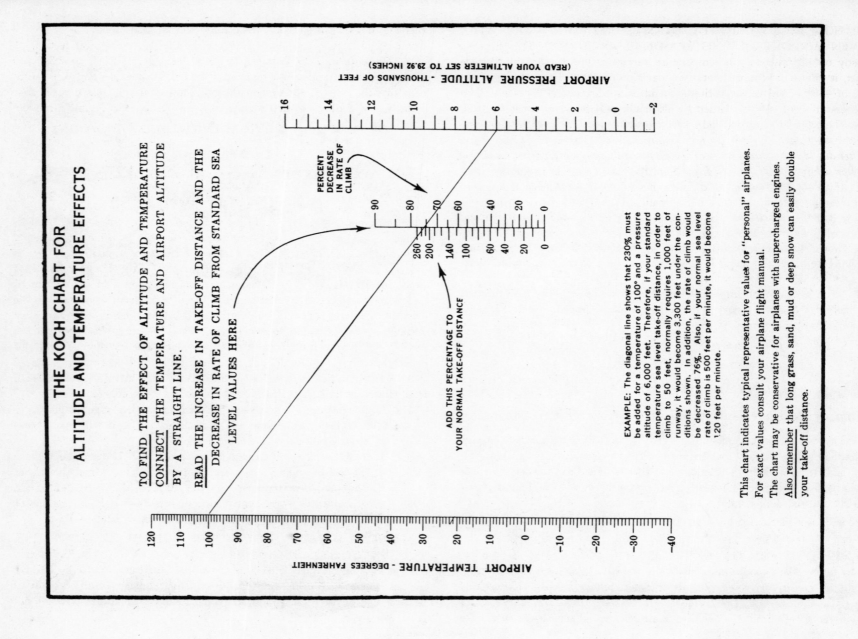

THE KOCH CHART FOR
ALTITUDE AND TEMPERATURE EFFECTS

TO FIND THE EFFECT OF ALTITUDE AND TEMPERATURE
CONNECT THE TEMPERATURE AND AIRPORT ALTITUDE
BY A STRAIGHT LINE.

READ THE INCREASE IN TAKE-OFF DISTANCE AND THE
DECREASE IN RATE OF CLIMB FROM STANDARD SEA
LEVEL VALUES HERE

AIRPORT PRESSURE ALTITUDE - THOUSANDS OF FEET
(READ YOUR ALTIMETER SET TO 29.92 INCHES)

PERCENT
DECREASE
IN RATE OF
CLIMB

ADD THIS PERCENTAGE TO
YOUR NORMAL TAKE-OFF DISTANCE

EXAMPLE: The diagonal line shows that 230% must
be added for a temperature of 100° and a pressure
altitude of 6,000 feet. Therefore, if your standard
temperature sea level take-off distance, in order to
climb to 50 feet, normally requires 1,000 feet of
runway, it would become 3,300 feet under the conditions shown. In addition, the rate of climb would
be decreased 76%. Also, if your normal sea level
rate of climb is 500 feet per minute, it would become
120 feet per minute.

This chart indicates typical representative values for "personal" airplanes.
For exact values consult your airplane flight manual.
The chart may be conservative for airplanes with supercharged engines.
Also remember that long grass, sand, mud or deep snow can easily double
your take-off distance.

AIRPORT TEMPERATURE - DEGREES FAHRENHEIT

4. HOW MUCH CAN THE DENSITY ALTITUDE VARY AT A GIVEN AIRPORT DURING SEASONAL EXTREMES? This depends mostly on the extremes in temperature variation. From a density altitude chart, it can be determined that at an elevation of 5,000 feet and a temperature of —6° F., the density altitude would be approximately 2,200 feet; at a temperature of 104° F., the density altitude would be approximately 8,900 feet. These figures do not include the increase due to a high relative humidity on the 104° day. *Do not let the performance of your airplane on a cold winter day lull you into a sense of security when taking off from the same airport on a hot, humid summer day.* (Note the pilot's remarks in the cartoon.)

5. If an airplane requires a distance of 1,200 feet for takeoff at sea level (to clear a 50-foot obstacle) under standard conditions, what distance is required at (a) an elevation of 5,000 feet, temperature —6° F.; (b) an elevation of 5,000 feet, temperature 104° F.? Refer to the Koch chart. (*Assume that pressure altitude and elevation are equal.*)

Problem A

The line joining 5,000 feet and —6° F. shows an increase in takeoff distance of 20 percent.

Increase in T.O. Distance = .20 x 1,200 feet = 240 feet
Total T.O. Distance = 1,200 feet + 240 feet = 1,440 feet

Problem B

The line joining 5,000 feet and 104° F. shows an increase in takeoff distance of 190 percent.

Increase in T.O. Distance = 1.9 x 1,200 feet = 2,280 feet
Total T.O. Distance = 1,200 feet + 2,280 feet = 3,480 feet

Difference in T. O. Distance = 3,480 feet — 1,440 feet = 2,040 feet
Under the above conditions presented in item 5, Problems A and B, it can be seen that the takeoff distance on the hot summer day increased *more than 2,000 feet* over that required on the cold winter day at the same airport.

BEWARE OF HIGH, HOT, AND HUMID CONDITIONS

Exam-O-Gram No. 12

The Magnetic Compass

The magnetic compass, in terms of its errors, limitations, and in-flight characteristics, is one of those aeronautical subjects in which consistently large numbers of pilots fare poorly on FAA written examinations. There is evidence that this veteran instrument—it was one of the first to be installed in an aircraft—is one of the least understood instruments in the cockpit of today's modern general aviation aircraft. Many pilots seem to operate on the premise that it is easier to ignore the errors of this instrument than learn them. However, it should be remembered that (1) this is the only direction seeking instrument in the cockpit of most general aviation aircraft, and (2) it is mechanically a simple, self-contained unit (independent of external suction or electrical power for its operation) that is likely to remain reliable at all times—reliable, that is, if the pilot understands its inherent errors.

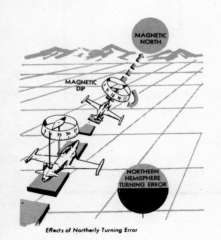

Effects of Northerly Turning Error

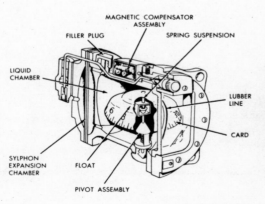

The Magnetic Compass

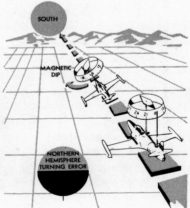

WHAT ARE SOME OF THE COMPASS ERRORS THAT THE PILOT SHOULD UNDERSTAND? The pilot should understand:

1. VARIATION—This is the angular difference between *true north* and *magnetic north* which is plotted on charts in degrees east or west. The pilot should understand perfectly *which to add and which to subtract* when converting from true headings or courses to magnetic headings or courses and vice versa. (Many pilots find such memory aids as "east is least and west is best" helpful in remembering that *east is subtracted* and *west is added* when going from *true* to *magnetic*.)

2. DEVIATION—This is the deflection of the compass needle from a position of magnetic north as a result of local magnetic disturbances in the aircraft. To reduce this deviation, the compass has a compensating device consisting of small adjustable magnets. The compass should be checked and compensated periodically. The errors remaining after "swinging" the compass should be recorded on a compass correction card that should be installed in the cockpit within the view of the pilot. (NOTE: Avoid placing metallic objects such as metal computers, flashlights, etc., on top of the instrument panel near the magnetic compass, since this practice may induce large amounts of deviation and seriously affect instrument accuracy.)

In addition to these errors, the pilot should have a *working knowledge* of the following in-flight errors:

3. OSCILLATION ERROR—The erratic swinging of the compass card which may be the result of turbulence or rough pilot technique.

4. MAGNETIC DIP—The tendency of the magnetic compass to point down as well as north in certain latitudes. This tendency is responsible for:

a. Northerly Turn Error—*This Error is the most pronounced of the in-flight errors*. It is the most apparent when turning to or from headings of north and south.

b. Acceleration Error—An error that can occur during airspeed changes. It is most apparent on headings of east and west.

As a quick refresher on this instrument's in-flight dip error, we invite you to accompany us on a simulated demonstration flight around the compass rose. Unless otherwise noted, we will limit our bank during turns to a gentle bank. Also, we will assume that we are in the northern hemisphere because the characteristics which we will observe would not be present at the magnetic equator, and would be reversed in the southern hemisphere.

DEMONSTRATION NO. 1. (Heading—North; Error—Northerly Turn Error.)

As we start a turn in either direction from this heading, we notice that momentarily the compass *gives an indication of a turn opposite the direction of the actual turn*. (While the compass card is in a banked attitude, the vertical component of the earth's magnetic field causes the north-seeking end of the compass to dip to the low side of the turn, giving the pilot an erroneous turn indication.) If we continue the turn toward east or west, the compass card will begin to indicate a turn in the correct direction, *but will lag behind the actual turn*—at a diminishing rate—until we are within a few degrees of east or west. One additional demonstration we will cover before leaving north is the Slow Turn Error. If, while holding a compass indication of north, we sneak into a very gradual shallow banked turn—say 3 or 4 degrees of bank—it is possible to change the actual heading of the aircraft by 20° or more *while still maintaining an indication of north by the compass*.

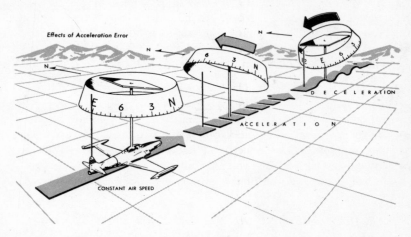

Effects of Acceleration Error

DEMONSTRATION NO. 2. (Heading—East; Error—Acceleration Error.)

The Northerly Turn Error that we previously experienced is not apparent on this heading (or on a west heading). However, let's see what happens when we accelerate and decelerate by changing the airspeed. With the wings level, we will *increase* the airspeed by increasing the power setting or by lowering the nose—or both. Result—although we are holding the nose of the aircraft straight ahead, our compass card erroneously indicates a turn toward *north*. On the other hand, if we *decrease* the airspeed by reducing the power setting or raising the nose of the aircraft—or both, the compass will give an erroneous indication of a turn toward *south*. (Because of the pendulous-type mounting, the end of the compass card which the pilot sees is tilted upward during acceleration, and downward during deceleration and changes of airspeed. This momentary deflection of the compass card from the horizontal results in an error that is most apparent on headings of east and west.)

DEMONSTRATION NO. 3. (Heading—South; Error—Northerly Turn Error.)

Again we are presented with the Northerly Turn Error problem that we encountered in Demonstration 1. Although the same set of forces that caused the erroneous indication when we banked the aircraft while on a north heading will likewise be working against us on this heading, the compass indications will appear quite different. For example, as we roll into a turn in either direction, the compass gives us an indication of a turn in the *correct direction* but at a *much faster rate than is actually being turned.* As we continue our turn toward west or east, the compass indications will continue to precede the actual turn—but at a diminishing rate—until we are within a few degrees of west or east. (It might be noted that the Acceleration Error is not apparent on this heading or on a north heading.)

DEMONSTRATION NO. 4. (Heading—West; Error—Acceleration Error.)

On this heading we encounter the exact same errors that we previously covered on a heading of east in Demonstration 2. If we *increase the airspeed,* we will get an erroneous indication of a *turn toward north.* If we *decrease the airspeed,* we will get an erroneous indication of a *turn toward south.* (A memory aid that might assist you in recalling this relationship between airspeed change and direction of the error is the word "ANDS"—*Accelerate-North, Decelerate-South.*)

WHAT ARE THE MAIN POINTS THAT SHOULD BE REMEMBERED CONCERNING THE FOUR DEMONSTRATIONS?

The points we are trying to get across are these: (1) WHEN TAKING READINGS FROM THE MAGNETIC COMPASS WHILE ON A NORTHERLY OR SOUTHERLY HEADING (for establishing a course, setting the gyro-driven heading indicator, etc.), REMEMBER THAT IT IS ESSENTIAL TO HAVE THE WINGS PERFECTLY LEVEL FOR SEVERAL SECONDS BEFORE TAKING THE READING. (2) IF YOU ARE ON AN EASTERLY OR WESTERLY HEADING, IT IS IMPORTANT FOR THE AIRSPEED TO BE CONSTANT SO THAT YOU CAN GET AN ACCURATE READING. (3) ON AN INTERMEDIATE HEADING, BOTH OF THE ABOVE CONDITIONS SHOULD BE MET. (*Note:* If your aircraft is equipped with a gyro-driven heading indicator, check it frequently with your magnetic compass.)

* * *

TURNS TO HEADINGS BY REFERENCE TO THE MAGNETIC COMPASS

For the pilot who would like a general set of rules for determining his lead point when making turns by reference to the magnetic compass, the following is submitted:

(Note: The angle of bank should not exceed 15° in order to minimize dip error.)

1. *When turning to a heading of north you must allow, in addition to your normal lead, a number of degrees approximately equal to the latitude at which you are flying. Example:* You are making a left turn to a heading of north in a locality where the latitude is *30° N.* You have previously determined your normal lead to be approximately *5°* for this particular angle of bank. In this case, you should start your roll-out when the compass reads approximately *35°.*

2. *When turning to a heading of south, you must turn past your normal lead point by a number of degrees approximately equal to the latitude at which you are flying. Example:* You are making a right turn to a heading of south in a locality where the latitude is *30° N.* You have previously determined your normal lead to be approximately *5°* for this particular angle of bank. In this case, you should turn past your normal lead point of *175°* (180° − 5°) by *30°,* and start your roll-out when the compass reads approximately *205°.*

3. *The error is negligible during turns to east or west; therefore, use the normal amount of lead during turns to an east or west heading.*

4. *For intermediate headings that lie between the cardinal headings, use an approximation based on the heading's proximity to north or south, the direction of the turn, and your knowledge of the compass's lead and lag characteristics in these areas.* In other words, use an "educated guess-timate."

We won't guarantee you that the above method will roll you out on exact heading every time—at best, it is an approximate method. But it will get you reasonably close to your desired heading, and this beats having no method at all.

KNOW YOUR MAGNETIC COMPASS

Exam-O-Gram No. 13

Weight and Balance

Loading the family automobile for a trip requires little serious planning. You can C-R-A-M as much luggage into the trunk as you have space, squeeze as many persons into the seats as you have room, and top off the gas tank with no thought given to gross weight or center of gravity. A similar approach to loading your "flying machine" could result in a serious accident.

WHAT IS EXCESSIVE WEIGHT? Assume that your airplane is a 4-place airplane with a baggage allowance of 120 pounds, a usable fuel capacity of 39 gallons, and an oil supply of 8 quarts. On a hypothetical flight you take on full fuel and oil servicing, toss the suitcases in the baggage compartment, and you and your three passengers eagerly climb aboard. This seems like a reasonable load, but if you had placed each of them on the scales you might have found that you and the passengers average 180 pounds each (720 pounds), and the four suitcases, 30 pounds each (120 pounds). The usable fuel load weighs 234 pounds and the oil 15 pounds. Assume, also, that the Weight and Balance Data for the airplane shows an *empty weight* of 1,325 pounds and a maximum allowable *gross weight* of 2,200 pounds. NOW, add the weight of the useful load to the empty weight and compare the total to the allowable gross weight. (1,089 pounds + 1,325 pounds = 2,414 pounds) ... *214 pounds excess!*

WHAT RESTRICTIONS ARE THERE ON WEIGHT AND BALANCE? In many civilian airplanes it is not possible to fill all seats, the baggage compartment, and tanks, and still remain within the approved weight and balance limits. If you do not wish to leave a passenger behind (a normal reaction) you must reduce your fuel load and plan on shorter legs en route or cut down on the baggage carried, or both. Frequently, restrictions are placed on rear seat occupancy with maximum baggage allowance aboard. By all means follow the Airplane Weight and Balance Form restrictions. The loading conditions and the empty weight of your particular airplane may differ from those shown in the owner's manual, especially if modifications have been made or equipment has been added to the basic airplane.

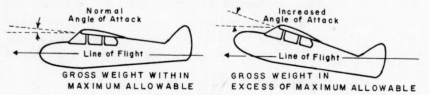

NORMAL
Angle of Attack

— Line of Flight —

GROSS WEIGHT WITHIN
MAXIMUM ALLOWABLE

Increased
Angle of Attack

— Line of Flight —

GROSS WEIGHT IN
EXCESS OF MAXIMUM ALLOWABLE

IS CRUISE PERFORMANCE AFFECTED BY AN EXCESS LOAD? At normal weight, the airplane requires a certain angle of attack to maintain straight-and-level flight at a given airspeed. To sustain a heavier load at that same airspeed, the angle of attack must be greater to provide the increased lift that is necessary. More power must be added to overcome the increased drag resulting from the increased angle of attack. Additional power, in turn, burns more fuel, thereby reducing the range of the aircraft.

IS CLIMB PERFORMANCE AFFECTED BY EXCESS LOAD? Time to climb to a given altitude is lengthened, because extra thrust required to carry the additional weight limits the rate of climb and may limit the climbing speed, since this depends on the surplus power available. The additional time in climbing at the higher power setting also increases the fuel consumption.

IS "G" FORCE TOLERANCE AFFECTED? Assume that your airplane has a limit-load factor of 3.8 "G's." If the allowable gross weight is not exceeded, this means the wings can safely support 3.8 times the weight of the airplane and its contents. In accelerated flight (pull-ups, turns, turbulent air) the actual load on the wings would be much greater than the normal load, which of course results in much greater stresses in the wing structure. Overloading, therefore, has the effect of decreasing the "G" load capability of the aircraft and thus could result in the wing being stressed to the point of popped rivets, permanent distortion, or structural failure.

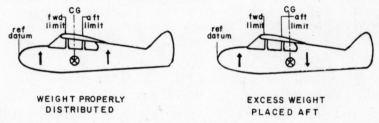

WEIGHT PROPERLY
DISTRIBUTED

EXCESS WEIGHT
PLACED AFT

HOW IS AN AIRPLANE BALANCED? An airplane, like a steelyard scale, is in perfect balance when the weight is distributed in such a manner that it remains level when freely suspended. In an airplane, however, as long as the center of gravity lies anywhere within specified limits, balance can be maintained in flight. Flight with the CG outside of this range results in unsatisfactory or *dangerous flight characteristics.* Loading an airplane, then, is simply a matter of distributing the load so that the CG falls within the allowable range. This can be accomplished by arranging the load in accordance with the center of gravity envelope provided for each airplane.

DOES IMPROPER LOAD DISTRIBUTION AFFECT SAFETY? YES!
When loading conditions cause the center of gravity to fall outside allowable limits, stability is adversely affected and erratic control forces may develop. Stalling speed, takeoff distance, and landing speed may be increased to the point of *actual danger*.

Due to the size of many baggage compartments there might be a tendency to fill them to capacity, ignoring the placarded baggage weight limitations.

This could produce a center of gravity aft of allowable limits and create a highly dangerous flight condition. The result would be a nose-high attitude that could lead to a stall from which recovery might not be effected because of inadequate elevator control.

AN AIRPLANE'S BEHAVIOR IN THE AIR
DEPENDS ON WEIGHT AND BALANCE!

EMPTY WEIGHT = empty wt of airplane
with all instruments +
unusable fuel

useful load = pilot, passenger, oil,
usable fuel, oil
baggage

gross wt = empty wt + useful load

APPENDIX II—ANSWERS TO EXERCISES

Exercise No. 1—

	WCA	TH	GS (mph)
1.	14° L	226°	124
2.	6° L	254°	115
3.	6° R	266°	178
4.	6° L	344°	107
5.	6° L	94°	191
6.	12° R	142°	147

Exercise No. 2—

	Percent Increase	Takeoff Distance (feet)
1.	95	975
2.	150	1,825
3.	70	1,632
4.	230	3,630
5.	160	2,210

Exercise No. 3—

	Ground Run (feet)	To clear 50-foot (feet)
1.	75	260
2.	1,062	2,019
3.	310	700
4.	666	1,296
5.	325	730

Exercise No. 4—

	TAS	Gal/hr	Flight Time
1.	158	14.2	3:52
2.	151	11.7	3:51
3.	107	7.0	3:34
4.	105	7.0	3:34
5.	158	13.4	3:44

Exercise No. 5—

1. 2 hrs 20 min
2. 2 hrs 36 min
3. 1 hr 28 min
4. 2 hrs 24 min
5. 26 min
6. 19 min

Exercise No. 6—

1. 150 mph
2. 120 mph
3. 98 mph
4. 108 mph
5. 120 mph
6. 154 mph

Exercise No. 7—

1. 4 hrs
2. 5 hrs 19 min
3. 5 hrs 18 min
4. 4 hrs 14 min
5. 2 hrs 52 min

Exercise No. 8—

1. 21 gal
2. 38.5 gal
3. 22.2 gal
4. 43.7 gal
5. 71 gal

Exercise No. 9—

1. 128 mph
2. 149 mph
3. 155 mph
4. 165 mph
5. 160 mph

Exercise No. 10—

1. 23 mph
2. 18.4 mph
3. 30 mph
4. 46 mph
5. 54 mph

Exercise No. 11—

	WCA	TH	GS (mph)
1.	10° R	020°	150
2.	0°	267°	164
3.	6° L	039°	143
4.	15° R	155°	131
5.	9° L	111°	122